ran
when
parked...

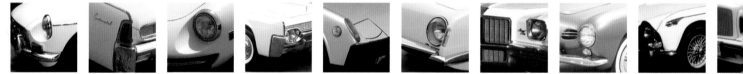

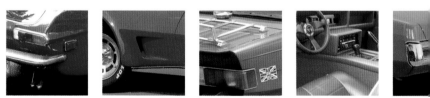

ran
when
parked...

Advice and
Adventures from
the Affordable
Underbelly of
Car Collecting

Rob Sass

PARKER
HOUSE

Parker House Publishing Inc.
1826 Tower Drive
Stillwater, Minnesota 55082, USA
www.parkerhousepublishing.com

ISBN-13: 978-0-9817270-4-2

Book and cover design: Diana Boger
Cover design concept: Chris Fayers
Editor: Kathleen Donohue

Manufactured in China through World Print

10 9 8 7 6 5 4 3 2 1

contents

forewords
by McKeel Hagerty and Keith Martin   6

introduction   8

1 buying a "right" car   10

2 look rich for cheap   18

3 credit card cars   48

4 american icons   68

5 practical classics   90

6 oddballs   140

acknowledgments   159

index   160

forewords

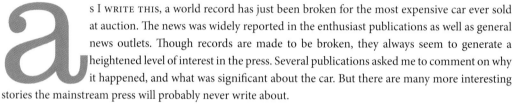

s I write this, a world record has just been broken for the most expensive car ever sold at auction. The news was widely reported in the enthusiast publications as well as general news outlets. Though records are made to be broken, they always seem to generate a heightened level of interest in the press. Several publications asked me to comment on why it happened, and what was significant about the car. But there are many more interesting stories the mainstream press will probably never write about.

For the most part, the media seems to focus on the tiny minority of collector cars that are capable of bringing stratospheric prices. And while it's understandable that this is where the spotlight generally shines, few press releases cover hobbyists' every day accomplishments…the baby boomer who fulfills his childhood dream, buying a Mustang convertible just like the one he'd admired decades ago in the neighbor's driveway. The hard work of a father and son—a beautifully restored MGB, returned to the road, and enjoyed and shared with other enthusiasts at weekend car shows. These are closer to my own car experiences growing up—much more in touch with learning to drive in a 1933 Ford truck than hanging out with the Bugatti crowd.

And these are exactly the types of stories that keep the hobby alive, stories filled with engaging people; parts suppliers, restoration shops, vintage tire suppliers, platers and upholsterers. There's a whole support system that has grown up over the last sixty years or so, servicing not just the top one percent of the collector car market, but the ninety-nine percent that most of us occupy.

Within these pages, you'll find stories that are closer to home—but they also provide "news you can use." Stories that show you how you can enjoy the collector car hobby while still paying mortgages, putting kids through school and meeting life's obligations—as well as the secrets of minimizing your outlay for things like maintenance, repairs and insurance while maximizing the fun (driving). This is the good stuff—the nuts and bolts of collector car ownership, seldom divulged in real-life detail as they are here.

All too often, an individual's first foray into the collector car hobby is his or her last. And the stories generally have an element of commonality to them—the wrong car bought without research, sight unseen. Lots of money spent to no good end, frustration and eventual sale at a loss.

There's no reason to learn these lessons the hard way when others have done it for you. Learn from those mistakes, buy the right car and enjoy a thousand sunny afternoon drives. Do what we all do, bookmark Craigslist, eBay Motors and other favorite websites mentioned within the pages of this book and start shooting e-mails back and forth to your collector car friends. You've got cars to buy and enjoy. Welcome to the hobby.

McKeel Hagerty
Hagerty Insurance Agency

EVERYONE'S GOT A HOBBY of one sort or another. Some people collect baseball cards, others like to fish and going to a flea market can be a perfect day for a bargain hunter.

Rob Sass's hobby is buying and selling cool cars at cool prices. And he's probably better at it than nearly anyone else on earth. When he was my Vice-President of New Business Development at Sports Car Market magazine, it seemed like he routinely put in 20-hour days driving the business forward, and the other four were spent scouring eBay Motors, Craigslist, Bringatrailer and every other cars-for-sale website imaginable. When he slept, I'll never know.

I still remember the staff meeting we were having when, like a bloodhound that's suddenly picked up a scent, Rob ran to the window and proclaimed, "1966 Volvo 122 passing by, white with tan, 'for sale' sign—I'll be right back." He bolted to his car, chased down the Volvo, and within a couple of days it was part of the SCM collection of cars.

For Rob, every day offers the opportunity to find a new car, and to sell an old one. He's not picky—a Datsun 240Z with a few needs, or a Maserati Mistral that's only a paint job away from a tidy profit, all fall within his sights. He has an uncanny ability to spot cars that have hidden value, where perhaps grime and neglect have obscured the gem beneath.

I've known Rob for many years, and I am perhaps proudest of the fact that by working for *Sports Car Market*, we helped launch his career as an automotive writer and at the same time allowed him to exit the "billable hour" world of an appellate lawyer that he came from. Make no mistake, Rob was a first-rate attorney, but his heart has always been with old cars. I've watched with pleasure as his writings have appeared in the New York Times and elsewhere.

While Rob tries to make money on his car deals, in the end I think he would be just as happy standing on a corner wearing a sign that said, "Will Sell Cars for Food." More than anyone I know, he gets a genuine pleasure out of being on the hunt; following up a tip by driving 200 miles to buy a decent example of an unloved model, like a Lancia Beta, is Rob's idea of a fun afternoon.

In fact, not long ago I was with Rob at the Bloomington Gold Corvette gathering outside Chicago, and Rob informed me he had found a decent 1978 Corvette nearby listed on Craigslist for only $8,000. He wanted to buy it and then sell it the next day at the convention. The only thing that stopped him was my asking him if he was prepared to drive it to Portland, Oregon, where our offices are, if he didn't find a buyer. It had never occurred to Rob that he wouldn't find a buyer, and in fact I should have let him buy the car.

Rob always manages to find the right car, at the right price, and he always manages to find a buyer. And he's a great guy as well. The stories in this book are just the tip of the iceberg of Rob's hobby, and it continues to evolve every time he boots up his computer.

Keith Martin
Sports Car Market magazine

introduction

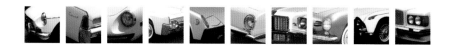

iAM CONTINUALLY AMAZED that so many people see the hobby of car collecting as the exclusive province of the very wealthy—one that is about as accessible to those of modest means as a string of polo ponies or a private jet.

Over the years, I've done my part to dispel this belief, through both words and deeds, commiserating with friends about what just popped up on eBay or extolling the virtues of Craigslist to readers of my pieces in *The New York Times* and *Sports Car Market*. No, I'm not a dealer, just a passionate car guy. I travel to old car events, I write about old cars and I tend to accumulate them the way deranged old ladies hoard cats.

And while it's true that a nine- or ten-figure net worth is a prerequisite if you simply must own a Ferrari Daytona Spider, I bristle at the notion that car collecting isn't just as rewarding for the rest of us. Honestly, to all but the most jaded, a very sexy 1972 Jaguar E-type V12 roadster worth about $45,000 will deliver at least half the enjoyment of the $1.5 million Ferrari. Half the fun at one-thirtieth the cost? I'm no math wizard, but that formula works for me.

I've put together diverse collections of interesting old cars for as little as nine thousand dollars. Don't believe me? Read on and have a look at the very pretty Lancia Beta Zagato Spider, Datsun 240Z and Volvo 1800ES. My total investment in these three vintage cars was about $9,000. They were all bought recently, and none were project cars—all were ready to enjoy with very little work. And, I'm not even a particularly shrewd negotiator, so the prices I paid are more a function of being able to spot a bargain rather than creating one.

For a bit more money, you can own nice examples of some really well-regarded classic cars that people have actually heard of. Ponder this hypothetical collection, all pulled recently from the annals of Craigslist: A 1966 Oldsmobile Toronado with no rust, 86,000 original miles, fresh paint done to a decent standard and a good original interior for $10,500. Want to add a ragtop to the mix? How about a 1984 Porsche 911 Carrera cabriolet—a close friend just sold one via Craigslist with 68,000 two-owner miles and all records for just $18,000. Add one more perhaps? You might consider a 1973 BMW 2002 with a sunroof, fresh paint and a recently rebuilt engine for $8,500—or best offer.

These are all cars that need no explanations and beg no apologies—still found at the price points and condition to provide immediate enjoyment. Each is an indisputable icon that has made countless auto journalists' lists of all-time greats.

For example, the Oldsmobile Toronado is a Bill Mitchell masterpiece and perhaps the last style tour de force to come from GM. It is in my opinion, the Cord 810 of its era and with a 425 hp V8, it's no slouch either; the Porsche 911 is perhaps the best-built and most enjoyable sports car of any era; and the cheeky 2002 put BMW on the map in the U.S.—the inspiration for the term "sport sedan."

Your total investment in this hypothetical collection of *three* incredible cars would have been about the cost of one fully-loaded Toyota Camry. And lest you think that these are finicky impractical toys, any one of the above (with the exception of the 8 mpg Olds) is capable of providing economical, reliable daily transportation in environments where road salt is not used. For that matter, the Porsche with its galvanized body can even stand up to road salt—the Kryptonite of old cars.

And while some maintenance will undoubtedly figure into the equation, unlike the new Camry, none of these cars will depreciate significantly. The Olds and the BMW will probably even appreciate at a modest rate.

This book won't purport to make you an expert on every car covered inside. No book is a substitute for the hands on experience that comes from getting out and looking at hundreds of cars over the course of many years or consulting with a true expert. You will note that I constantly repeat the advice that before you part with any money, have an expert familiar with the marque thoroughly inspect the car. The point of the book is to debunk myths (or, conversely, to give support to assumptions when appropriate), to get you thinking about what's out there, and what works for budget-minded enthusiasts.

The worst thing to do is succumb to the pressure to buy something to satisfy a sense of immediate gratification. It's what magazine publisher and TV commentator Keith Martin calls "the red mist" or "car horniness." It descends when you really want a car and robs you of your faculties and common sense. Take a pass if you're not absolutely comfortable with a car. It's never the last one—something else better nearly always comes along. It always helps to bring a friend along to serve as the voice of reason if something doesn't feel quite right about a car you've always wanted.

Finally, old cars simply aren't for everyone—especially those who can't deal with the occasional breakdown. You really do have to be somewhat sympathetic and in-synch with mechanical things—let the car warm up before zinging it to the redline, keep an ear open for odd noises, be wary of odd smells and keep an eye on your vital gauges. And if something isn't right, shut it down and call a flatbed. The car isn't to blame if you're not paying attention to the temperature gauge when it overheats, then repays your inattentiveness by blowing a head gasket. It's no secret that old cars break occasionally, and it's up to you to mitigate the consequences by taking care of things at the earliest opportunity.

Be smart, keep your wits about you, and learn from your mistakes—and mine, which are abundantly and unashamedly documented here. This is a great and rewarding hobby full of extraordinary cars and fascinating car people—all ready to be your enabler or the voice of reason as the situation requires. As famous collector car auctioneer Dean Kruse is fond of saying: "Buy a car and change your life!"

buying a "right" car

"A car is either a 'right' car or it isn't."

Paul Duchene.

mY FRIEND AND ESTEEMED COLLEAGUE Paul Duchene, the Executive Editor of *Sports Car Market* magazine, has perhaps the simplest classification system of any old car lover I know: According to Paul, a car is either a "right" car or it isn't. Unfortunately, knowing exactly what constitutes a "right" car appears to be the result of years of looking at good and bad cars… tempered with a finely-tuned gut.

Ironically, Paul, an otherwise prolific writer, has never gotten around to quantifying in writing what constitutes automotive "rightness." I'm hoping he'll rectify that omission one fine day. But having looked at a healthy share of old cars both good and bad with him, I'm willing to take a stab at it.

What makes a "right car?"

A right car is an honest car; it's not hiding anything, nor is it trying to be something that it isn't. A well-preserved, unrestored car almost always qualifies as a "right" car, but that doesn't mean that a freshly restored car or even an aging older restoration cannot be.

Wavy or lumpy bodywork immediately disqualifies a car from being a right car. It's the most obvious thing that you can see, and if the owner couldn't get that part right, you can bet that what you can't see is far worse. Always look down the side of a car when it's parked in the shade. Lumps, waves, ripples, bubbles, poor fit of the doors trunk and hood are never a good sign.

Conversely, honest patina on old paint is a good thing. I'd much rather see a few scrapes, dings and chips on original paint or on a nicely mellowed old respray than indifferently applied but shiny new paint covering up heaven knows what.

Most body professionals will tell you that 90 percent of a successful paint job is in the prep work. Good prep work means taking things apart—removing lights, door handles, glass and other trim items before doing body work, guide coating, block sanding, painting and then putting it all back together

afterwards with fresh rubber gaskets. Few things turn me off quicker than overspray on rotten rubber seals. It's one of the most obvious signs of a wrong car.

The engine compartment of a right car will be largely original with a bit of a shine left on the paint on the inner fenders. A little dirty is just fine, honest seepage or minor leaks acceptable. No badly spliced wires, cheap aftermarket air cleaners, rusty shock towers or battery boxes please. If it's restored, it should be restored to the point where it was clear that the engine was out and every firewall accessory was removed with no overspray on the wiring harness, wiper motor or anything else.

Attempts at cutting corners in the engine compartment always announce themselves like a Hawaiian shirt at a black tie event. The infamous "rattle can detail" beloved of "fluff and buff" artists looking to turn a car at a quick profit is a prime example. It's nearly impossible to achieve anything resembling a good result using a can of Krylon—trying to mask the un-maskable, like a wiring harness or brake master cylinder. A right car will rarely be one that has been treated to a poor rattle can detail.

Nothing is more dishonest than an engine compartment that looks like a bomb of flat black paint went off inside it. The *piéce de resistance* is usually a coating of gooey black undercoating on the underside of the hood. Unless it's a car with inner fenders that *came* painted flat black, an all black engine compartment usually indicates that the car has had a very bad color change. Part and parcel of most bad color changes is

Saleproof—an otherwise lovely but color-changed MG Midget nobody wanted.

a trunk also painted flat black or even worse, left the original color along with the door jambs. Few things look worse than a red car with brown door jambs and a brown trunk. Not the sign of a right car.

While successful color changes do exist, doing it right involves stripping the car to a shell, removing doors and glass and painting everything that was painted by the factory in the new color. More often than not, especially in the inexpensive cars covered in this book, a color change is not carried out as described above. It's especially disappointing when a non-factory color is selected. In any event, a color change is a story and generally, buyers of collector cars like to hear as few of them as possible.

A less than perfectly executed color change will always come back to haunt you at resale time, as it did with an otherwise very nice MG Midget I once owned. Changed from white to Damask Red, a very pretty factory color, the engine compartment had been re-painted flat black and there was a little strip of the original white paint on the top of the dash between the edge of the crash pad and the windshield that couldn't be painted without removing the windshield (which the former owner clearly had no desire to do).

Even though the paint job on the Midget was truly excellent (much better than new in fact) and the car showed and drove very well, when I sold it I got about a third less than what I would have if it had been repainted in its original white. Everyone who looked at the car knocked the color change.

Finally, a right car never tries to be something that it isn't. The best example I can think of is the fate of a large number of early Porsche 911s. Early 911s are hot in the collector car market now because so few survived unrusted, uncrashed and unmodified. The vintage touches on the early cars like chrome or polished stainless steel trim, pretty low-back seats and Fuchs alloy wheels with bare (rather than black anodized) aluminum spokes give them some of the charm of the earlier 356.

But when these cars were cheap, they were bought in droves by people who wanted a new Porsche but couldn't afford one. Juvenile buyers tried to "update" the looks of the cars by blacking out chrome trim, adding fender flares, high back seats, phony whale tails and fat low-profile tires with black center wheels. It was a bit like buying an old house and removing all the charming bits like the crystal doorknobs, leaded glass windows and crown molding. You're left with the worst of both worlds—none the charm but all of the problems of an old house. Just in case you were one of those juvenile buyers and you're now feeling embarrassed, join the club. Unfortunately, I did most of the above to a '72 911S when I was in college.

These "updated" cars look awful today and are worth a fraction of a "right" car. Stock unmodified "right" cars are generally the best investments. The same goes for "clones", "tributes" and replicas, few of these cars with stories will increase in value in the long run the way a "right" car will.

Separating the wheat from the chaff
The initial phone call to the seller

The primary purpose of your first phone call to a seller is to determine whether you are going to spend more of your valuable time pursuing the car in question. Start with the basics—the things that are deal killers—and work down. Obvious active rust, a non-professional color change (especially one to a non-factory color) will probably lead to a polite "thank you very much" and crossing that car off your list.

Assuming things sound promising enough to stay on the phone, there are some basic questions you should ask. What are the car's immediate needs? What work has the seller done? ?Are there tools, manuals, receipts and records present? How long the current owner has had the car, whether it's registered in their own name and the condition of the title are all important.

Although several states allow cars beyond a certain age to be sold on a "bill of sale," most states require a title to pass as evidence of ownership. Always insist on seeing a copy of the front and back of the title before parting with a deposit. Most liens against a car will be recorded on the title itself; an empty lien box on the title usually indicates a "clear" title. If you purchase a car that the seller owes money on and you pay the seller directly, and he or she fails to pay the lender, the lender can come after you for the balance owed by the seller.

When there is a lien on the car, it's best to deal with the lender and the seller together. You pay the balance owed directly to the lender and the remainder to the seller. The lender takes care of releasing the lien and letting the DMV know that it's okay to issue a title to you free and clear of their now-satisfied lien.

Before completing a transaction, always make sure the VIN on the title and the car match. Ask to see the seller's ID so you can verify that you are dealing with the person named on the title. If the person is purporting to sell the car on behalf of a deceased person, insist on verifying that he or she is the executor and insist on keeping copies of all relevant affidavits and probate documents.

Finally, salvage titles are not uncommon in the old car world, especially at the price point of most of the cars in this book—it's not always a deal killer. A salvage title simply means that at some point, an insurance company has declared the car a total loss, taken title to the vehicle and sold the remains or the "salvage." When someone purchases and re-registers the car, it gets branded with a "salvage title." Given the cost of parts and repair versus the values of inexpensive collector cars, it happens more often than you would think.

As a general rule, when repairs total around 70 percent of the value of a vehicle, the insurance company will declare it a total loss. For an MGB that was worth $1,200 in the early 1980s, a $750 fender bender would have rendered it a total loss and that car today would likely still carry a salvage title if it was subsequently repaired and put back on the road.

I'm less forgiving of salvage titles with unlikely explanations, those on more valuable cars and those where the salvage notation occurred in the more recent past. For example, an Opel GT that acquired a salvage title twenty years ago is probably okay,, though I would probably run screaming from any Porsche 911 with one. An exception to all of this is when flood rather than collision was the reason for the total loss. I would never touch a car that had once blown its ballast tanks and done its best impression of the U-505. It's always risky business.

Finally, in my experience, most sellers aren't particularly dishonest; rather, they just aren't particularly knowledgeable. Assuming your seller is not the Michelangelo who sculpted the rocker panels out of Bondo, they just may not recognize the tell-tale lumpiness or cracking as a sign that the panel is made out of plastic rather than the preferred ferrous metal. For obvious reasons, I've generally had better luck when the seller is clearly an enthusiast who "gets it" rather than a non-car person.

Inspection

By now, it should be obvious that a hands-on inspection of a prospective purchase is a must. Spend the $400 to fly in and have a look—or, if this isn't possible, there are resources such as Buyer's Services, LLC (www.automobileinspections.com). For a modest fee, they'll send a qualified inspector to drive, photo-graph and note and any issues with the car. For a more expensive car, a USPAP (Uniform Standards of

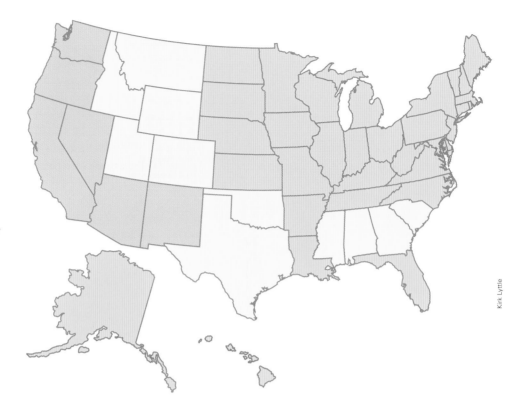

A simple guide to the automotive rust belt. Although West Texas is quite dry, the state as a whole gets a yellow for caution thanks to the salty, humid Gulf Coast. Ditto for Louisiana and Florida, which earn reds for their humid coastlines. Colorado, Utah, Idaho, Montana and Wyoming, while snowy, tend to use sand and gravel rather than salt and have low humidity in the summer.

Kirk Lyttle

Professional Appraisal Practice) compliant appraiser will travel to the car (for expenses and a daily rate) and give you a detailed report is a good option. Dave Kinney and Donald Osborne who helped on the values in this book are among two of the better-known high-end appraisers. If this isn't feasible, car club members are often willing to help.

With inspections, it helps to understand that few appraisers can perform a mechanical inspection and few mechanics are qualified to judge the quality of bodywork. And while it may seem unnecessarily complicated, in addition to having a qualified person eyeball the general condition of the car and body, a thorough pre-purchase inspection by a mechanic familiar with the marque is important as well. A $100 spent this way has saved me thousands. This is not a lesson you want to learn the hard way.

Common sense should always be your guide. The above is particularly sound advice when looking at a Porsche, BMW or Mercedes with a $20,000 or better price tag. The downside of choosing poorly here is potentially large—a Porsche 911 with a head stud issue will immediately set you back $6,000 or more. But for something like a $4,500 Triumph Spitfire, you may be perfectly fine paying a knowledgeable local Triumph club member $50 to give you his or her opinion of the car.

Where the right cars live

Until quite recently, the science of rust prevention was largely unknown. Back in the day, even high-quality cars like Porsches and Mercedes-Benzes would rust as badly as a common VW. Salt is Kryptonite to old cars. Whether it's in the air or spread on the road in the wintertime, salt makes automobile bodies dissolve. You will *always* regret buying a rusty car. In addition to the obvious tetanus risk, cars with severe rust or poorly repaired rust are unsafe, difficult and costly to put right and will almost always be worth less when you sell them.

In general, the best preserved cars come from dry areas away from the salt air of the coast and where road salt isn't used in the winter. Places like Arizona, Nevada, New Mexico, West Texas and inland California are chock full of solid, largely rust-free old cars. Much of Utah, Eastern Washington and Eastern Oregon is quite arid as well.

Surprisingly, cars from Seattle and Portland are often very good too. Although winters are wet there, it snows infrequently, and road salt isn't used. Water alone (unless it gets inside the car and saturates carpeting and floors long-term) seldom does much damage. One more red flag: Be careful with Florida and coastal Southern cars. Although it doesn't snow, the humid, salty air can eventually dissolve sheet metal just like road salt.

The Midwest and East Coast are generally very tough on cars. Salt is the state mineral of Michigan and Illinois, and I've seen some hideous Missouri rust buckets in my hometown of St. Louis. This isn't to say that the East Coast, South and Midwest don't have solid unrusted cars; they simply aren't as common as they are out west. Most of the rust-free cars in the Midwest and Northeast invariably either lived somewhere else or were stored in the winter. The same goes for Canada.

You should scrutinize a car from the Midwest, the East Coast or Canada carefully—not just for active rust but for bad repairs, especially in a car with mileage high enough to indicate that it probably was not stored during the winter.

How to find a right car

Of course, you can still find cars the old-fashioned way, in print in places like *Hemmings Motor News* and in newspaper classifieds, but the Internet is the key to tapping into the national market in a timely fashion. There are numerous small sites that advertise collector cars, but most of the time (especially when I'm searching for an oddball car) I tend to go back to the majors: eBay Motors, Hemmings online, AutoTrader Classics and Craigslist. BringATrailer.com, a newcomer that posts interesting ads and combines them with user-generated comments, is also great fun.

Unlike the other websites, the editors of BringATrailer.com scour listings from all over the Web and choose their favorites of what's fresh in the market, adding well-written and intelligent commentary on the ads. There are also user generated comments that can be quite insightful and useful. While there are far fewer listings than on other websites, what's there is always interesting.

A complete review of the nuances of eBay Motors is well beyond the scope of this book and in fact, several good books have been devoted solely to the topic of buying on eBay. Suffice it to say, it's the single largest marketplace for collector cars on the planet—eBay Motors lists over 10,000 collector cars each week. If you look long enough, eventually it—whatever "it" is—will turn up on eBay. And if you're a fan of oddball makes, you shouldn't skip the "Other Makes" category, the North African souk of eBay Motors.

Several years ago, my friends on the West Coast started talking about Craigslist, a no-frills Internet take on the old "*Trading Times*" local classified paper. What started in 1995 as one man's email list of San Francisco events has morphed into a worldwide unlimited resource for all life's necessities: jobs, housing, dating, and for our purposes, cars. As of this writing, Craigslist has a presence in 50 countries and counting. If you live in or near a city of reasonable size, you probably have your own Craigslist. It's free, the listing process is simpler than eBay and the locally oriented ads are less anxiety-inducing than the potentially far-away cars and auction format of eBay.

The main downside of Craigslist is that it's a decidedly local resource—in fact, the site actually discourages sellers from dealing with non-local buyers. Some sellers heed the advice and won't deal with out-of-towners, but most will. Because of Craigslist's "locals only" philosophy, there is no way on the site to search more than one city's Craigslist at a time. Consequently, most of my time was spent on the most target-rich cities such as LA, San Francisco, Seattle and Portland.

Necessity being the mother of invention, a number of universal Craigslist search engines have recently popped up, the most effective of which is probably www.zimkiv.com.

These sites allow you to search multiple Craigslist cities at one time, thus making it easier than ever to find that AMC Marlin hiding out in Yreka, California.

Deciphering the ads

There are only so many different permutations and combinations of descriptive verbiage that can be used to create a car ad. Look at enough of them and they all start to look the same. Here's a quick glossary of commonly used phrases and what they actually mean:

Barn Find: Any car that has been in undisturbed, indoor, long-term storage—although not necessarily in a barn. A parking garage, basement, shed or storage lockup will do. Barn finds have a time capsule quality to them that many people find extremely charming, particularly when the cars are full of other period items such as yellowed newspapers and magazines or even ration cards. See also, "Needs Everything."

Black Plate Car: In California and in a few other states, license plates stay with the car when it is sold. So a car that has been continuously registered in California its whole life should have the plates that it was first registered with. Cars registered in the 1960s will have six-digit black plates with yellow characters. Those from the 1970s will have blue plates with yellow characters (six characters in the early part of the decade and seven in the latter part). Original black or blue plates are considered a major selling point.

Diamond in the Rough: Emphasis is always on the "rough" part. See, "Needs a Little TLC."

Needs a Little TLC: See "Needs Everything."

Needs Everything: If a seller is this candid, you can be certain that the paint and chrome as well as every bushing, hose, rubber piece, soft trim item and major mechanical system is well and truly shot. And if you are fortunate enough to be able to entertain a project of this magnitude and certain expense, you might ask yourself why you're reading a book on "affordable" classics.

No Stories Car: No stories means just that, no engine replacements, no color changes, no major accidents, no major rust repair, no gray market or title issues, etc. This is not a term generally used by amateurs, so it's safe to assume that anyone asserting this in their ad is either an experienced collector or a dealer, so be on your guard to ensure that this is actually the case.

Original: This term implies that at the very least, the engine is original to the car, and the finishes and interior are factory applied and installed (see "Survivor"). Yet I constantly see restored cars being advertised as "all original." The term has become so misused and abused as to have lost any meaning. With a few probing questions, you uncover what their definition of original is.

Ran When Parked: Means that the car struggled into a field/alley/steel building/barn/garage ten years ago and then expired. Waking up a car that has been asleep for years is never simple, and it's always more expensive than you think it will be. Anyone who disagrees with this probably believes that one day we will cryogenically freeze a person with a dire disease and successfully wake him up in the future when the disease can be cured with a fifty-cent pill. In reality, the malady that probably got the car parked ten years ago is still expensive, difficult to put right and is now compounded by years of slumber. Prolonged improper storage is about the worst thing that can be done to a car. It is ruinous to fuel systems and hydraulics. More often than not, the long-term layup was caused by either an unavailable or hideously expensive part essential to the operation of the car. Do yourself a favor—let sleeping cars lie.

Smokes a Little: These usually turns out to be chain smokers with a quart-a-day habit. Exhaust smoke is never a good sign, especially for an old Porsche, BMW or Mercedes. It almost always signals some expensive engine work, most likely valve guides or rings.

Surface Rust: This is one of my favorites. Most cars tend to rust from the inside out when moisture, salt and road grim become trapped in boxed sections without adequate drainage. What you see on the surface is invariably worse underneath. True surface rust is generally seen only in very arid climates where the old paint and primer has become so thin that a light coating of rust is able to form on the sheet metal beneath. It's superficial and easily dealt with but the majority of what is described as surface rust is anything but—it's rust from the inside that is now emerging through the surface of the metal.

Survivor®: Unbeknownst to most collectors, "Survivor" is actually a trademarked term of the Bloomington Gold organization which for many years has been certifying the authenticity of Corvettes. In general, a Survivor is an automobile that has been certified by Bloomington Gold to be nicely preserved and mostly unrestored, un-refinished, and unaltered. Much to the chagrin of Bloomington Gold, their trademark is widely abused. The most common misconception is that any car of a certain age is a "survivor"—no matter how altered or compromised it is—simply by virtue of the fact that it hasn't been crushed, rusted or junked.

A note about the ratings used

As you will note throughout, each car profiled is rated on a five star scale (✪✪✪✪✪) on the following attributes: How available parts are, expense of maintenance, investment potential, and how fun they are to drive. These are somewhat subjective ratings, and as a general rule, American and British cars will be less expensive to maintain than German or Italian ones simply because the parts are cheaper. The parts availability ratings are biased toward how easily obtained the essential maintenance items are, but a car that you can't get switches, rubber and glass for readily will certainly get few stars. Nobody likes having to adapt a hardware store switch to substitute for an unavailable wiper switch.

For easy reference, each car is also rated on a price scale that works as follows:

$$$$	$15,000–$25,000 US
$$$	$10,000–$15,000 US
$$	$5,001–$10,000 US
$	$5,000 US and under

Finally, I like effective air conditioning. It's a great thing to have in an old car and is almost essential to use one on a regular basis in many climates. Those cars that had effective A/C available as an option are noted with this symbol: ❄ In general, these will be American cars or Japanese cars. Italians, Germans and British didn't seem to get the hang of effective A/C until quite recently.

 **chapter two**

look rich for cheap

Icons of style made affordable by the miracle

of depreciation, but beware, the purchase price

is often just the entry fee

I T IS AXIOMATIC that those who can afford to maintain used semi-exotics can also afford the newest model (which they'd rather be seen in anyway). Unless and until they reach true collectible status, older semi-exotics languish like last year's Christmas presents, selling at seemingly bargain basement prices.

While it is possible to pick up a "look rich for cheap" bargain and enjoy the once ultra-expensive cars of oil barons and the other "greed is good" types you remember fondly from "Dallas" or "Dynasty" without fiscally imploding, the key to surviving life with these complex and expensive to maintain cars is to be very, very picky about the one you buy.

Why is that Porsche 928 so cheap?
The downward spiral of depreciation

Lenders and car care professionals are fond of saying that "your house and your car are your two biggest investments." I beg to differ with the use of the term "investment" for the latter. Late model cars are not investments, at least not the appreciating kind.

To wit, it is highly unlikely that in ten years, you will be able to buy the $2.5 million starter castle going up down the street from you for $500,000. But, ten years from now, you'll probably be able to pick up the new $85,000 Range Rover currently parked in its eight-car garage for about $15,000. It's the miracle of depreciation.

There's a reason why the values of European luxury and semi-exotic cars take such a huge hit—in general, they age rather expensively. While their body shells may be more rust-resistant than cars of the 1960s and their engines may be capable of over 200,000 miles, cars built in the last 15-30 years are a complex myriad of computers, electronics, accessories, wiring and convenience features.

No breaks when things break

And when these things break, you can bet there will be no breaks when it comes to parts and labor prices on BMWs, Mercedes-Benzes, Porsches and Jaguars. Just ask anyone faced with the prospect of a $2,000 bill to replace a water pump on a 1978 Porsche 928 worth about $5,000.

Porsche 928—a lovely car with potential annual maintenance costs greater than the GDP of several island nations.

It's precisely the reason that these once expensive cars are rapidly disappearing from the roads. They're not rusting, and they're not all getting wrecked—but when something expensive gives out, they become parts cars or a donation to the Kidney Foundation.

This Sword of Damocles, in the form of crippling repair and maintenance costs, is what drives the downward spiral in values for used semi-exotics and luxury cars—and it's why they're so cheap. Buying a high-mileage semi-exotic with no records is like playing Russian roulette with five of six chambers loaded.

Insist on documents, documents and more documents

With any used car, but especially a used semi-exotic, your ultimate goal should be to find the one owned by the anal-retentive airline pilot or obsessive-compulsive engineer who kept every receipt and record. By this I mean not just a few receipts for stuff done by the current owner, you want records going as far back as possible, preferably to the original owner. Documentation like this writes the story that you want to read about your potential purchase.

Paydirt—a binder with all the car's records from new.

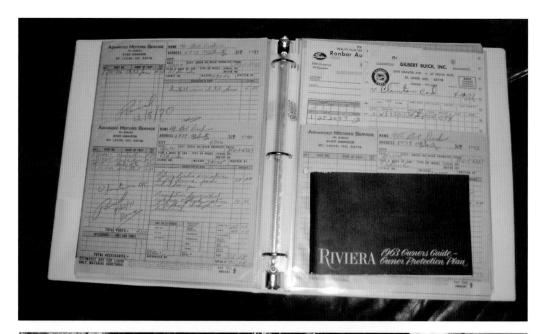

When you find an over-the-top example of a relatively ordinary car like this 1973 Alfa Spider, count your blessings, pay the full asking price (in this case $10,000) and be happy about it. You'll never make a $4,000 example look and drive this nice for $6,000.

This story should be one of an owner (or a few owners at most) who maintained the car at a reputable shop, attended to things as they broke or wore out. Our meticulous owner(s) never seemed to get behind or give up on things or take the car off the road for an extended period of time. Continuous registration and license plates of the proper vintage for the car are evidence of this. Window stickers, warranty booklets and owner's manuals with delivery notations and service stamps are also desirable pieces of a car's history.

After you've found a car like this, be prepared if you must to spend in excess of what the price guides say the car is worth. Nobody ever complains about paying too much for a great car. And if you take away nothing else from this book, remember that paradoxically, the most expensive examples of the affordable classics in this book wind up being the cheapest to own in the long-run.

ran when parked...

BMW coupes

2800CS 1968-71, 3.0CS 1971-75			❄
Parts availability ✪✪✪	**Inexpensive to maintain** ✪	**Investment potential** ✪✪✪	
Fun to drive ✪✪✪✪	**Price category** $$$$	Nice driver, $16,000; Show winner, $38,000	
Performance 0 to 60 in 9.3 seconds; ¼ mile in 17.4 seconds at 82 mph (*Road & Track* 2/70)			

630 CSi 1977-78, 633CSi 1978-84, 635CSi 1985-89, M61987-89			❄
Parts availability ✪✪✪	**Inexpensive to maintain** ✪✪	**Investment potential** ✪ (✪✪M6)	
Fun to drive ✪✪✪ (✪✪✪✪✪M6)	**Price category** $$	Nice driver, $8,500; Show winner, $15,000 (635CSi)	
Performance 0 to 60 in 8.4 seconds; ¼ mile in 16.8 seconds at 84.5 mph (*Road & Track* 9/78)			

Parts Maximillian Imports, www.bmwmobiletradition-online.com; Bimmer Parts, www.bimmerparts.com

Club BMW Car Club of America, www.bmwcca.org

BMW has a long history of producing elegant and attractive sport coupes. Strangely, they got off to a very bumpy start in this segment. In 1966, BMW introduced the 2000 CS styled by the famous Wilhelm Hoffmeister. It was a pillarless coupe with lots of glass and some very pretty details like the C-pillar vent disguised as a BMW roundel. The rear three-quarter view was stunning, but the face was one only a mother could love. Squashed and grille-less (besides the obligatory twin kidneys), it had odd covered headlights that gave it a kind of a blank stare, like a cartoon character out of the Pixar film "Cars."

And for a coupe with sporting pretensions, a 130 hp 2.0 liter four cylinder just wasn't going to cut it against competition from Mercedes-Benz or Jaguar. BMW figured things out in very short order, keeping all that was good (the looks aft of the cowl and the luxurious wood-trimmed interior) and added six inches to the front, a powerful six-cylinder engine and a handsome, aggressive shark-like nose.

The result was one for the ages: known internally as "E9" coupes, the 2800CS and later the 3.0 CS were perennial favorites of all the enthusiast publications. *Road & Track* found its greatest virtues to be "all around balance, fine finish, precision mechanicals and some of the nicest sounds ever to delight an enthusiast's ear." They named it one of the ten best cars in the world. Writing for *Playboy* magazine, respected auto journalist Ken Purdy called it *the* best car on the planet.

The 1971 BMW 2800CS— it's difficult to imagine any design from the Chris Bangle era at BMW looking this good in the year 2040.

The E9 came in several versions, all of which looked visually similar: The 1968-71 2800 CS with 170 hp; the 1971-75 3.0CS 180 hp added 200 ccs and rear disc brakes; the 1971-75 3.0CSi; and the 1971-75 3.0CSL were both fuel injected with 200 hp and sold new only in Europe. The CSL (the "L" stood for "leicht" or "light" in German) added some alloy panels, a front spoiler and a large side stripe. They were the birth of the now-famous "M" cars. The looks of the 1974-75 cars were somewhat spoiled by 5 mph impact bumpers.

Rust, rust and more rust

All E9 coupes suffer from the same basic maladies, the most serious of which is rampant rust. Karmann built the bodies for BMW, and they were grievously rust-prone. With numerous enclosed nooks, spaces and cavities in the final welded unit (none of which Karmann gave any thought to adequately rust-proofing), E9 coupes rust from the inside out. You can be assured that rust you can see is literally the tip of the iceberg—and what's under the surface is ready to rip a fatal gash into the side of your wallet.

Nearly anyplace is fair game for rust on an E9. Serious damage to shock towers, floors and rockers can be terminal. Be wary of even the few bubbles on the lower front fenders and door bottoms that are common on an E9. A seriously rusty BMW coupe should trigger the same flight mechanism in you that a saber tooth tiger triggered in your Cro-Magnon ancestors. Unless you want a parts car, free is too expensive for a rust-bucket.

Buying an E9 coupe that is either wrecked or missing pieces is also generally not a very smart move. While most mechanical bits can be found from various specialists and even BMW Mobile Tradition, body panels, some smaller trim items including grilles, bumpers and some lenses are nearly unobtainable.

From a mechanical standpoint, BMWs are reasonably robust, but when things break, parts are generally not cheap. If E9 coupes have an Achilles heel, it is probably the cylinder head which is prone to warping and cracking when overheated. Consequently, a large number of E9 coupes have had replacement heads or entirely new engines.

Often, engines are replaced with larger units from later cars, like a 3.2 or a 3.5 liter from a 633i or 635i. 5-speed transmission swaps are common too. I suppose there are people who value originality above all else, but I haven't talked to very many people for whom a 3.2 (without EGR and thermal reactors) or a 3.5 liter with a five-speed conversion would be a deal breaker. Any potential E9 purchase should be heavily scrutinized both mechanically and by someone familiar with where the rust hides.

Grand tourers par excellance

As high-speed touring cars, E9 coupes are just sublime with adequate power and a superb exhaust note. I took a 2000 mile road trip in mine, and enjoyed every minute of using the car the way it was designed to be used. The results are evident from the photo, left.

The suspension of a 2800/3.0CS is relatively soft; it soaks up most bumps and road irregularities with aplomb. In spite of the decent ride, E9 coupes corner well enough, and the power steering has a reasonable amount of road feel—although some may find the stock steering wheel way too large. There is some body roll and they can be a bit tricky at the limits, but the car was just wonderful both as a high-speed tourer on the interstates and on the two-lane mountain roads of Wyoming and Idaho.

Later, I drove the car from Portland, Oregon to Monterey for Pebble Beach weekend. Even in that environment of over-the-top automobiles, the CS generated quite a bit of favorable comment and more than a few looks, illustrating that good taste and fine design don't always have to cost a fortune.

The only problems that I had on these trips—which totaled over 3,000 miles—was an A/C evaporator core that frosted up worse than the inside of an old Norge freezer, and a failed oil-pressure relief-switch that caused the car to do its best impression of the Exxon Valdez. It had me stopping every 100 miles to rent a quart of oil. I'm ashamed to admit that I left I-5 between Portland and Monterey looking the way Captain Hazelwood left Prince William Sound.

The market

As collectibles, I've always expected E9 coupes to generate more excitement in the market than they do. They are good performers, very pretty, they have street cred in the form of several European touring car racing championships. And, they were quite desirable when new. To date, they haven't created much buzz. That doesn't mean that they never will, but even in the relatively superheated market that just recently ended, not much happened, at least not openly.

I think the market's relatively cool attitude is the result of several things: First, good examples are quite rare and they don't seem to sell publicly—the really great ones are jealously guarded by club members and trade among the in-crowd. And while I'm sure that a real number one condition 3.0 CS might bring into the fifties (even more for a CSL), it's the marginal to average examples that seem to appear at auction. The mid-twenties is all the money for a good driver quality car, so consequently, that's where the market pegs these cars.

The other problem with the ultimate collectability of the E9 is that they are all coupes. The old adage is, "the price goes up when the top goes down." If BMW had made a factory cabriolet, we might be seeing prices for them similar to the six-figures garnered by a Mercedes 280SE 3.5 cabriolet. But they didn't, so we're not. And that's that.

As an aside though, E9s have no side pillars; with the windows down and the sunroof open, it's a very open and airy car. Consequently, a sunroof is a *very* desirable option on any E9. Air conditioning is both common and desirable as well. Conventional wisdom holds that BMW A/C was ineffective until very recently. However, mine worked just fine even on days approaching 100 degrees.

Colors and years really do make a difference. Collectors seem to prefer the 1971-73 3.0 CS with rear disc brakes to the 2800 CS with its rear drums. Less favored is the U.S. version of the 1974-75 3.0 CS with its bulky 5 mph impact bumpers.

Polaris Silver and Fjord Blue with navy leather and Malaga (a burgundy with a hint of purple) with a tan interior seem to be among the more popular E9 color combinations. Regrettably, both metallic brown and automatic transmissions are quite common in later years. Automatic cars will always be a much tougher sell, and the ZF autobox is also getting tough to find parts for.

In all likelihood, with the exception of the ultra-desirable "Batmobile" CSLs—a discussion of which is beyond the scope of a book on affordable classics—E9 coupes will continue to appreciate at a modest rate and the best will always find ready takers among the cognoscenti. Buy a great example of one of the most elegant coupes ever built, simply enjoy it without obsessing about appreciation, and you will likely be quite happy.

E9 coupe summary

If you can find one of the rare truly great examples, pay the price and buy the car. As for the mediocre cars, don't bother. The car might look great from fifteen feet, but it will nickel and dime you to death. Once the rust process starts, it's an inexorable march to some very expensive sheet metal work.

Enter the 6-series

By the mid-seventies, elegant as it was, the E9 was getting decidedly long in the tooth. BMW was engaged in a wholesale redesign of its line with the 3.0S and Bavaria sedans that the coupes shared so much with being replaced by the 5-series and 7-series sedans.

Much of what was outstanding was retained in the E9's replacement, which was sold in the U.S. as the 630CSi, 633CSi, L6, M6 and 635CSi.

Paul Bracq designed the second generation of modern BMW coupes, popularly referred to as the 6-series and known internally as "E24." Although not as finely detailed or elegant as the E9 coupes, the "sixer" was handsome nonetheless, and very desirable in its day.

Most of the design elements that BMW was known for (prior to Chris Bangle doing for BMW's styling department what the Luftwaffe did for Coventry) were present in the E24. Ample overhangs, a relatively tall, airy greenhouse and a low, aggressive and steeply-angled nose with four round headlights.

Unfortunately, the interior style of the day dictated lots of inelegant black plastic, sharp angles, warning lights for everything, and little of the tasteful use of wood trim found in the E9 coupes. Still, the new car was a quantum leap in terms of comfort, ventilation and crashworthiness. The European version of the car was just sublime—the U.S. version, not so much—at first.

In regard to style innovation, the mid to late 1970s were trying times for just about every industry. Fashion had the leisure suit, music had disco, and the best that the novelty industry could come up with was the pet rock. The creative visionaries who came up with the lava lamp were missing in action having no doubt spent their bonanza on a lot of Northern California sensimilla. The auto industry was hit especially hard. U.S. emission regulations played havoc with every manufacturer, including BMW, whose solution to a clean tailpipe was uncharacteristically clumsy.

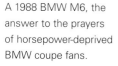

A 1988 BMW M6, the answer to the prayers of horsepower-deprived BMW coupe fans.

Writer Mike Miller described it best in his blog: "What happened to U.S.-spec E24 engines was just a sin. American emissions laws mandated use of a positively horrible exhaust-gas recirculation (EGR) system, incorporating an air-injection system component that was akin to bolting a two-by-four board across the cylinder head exhaust ports. High-compression pistons were out of the question, and, in fact, low compression was the order of the day, due not only to the EGR system but also to the demise of serious high-octane gasoline—this was way before the knock-sensing ignition emerged to save the day for compression ratios. The result was that horsepower and torque nosedived. Due to the thermal reactor exhaust manifolds, cylinder-head warpage problems in the E24's M30 engine appeared almost instantly in the heat of American summers."

For these reasons, stock 1977-79 630s and 633s are best avoided like a French public restroom. Sure, there are some running around that have been de-smogged, but with the emission laws of some states now requiring even cars this old to pass smog exams, it's just not worth it. Mercifully, most of these examples from BMW's darkest days in the U.S. have simply rotted away.

1980 finally brought the miracle of the Bosch oxygen-sensor and catalytic-converter which allowed BMW to finally dispense with the reviled thermal reactors and EGR. Around the same time, leather and A/C became standard in the 6-series, but in practice, I have rarely seen one without both options.

Bosch continued to improve electronic fuel-injection technology by replacing the L and K-Jetronic systems with the fully computerized Motronic system in 1983. The Motronic box controlled not just the mixture but timing as well. The only disadvantage to the early Motronic systems is they cannot be chipped like the later units for additional horsepower. A Getrag 5-speed was also finally added just before the 633CSi became the 635CSi in 1985.

The 635CSi is undoubtedly the best of the normal 6-series. Most cars you see still on the road are 635s. The L6 of 1987 was simply a more option-laden version of the normal 635. The most notable added luxury was the full leather interior. Like similarly equipped Porsche 911s, the leather tends to perish on surfaces that get a lot of sun—like dashboards. An L6 owner who did not routinely care for the leather or purchase a dash cover was soon faced with a dried, shrunken mess.

One caveat involves the ill-fated experiment with Michelin TRX tires. A TRX equipped car has wheels sized in millimeters rather than in the traditional inches. So, rather than a fourteen or a fifteen inch wheel, you got a 390mm wheel. The upshot is that only 390mm Michelin TRX tires will fit on TRX wheels. TRX tires are scarce, expensive and several generations behind modern tire technology. The only practical solution is to dump them in favor of a set of fourteen, fifteen or sixteen-inch alloys.

U.S. enthusiasts finally got a taste of what Europeans enjoyed when BMW at last tired of its new role as "the ultimate fashion accessory." The 1988 M6 was the answer to real Bimmerphiles' prayers. Available only with a manual transmission, its 256 hp six was only 30 hp shy of the Euro model. Although it doesn't seem like much today (a base 3-series will make almost as much horesepower) it was a revelation in 1988. While irrelevant to country club wives and gold chain wearers, the M6 (along with the new M3 and M5) brought credibility back to BMW after a series of successively softer new models.

By the end of the E24's run in 1989, the car had become fully sorted and not prone to any particular failures such as the head-warping of the earlier cars. Even BMW rust-proofing had improved considerably. Nevertheless, these are complicated cars with numerous power accessories. Motronic boxes do fail occasionally, and can be somewhat expensive to replace, but it's not a frequent occurrence even in high-mileage cars. The same goes for Bosch ABS systems with its sensors and large pump.

Electronics can become especially troublesome with age. Wiring, instrument clusters, blower motors and power window motors all eventually fail and just getting to them can be expensive and time consuming to say nothing of the part cost and availability. The key here is to be very particular, pay up and buy the best low-mileage example on the market.

The market

The good news is that even the best E24 coupes (M6s excluded) are not expensive. They still inhabit the nether region between used car and collectible. Since they were built for over a decade and in large numbers, it is doubtful that they will see serious appreciation any time soon.

Case in point, the outstanding '87 635 I looked at in 2006. A friend found it listed on eBay Motors, saw it was in my hometown and asked me to have a look. It showed only 68,000 miles, and every tenth of that was documented by its only owner, an anal retentive, retired TWA pilot. I'm not exaggerating. Every fill up, oil change and service item was documented. The owner's manual showed dealer service stamps up to the 60,000 mile service.

The factory applied white paint was nearly flawless; the oxblood leather interior showed just the slightest wear on the driver's seat bolster. I was on the phone to my friend advising him to buy the car when another savvy eBayer hit the $8,500 "Buy it Now."

It seemed like an utter giveaway—a big, elegant BMW coupe for the price of a used Kia Rio. Just accept the fact that the purchase price is merely the cost of admission. Maintenance costs even for an excellent car are likely to be rather steep.

Case study

1971 BWM 2800CS		
Purchase Price $11,000	**Sale Price** $13,000	**Owned for** 1.5 years

Golden spike be damned, E9 coupe is a better way to cross the plains than the transcontinental railroad.

I did nearly everything wrong with this car. I'd wanted a BMW E9 coupe in either Polaris Silver or Fjord Blue (a very pretty light metallic blue) ever since I went on a test drive in one with my dad when I was eight. Finding even a half-decent one isn't easy.

This one had all the signs of a questionable car and few of the signs of a "right" car: First of all, it was an unofficial "gray market" import, as evidenced by the speedometer with typeface that didn't quite match the other gauges (it had been converted from a KPH unit) and the added DOT side marker lights. It was also a color change (it started life an orangish-yellow color called "Colorado") it had some rust and it came with no records beyond a blue California license plate and California title.

As a rule, I don't like gray market cars for several reasons: First, because of the rust issue: They salt the roads in Europe. Other than Spain or Southern Italy, the climates are generally harsh, and salt air often isn't far away. Also, Euro cars tend to lack nice amenities like A/C and leather.

Color changes also bother me because really cool period colors get lost forever. Often, the change is to an incorrect color and the old color almost always manages to show up in the door jambs, trunk or engine compartment. Quite nasty.

ran when parked...

My car had A/C, but no sunroof, and a black vinyl interior. Somewhere after the original orange but before the silver, it had been light blue. Nevertheless, at around the late Cretaceous level in the paint strata, the orange paint showed up in a few annoying spots. But if this coupe wasn't "Mr. Right", it was "Mr. Right Now"—it was very much for sale when few others were on the market. I let the red mist and general car horniness get the best of me.

I kept it for about a year and a half and wound up footing the bill for all of the deferred maintenance—a water pump, alternator, brakes, new carburetors, tires, a front end, power window motors, etc. When the throw out bearing started making noise, I replaced the clutch and called it a day. It was one of the few cars I lost money on. I purchased it for $11,000, put about $4,000 in it and sold it for $13,000.

Lessons learned? Old BMWs are complicated cars with accessories like power windows, power steering and A/C not found in old British cars. Not to mention the normal replacement items like water pumps, fan clutches, alternators, etc. All this stuff eventually breaks, and it's not cheap to put right—the way it generally is with an American car. In the absence of records, you can assume that none of this stuff has been done. I would have been far better off paying more and holding out for a better car with extensive records.

Bentley

Turbo R 1989-97		❄
Parts availability ✪✪½	**Inexpensive to maintain**	**Investment potential** ✪✪
Fun to drive ✪✪✪✪	**Price category** $$$$	Nice driver, $35,000; Show winner, $50,000
Performance 0 to 60 in 6.8 seconds; ¼ mile in 16.3 seconds at 91 mph		

Parts Flying Spares, www.flyingspares.com
Club Bentley Driver's Club, www.bdcl.org; Rolls-Royce Owners Club, www.rroc.org

I wrestled with including the Turbo R in a book on affordable classics, because more than any other car in this book, the Turbo R has the ability to inflict fiscal ruin upon its owner. Not just a shocking bill or two, but real Old Testament wrath of God stuff that makes the ten plagues of Egypt look like a mild case of heat rash. Still, the Turbo R is such a special car, and owning one can be extremely rewarding—but only if one is extremely careful about the example purchased.

By the 1980s, Rolls-Royce finally sensed that there was a market for a Bentley that was more than just a badge-engineered version of its own cars. The Mulsanne Turbo was their first stab at trying to reclaim some

Turbo R is almost too imposing to function.

Left: Wool rugs, fine wood and Connolly leather with contrasting piping. All very nice. Right: Turbo R components are complex and inaccessible. This book should charge you $100 just for looking at the photo; your mechanic certainly would.

of Bentley's 1930s-1950s glory. The Mulsanne was based on the Silver Spirit body which was itself based on the platform of the earlier Silver Shadow. There was obviously nothing sporting about it—including the 6.75 liter V8.

Turbocharging did wonders for the under-stressed Rolls V8, and although power output was always quoted simply as "adequate," most magazines reckoned the car to have somewhere around 275 to 300 hp. The Turbo R was an improvement over the Mulsanne in nearly every area (except, perhaps, the name). Bosch Motronic injection added more torque and horsepower. The suspension was upgraded with increased anti-roll bar rates front and rear, the addition of a Panhard rod, stiffer shock absorbers and wider wheels and tires. Changes were few and limited to a new four-speed automatic transmission and improved fuel-injection in 1995.

At nearly 5,000 pounds, the Turbo R was anything but nimble. *Hagerty's Cars That Matter* price guide publisher and Turbo R owner Dave Kinney calls the car "athletic in the way that William 'The Refrigerator' Perry was athletic." The Turbo R also pegs the swagger meter—Kinney has watched valets move late model S-Class Mercedes-Benzes to make room for his Turbo R. According to Kinney, the feeling of absolute security in nearly every driving condition is something that few modern cars can even approach.

Some have speculated that it took hundreds of hours more for the skilled work force at Crewe to assemble a Turbo R than it does to put together a new Continental GT. Paintwork, body gaps, interior fit and stitching and woodwork were as fine as anything ever done in the automotive world; any example you consider should be up to factory spec in all of these areas.

Of course, all of this comes at a steep cost. The price you pay for the car is just the entry fee. Buy a cheap and nasty Turbo R and you might as well have the seller throw in Alvin the deep sea submersible, you will be that far under water. Things like re-bushing the suspension at $1,000 or brake rotors at $600 each are just the tip of the iceberg. Because of tight access, servicing anything under the hood is a time consuming nightmare.

Common areas to scrutinize are, of course, body rust in the sills, around door locks and lights. Hydraulics can also be a problem; rear suspension spheres can leak and go stiff. Only approved mineral-based fluid can be used in the hydraulic system. Using the wrong fluid will have dire consequences, as will not doing a fluid change every two years and a major service every eight years. Turbo, power steering pump, differential, brake disks and calipers, central locking and window and HVAC controls are expensive to deal with as well.

Assuming that none of the foregoing has scared you into a Triumph Spitfire, it cannot be overemphasized that the only Turbo R to consider is one like the example owned by Dave Kinney. Kinney's Turbo R was owned by the notoriously disagreeable wife of the dealer. In an effort to keep their interactions to a minimum, the service department kept on top of everything from the flying "B" emblem to the exhaust tip. Everything was documented. Buying a car with service records that are the size of the Dubuque, Iowa phone book as opposed to the Los Angeles one would be very foolish indeed.

The market

Turbo Rs have still not made the leap from interesting used car to collectible. And if you subscribe to the common notion that a car is not truly considered collectible until its value exceeds its original price, perhaps it never will. Still, the Turbo R is about at the bottom of its depreciation curve. It is unlikely that nice examples will get much cheaper.

The likelihood of owning a Turbo R for a long period of time without spending significant sums of money in upkeep is slim. Even the purchase of a right car will not absolve you shelling out large sums of cash from time to time.

In summary, Turbo R ownership will entail paying top dollar for a great example, spending additional money for upkeep, and selling the car at a hopefully small loss when it's time to move on. Because the Turbo R market isn't going anywhere any time soon, there is truly no upside to be found here, only a mitigation of the downside by buying the best example possible and crossing your fingers

Porsche

911SC/Carrera 1978-83, 911SC/Carrera 1984-89		❄
Parts availability ✪✪✪✪✪	Inexpensive to maintain ✪✪½	Investment potential ✪✪
Fun to drive ✪✪✪✪✪	Price category $$$	Nice driver, $15,000; Show winner, $25,000
Performance 0 to 60 in 6.3 seconds; ¼ mile in 15.3 seconds at 94 mph (*Road & Track* 4/78)		

Parts: Stoddard Porsche, www.stoddard.com; Pelican Parts, www.pelicanparts.com

Club: Porsche Club of America, www.pca.org

Paul Duchene

Paul Duchene

Left: A classic Guards Red 1978 911SC coupe. Right: Coupe is the prettiest of 911 body styles.

If you are predisposed to dislike air-cooled Porsches (like stock car legend Richard Petty, who once called them "ass-engined Nazi slot-cars"), skip this section. Any semblance of jaundice or objectivity goes out the window in it—quite simply, the Porsche 911 is one of the five cars you will meet in sports car heaven. If you can own just one car in the book, the 911SC or 3.2 liter Carrera should be it. Period. There, I've said it.

It isn't just the steering, perfectly weighted with just the right amount of feedback, or the Hand-of-God brakes, the flat-six howl and the Tiger tank solid structure. These are nearly indestructible, heirloom quality cars that are simple and very reliable. Like the famous Patek Philippe watch ad, you don't own a 911, you simply look after it for the next generation. With care, it should outlive you.

Early 911s—fragile rust buckets

It wasn't always that way. The first 911s from 1965 were tricky handling, torqueless, fragile rust buckets with some rather serious design flaws. While beguiling in many ways with many vintage touches reminiscent of the 356, these early short wheelbase 911s are an acquired taste, and have gotten quite expensive.

Later long-wheelbase, pre-safety bumper cars built from 1969-73, have also gotten expensive (especially in potent S form) and suffer from rust, finicky carburetors, and mechanical fuel injection.

By 1974, 911s came with Bosch electronic (CIS) fuel injection across the board. Unfortunately emission control from 1975 was via EGR, an air pump and thermal reactors. The latter created the extreme heat that lead to problems with cylinder head studs pulling out from the engine case. Nasty business. To make matters worse, in many states, these cars still have to pass emission tests; removing the smog gear is out of the question. For these reasons, the 1975-77 2.7 liter cars are best avoided. Finally, any pre-1976 911 could rust with the best of them.

The 1990 Carrera 2 and Carrera 4 (964 in Porsche-speak) introduced in 1989 got heavier and more complex, with power steering, optional all wheel-drive, unattractive wheels and front and rear fascias. Early examples of these could be troublesome.

The 1978-89 cars are the Goldilocks 911s—they're just right. Rust had been a Porsche problem almost from the beginning. It was truly ironic that such exquisite and carefully crafted cars would simply dissolve after a few East Coast winters. Porsche research into "lifetime" cars culminated in a zinc galvanizing process that Porsche pioneered. Initially just confined to the pan, by 1976, the entire body shell was galvanized. Rust issues became largely a thing of the past.

The head stud problem mentioned above turns up once in a while in post-1977 cars, although is far less common in the 3.0 liter 911SC and virtually unheard of in the 3.2 liter Carreras. In any event, post-1979 911s which came with a Bosch oxygen sensor and catalyst are probably a better bet simply because the heat of the EGR and thermal reactors isn't present.

By 1980, the 911 was nearly perfected with two relatively minor exceptions: The timing chain tensioners continued to rely on their own internal oil supply to keep them taut. Eventually, the tensioners would collapse with dire consequences for anyone who didn't immediately power down. For $1,000 or so, SC tensioners can be upgraded to oil-fed Carrera chain tensioners. At least a third of the SCs I've looked at have had this done. I would always recommend this modification.

Less potentially ruinous were the plastic air boxes that were part of the intake system. A backfire on startup could crack this $500 part, and possibly damage the throttle body too. A simple toilet seat shaped pop-off valve is the cure. Both of these issues were finally solved with the introduction of the 3.2 liter Carrera in 1984. Other minor issues would persist—alternators go poof every 30,000 miles or so, turn signal switches and fresh-air blowers go out frequently and targa tops eventually leak. Until about 1986, air conditioners were marginal at best.

Arguably, the best years were 1987-89. The slicker-shifting G50 gearbox became standard in 1987, and air conditioning was improved by increasing vent size and fitting a better compressor. Several aftermarket vendors sell A/C upgrade kits for all years that can turn marginal systems into effective ones.

Simplicity, durability, reliability and Tiger tank-like strength

The beauty of the 911 is its simplicity. No radiator, no water pump, no heater core, no power steering pump to go wrong. To be sure, Porsches aren't inexpensive to fix, but the parts aren't Ferrari money and they don't break very often. Buying a well-maintained example will put you way ahead of the curve.

And then there's the durability aspect. The years that are the subject of this section will easily do well over 200,000 miles without attention to the engine or gearbox. Cars still running strong with 250,000 or even 300,000 miles are by no means unusual. These are the Volvo 240 of sports cars.

The safety and strength of the 911 is well-documented. In a famous episode of the BBC show "Top Gear," host Jeremy Clarkson tried to destroy a 911 by various means including crashing it into a brick building at over 30 mph, dropping a grand piano on it, dousing it with acid and setting fire to it. After each insult, the car started and ran just fine and Clarkson (no doubt to the chagrin of his detractors) remained unscathed. The 911 was simply unkillable.

This indestructibility, of course, assumes a modicum of sympathetic maintenance, such as valve adjustments every 15,000 miles and regular 11 quart oil changes. A cylinder leak-down test that shows even compression across the board, accompanied by no odd noises or smoke is usually the sign of a healthy car. The factory paint was high quality and thus, original paint is still often seen even on thirty year-old cars. Purported low mileage cars with fresh paint are an anomaly that should prompt further investigation.

Paul Duchene

Steve Haas

Three different body styles and options galore (most you can live without)

1978-89 911s came in three different body styles: Coupe, Targa (a lift off folding roof center section) and, from 1983, a full convertible or "cabriolet" in Porsche-speak. It's a matter of personal preference, but I consider the Targa to be a compromised design from a style and function standpoint—the roofs can leak both air and water, and the large rollover bar and wrap-around rear window just aren't particularly attractive. Even the car's designer, Butzi Porsche, admitted as much.

A coupe is prettier, quieter and more rigid. Get one with a sunroof and forget the Targa. If you must have an open Porsche, the very pretty 911 cabriolet is the one to own. Just don't be the person who has to replace the top—it can run into thousands.

Popular 911 options included front and rear spoilers, sport seats, full leather interior and 16-inch forged alloy wheels. I'm not really a fan of any of these. A whale-tail rear spoiler to me looks silly on anything but a turbo. Front spoilers seem to get chewed up with regularity, and 16-inch wheels which come with stiffer shocks just seem to degrade the ride quality. The alternative, 15–inch Fuchs or ATS "cookie cutter" alloys in 7- and 8-inch sizes look quite good. Full leather interiors mean leather covered everything—including the dash—I've never seen an old 911 with this option where the leather hasn't shrunk and pulled away from the dash vents. Finally, the standard seats are more than supportive enough. Sport seats are confining and make ingress and egress more difficult.

As mentioned above, a high-mileage 911 is nothing to be afraid of, assuming regular maintenance. I would have no qualms about buying a 150,000+ mile car provided it passes a pre-purchase inspection and a leak down test performed by a 911 expert. The latter is essential along with a careful read of Peter Zimmermann's book, *The Used 911 Story*. The consequences of choosing poorly can be disastrous. Complete engine rebuilds often exceed $15,000.

Cars that give a good initial impression will have no obvious paintwork, no overspray on the weatherstripping and fender welting (the black vinyl piece that fills the seam between the cowl and the top rear of the front fenders) and worn in but not worn out leather interiors. Panel gaps should be even and uniform as they were when new. A right car should start up quickly, idle smoothly (if not always evenly— K-Jetronic 911s do some idle hunting) with no smoke, other than perhaps a puff on startup. Touched up chips on the bumper and front of the hood are expected, with no grille in front, these areas are vulnerable to rock damage.

A full service history with records, owner's manual and tools present are important. Don't forget that the car should include a compressor to fill the space-saver spare. For SCs, updated chain tensioners and an airbox pop-off valve are big pluses. One point should be noted: The mid-1980s were a high point for the value of the U.S. dollar. Consequently, a fair number of "gray market" Euro-spec cars found their way to the States. An added side repeater light on the front fender just behind the wheel well is the giveaway. Since these cars will have to pass smog regulations in many states, make sure that a current smog certificate and/or EPA/DOT releases accompany any gray market car.

Left: There actually is a 3.0 liter flat six under the airbox and a/c compressor and with care, it will likely outlast you.
Right: A 1985 Porsche 911 cabriolet in wonderful colors—so much nicer than a Targa.

Condition and history—the main considerations

Buy solely on condition and ownership history. Color should be a secondary consideration. Be aware though that Guards Red (the bright orange-ish-red pictured) with a black interior is probably the most common color combination. Some people love Guards Red, others think it's a bit cliché. Finally, while it's rare to find a rusty post-1976 911, the heat exchangers can and do rust. Heat exchangers are the ducts that convert engine heat into cabin heat. Badly rusted ones mean no heat and worse, carbon monoxide fumes seeping into the cabin. Budget around $2,000 to replace them with stainless steel parts.

On the road, you can't help but be impressed by the flat-six grunt, the howl it makes at 6,000 rpm and the feeling of quality that the 911 exudes. Doors shut with a click and potholes and speed bumps pass with a muffled "thump." 911s just feel expensive. Recent 911 convert, auto journalist Paul Duchene, freely admitted that before he bought a red '78 coupe, he couldn't understand all the fuss over 911s. "Now I get it. This is really all you need in a car."

Contemporary road tests pegged the SC/Carrera's performance at between 5.9 and 6.7 seconds 0-60 and with a top speed of between 132 and 139 mph. Not particularly fast by today's standards when a Hyundai Tiburon will do at least as well, but at the time, it was A-list performance and even today, it's more than adequate. You can console yourself with the knowledge that long after the Tiburon has become part of the automotive fossil record, your 911 will still be someone's treasured possession.

Left: A later 3.2 liter Carrera interior with power seats and large dash vents.
Right: Self-taught aerodynamics expert Malcolm Sayer designed a shape for the ages.

The market

A 911SC or Carrera is one of the few old cars that really can act as your only car no matter what climate you live in. They're reliable, not particularly thirsty, safe and reasonably straightforward to maintain. With a set of four snow tires, they even do pretty well in bad weather. Best of all, they have reached the bottom of their depreciation curve. This isn't to say that they're going to experience any rapid appreciation soon, there were just too many made and because of their galvanized bodies, the survival rate is quite high. But it's a cinch that they're not going to get much cheaper.

The enthusiast who buys a sound SC or Carrera today will enjoy one of the greatest automobiles ever made, probably have to put little into it and get back most if not all of his or her money when it's time to move on. Old car experiences don't get much better for most of us.

Case study

1983 Porsche 911SC		
Purchase Price $21,000	**Sale Price** $13,000	**Owned for** 6 years

I bought a black 1983 911SC sunroof coupe in 1989, right after I got out of law school. It was the newest car I'd ever owned with just 23,000 miles on the clock. Options included 16-inch forged alloys and Bilstein shocks (which I replaced with 7- and 8 x15-inch Fuchs wheels and softer Konis shocks), front spoiler and full leather. I traded a 1973 ½ 911T plus cash to a dealer. It came with all records from new including the window sticker, tools, manual and warranty book.

In six years and nearly 80,000 miles, I replaced the clutch (it still had the original rubber diaphragm disc when I got it) an oxygen sensor or two and several alternators. I also installed a set of oil-fed Carrera-style chain tensioners, replaced the tires, performed regular oil changes and valve adjustments. That was it. It was an amazingly reliable car and even with over 100,000 miles on it, showed few signs of wear and it was worth over 60 percent of what I paid for it. I missed it the day it left—and nearly every day since.

For once, I did everything right and actually followed my own advice. Since there are always plenty of 911s on the market, I was patient. I held out for one with one owner, all of its records from new and an obviously fastidious Porsche Club owner. I had it examined by a Porsche specialist and the car returned favor by giving faultless service.

You may note that I did lose money on this car which is something I generally try to avoid. The circumstances were a bit different with this car. I bought the 911 as a daily driver back in 1989, before the car had reached the bottom of its depreciation curve, so I paid quite a bit more than I would have today. Great 1983 SCs today generally trade in the $15,000 to $16,000 range.

Lessons learned? Certainly none the hard way. Simply that, from a standpoint of safety, performance, durability, quality and practicality, the 1978-89 Porsche 911 is the best this book (or any other you're likely to read on the topic) has to offer.

Jaguar

E-type Series I & Series II 1961-67 (Series I) 1968-71 (Series II)		
Parts availability ✪✪✪✪✪	**Inexpensive to maintain** ✪✪✪	**Investment potential** ✪✪✪✪
Fun to drive ✪✪✪✪✪	**Price category** $$$$	Nice driver, $38,000; Show winner, $90,000 (Series I coupe)
Performance 0 to 60 in 7.4 seconds, ¼ mile in 15.2 seconds at 94 mph (*Road & Track* 2/70)		

Parts Terry's Jaguar Parts, www.terrysjag.com; XKs Unlimited, www.xks.com; SNG Barratt, www.sngbarratt.com; Moss Motors, www.mossmotors.com; Original Specification Jaguar Interiors, www.osji.com

Club Jaguar Club of North America- www.jcna.com

At first glance, one might quibble with the inclusion of the Jaguar E-type in a book on *affordable* classics. "Affordable for whom?" you might ask. Yes, I'm well aware of the perfect Series I convertibles (OTS or "open two-seater" in Jaguar-speak) that have sold for over $140,000 and coupes have approached $100,000. But these are perfect cars that have had nut-and-bolt restorations that cost nearly as much as the prices these cars fetch.

Great E-types still around for a song

There are still E-types around for under $40,000 (in some cases, well under $40,000) that are by no means ratty or bastardized cars. The most desirable Series I cars are perhaps thin on the ground in that price range and a Series I convertible you'd want to own may be a stretch. But good Series II convertibles, Series I coupes and 2+2s are out there for reasonable prices. They are amazing bargains—to trade up substantially in performance and cachet, you're looking at things like a Ferrari 275 GTS, or a Mercedes-Benz 300SL roadster, both of which cost over a quarter million more.

The most compelling reason for owning an E-type is purely visceral—it is one of the sexiest cars ever. Noted auto journalist Henry N. Manney III called the E "the greatest crumpet catcher known to man." As nearly as I can ascertain, "crumpet" was Manneyese for "hottie", and assuming he was speaking from experience, no one would ever again doubt the E-type's powers in this regard—the bearded, funny hat wearing, pipe-smoking, crooked-toothed scribe was no Cary Grant.

The roadster (OTS) is more collectible but the coupe (FHC) is prettier. Opalescent Silver Blue a particularly lovely color. Plain "Jaguar" badge on the hatch makes this a 3.8 liter car.

History

At this point some E-type history would be appropriate—it's about as straightforward as the rise and fall of the Roman Empire—including its interim division into the Eastern and Western Roman Empires, and subsequent revival, in name only, as the Holy Roman Empire.

The E-type was a direct descendant of the Le Mans winning D-type racer, sharing the XK straight-six, disc brakes and semi-monocoque chassis design, with a stressed "tub" making up the passenger compartment and a square tube subframe supporting the engine and front suspension. The Series I was built from 1961 through 1967. The earlier cars (1961-64) came with 3.8 liter engines rated at 265 hp and a sadistic four-speed Moss gearbox with an unsynchronized first gear. Later (1965-67) cars had a 4.2 liter with a very pleasant all-synchro box. 4.2 liter cars also had more comfortable (but less attractive) seats, and since the engine was now stroked to within an inch of its life, it was less revvy than the 3.8.

Series I cars the Marcia Brady of E-types

The stylistic hallmarks of a Series I car included glass covered headlights, a small oval air inlet or grille, split bumpers front and rear, dainty, small tail-lights above the rear bumper and nifty toggle switches on the dash. These features, plus the triple SU carbs, real horsepower and no emission controls are the reason why the Series I is the prom queen—the Marcia Brady of E-types.

Earlier, I promised confusion—it starts in late 1967. Some late 1967 Series I cars lost their glass headlight covers. New vehicle lighting regulations passed in the U.S. rendered this feature illegal that year. These cars are otherwise standard Series I with toggle switches and triple carbs.

The so-called Series I ½ cars were interim cars produced for the 1968 model year. According to the factory, they're officially Series II cars but they look more like a hybrid of the Series I and II cars, hence the enthusiast's made up Series I ½ designation. They retained the small bumpers, small air inlet and small tail-lights located above the rear bumper, but lost their triple SU carburetors (along with 20 hp) in favor of emission-friendly dual Zenith-Strombergs. The cool fighter-plane toggle switches on the dash were replaced by "safety" rocker switches and a conventional column-mounted key-starter in place of the old starter button on the dash.

Series II cars more user-friendly

The "real" Series II cars started in 1969. They were the Jan Brady of E-types. More practical and less high strung…but just not as attractive. Headlights repositioned further forward with no covers gave the cars a bit of a pop-eyed look. The larger front air inlet, huge front marker lights below the bumper, stouter wrap around bumpers and larger tail-lights below the rear bumper also did nothing for the appearance of the car.

ran when parked...

Above left: Rear bumper guards were dealer accessories that protected the car but did nothing for the looks.
Right: Rather pop-eyed front of a 1970 Series II coupe.
Left: Series I interior with cool fighter plane-like toggle switches.

But all wasn't negative. Brakes, cooling and electrical systems were all improved and power steering and air conditioning became available for the first time. The Series II is a more user-friendly, if slightly less potent and attractive car.

There was of course a Series III car that was built from 1971-74, but it was a very different animal. With a new aluminum V12 and a longer wheelbase, it was quite complex and had an appalling reputation for reliability. Series III Coupes can certainly be inexpensive and with enough expert sorting can be made usable, but a quick look under the hood compared to a Series I or 2 machine should be enough to scare almost anyone back into a six-cylinder car.

Coupe, convertible and 2+2

Body styles were at least straightforward. Initially, the E came as a roadster or a two-seater coupe (in Jag-speak, OTS for "open two-seater" and FHC for "fixed head coupe" respectively). Because the top goes down, the roadsters will always be more valuable, but the coupes are prettier. A third body-style, a long wheelbase 2+2 coupe was added in 1966. Until the Series III, the 2+2 was the only body-style available with an automatic transmission—a guaranteed deal breaker.

The least expensive E-types will generally be 2+2s. They're often derided because of their longer wheelbases and a roofline that looks somewhat ungainly in comparison to the über-graceful two-seater coupe, and a high percentage of them were ordered with lazy three-speed Borg-Warner automatics. E-type snobbery aside, even a 2+2, especially in Series I form, is still a sexy car. And given the choice between a doggy coupe and a nice 2+2, the choice should be to go with the better car, unless it's an automatic.

Not as unreliable as you've been led to believe

Primarily based on the ghastly reputation of the Series III cars, all E-types are viewed as rather unreliable cars with some misguided owners even going so far as to replace the brilliant and nearly unbreakable XK six with an American small block V8. In fact, the six-cylinder Series I and Series II cars are not particularly troublesome. An up-rated alternator, modern solid-state fuel pump, electronic ignition, wiring in good condition and a cooling system in top shape generally take care of problem areas.

Also pleasantly surprising is the fact that E-type parts are both readily available and for the most part relatively inexpensive—certainly more like TR6 parts than Porsche parts in price. The main difference from a parts standpoint between a TR6 and an E is the fact that there are simply more of them in an E-type—three carbs to rebuild instead of two, six shocks instead of four, four calipers instead of two, etc.

If there's a difference in upkeep expense, it's primarily because of the greater complexity of the Jag. The clutch and rear brakes illustrate this point—replacing a clutch on an E is about as pleasant as replacing a propeller on the QE2. Although a dry dock isn't involved, it might as well be. The huge bonnet has to come off and the engine and transmission need to come out. There is no way around this. Rear brakes aren't particularly fun either, because they live inboard next to the differential. To do the job properly, the entire cradle that holds the rear suspension must be removed.

Most Series I and II E-type problems arise either poor owner modifications, or lack of use. The most reliable E-types are the ones that are used regularly. Cars that sit wind up with gummed-up fuel systems, clutch and brake pedals with no pressure and flat batteries. Use the car and don't let a mostly undeserved reputation for trouble stand in the way of E-type ownership.

What you should steer clear of are rusty cars. E-types are rusters of the highest order. Sills (inner and outer), floors, rear fender wheel arches, boot floors and rear suspension mounting points are all fair game and all are stressed parts of the monocoque structure. Bad rust repair with poor metal work and excessive use of plastic filler is not uncommon, as are ill-fitting opening panels and bonnets. Again, there is no substitute for an expert's opinion of a prospective purchase.

Replacement engines, cylinder heads and transmissions are not uncommon and as long as they're not the aforementioned small-block Fords, it's generally okay. Since one XK six was pretty much like the next, I'm not sure I understand the obsession with a matching numbers E-type. And in fact, a 3.8 liter car with a later all-synchro box is a nice combination. Be aware though, that collectors are starting to care about E-types with matching numbers; non-matching number cars do trade at a discount.

Poor color changes are common with colors like pale primrose yellow, sable brown and willow green (think split pea soup) falling out of favor by the 1980s. A red car with black subframe tubes almost certainly started out one of these colors. Many cars were done this way in "resale red" to cash in on the first wave of E-type appreciation in the mid-1980s. Cars like this are best avoided because poor quality resprays are almost always the tip of the corner-cutting iceberg. A certificate from the Jaguar-Daimler Heritage Trust can confirm any E-type's original color scheme.

E-types go as well as they look

Like the scandalously infrequent discussions of Marilyn Monroe's rumored 160-plus IQ, few people talk about how E-types actually drive. For the record, they're really quite entertaining. While the 265-rated horsepower was measured in gross rather than today's net system and optimistic at that (I've heard 200 is nearer to the truth), the E-type was compact and relatively light car. So the power to weight ratio was quite good, although the famed 150 mph top speed was actually attained by a specially prepared works car and not repeated by any contemporary magazine.

Advertised 150 mph top speed was optimistic

Contemporary tests pegged the 0-60 time at anywhere from 6.7 to 7.4 seconds, with the quarter-mile coming up in about 15 seconds—quite respectable, and generally a match for a small-block Stingray. Where the Jag would pull away, even from a big-block car, was in the top end. The slippery shape, courtesy of aerodynamicist Malcolm Sayer, was responsible for its 140-plus mph performance.

The E-type's ride is quite good, and under most conditions the handling isn't bad—light and responsive rack-and-pinion steering make the car easy to place in corners. Things are less wonderful at 9/10, where the limitations of skinny tires and the less-than-rigid rear suspension attachment points make themselves apparent. But other than perhaps hooligans like Jeremy Clarkson, nobody really pushes an E-type that hard.

But E-types were built to a price. While they looked and performed like Astons and Ferraris, they were priced like a loaded Corvette. Those who expect vault-like solidity and careful construction will be disappointed. It's not an issue of age or improper restoration, the cars just weren't very tight when they were new.

The heart of a Series I E-type, the Le Mans winning XK six—accept no small-block V8 substitutes. Sir William Lyons was directly responsible for the lovely presentation of the engine compartment. His philosophy—it costs no more to make it pretty.

Road & Track said back in 1967 that "the body of our test car was so full of rattles and squeaks that it almost made us laugh."

Recently, the market has been all over the place on E-types. The best Series I convertibles are stable at $125,000 to $140,000, but the lesser cars (like mine) took about a 15- to 20 percent hit in the wake of the subprime mortgage market meltdown, stock market dump and the ensuing recession in late 2008. For those with liquidity, the opportunity now exists to find a sound but slightly scruffy car at a bargain price that can be improved significantly without spending a fortune.

The hierarchy of desirability is a bit subjective but few would argue that the S1 convertible is at the top of the heap. Don't worry about "flat floors" and "outside bonnet-latches" (some of the features that set very early production cars apart), they're curiosities for hardcore E-type weenies—and people who find double stamped pennies and upside down airplane postage stamps fascinating.

After the S1 convertible, I'd have to give a slight advantage to the S1 coupe over the S2 convertible. Next would probably be the S1 2+2 (with manual transmission) then the S2 two-seater coupe followed by the S2 2+2. An automatic is a deal-breaker.

Case study

1967 Jaguar E-type Series I OTS		
Purchase Price $28,000	**Sale Price** N/A (still owned)	**Owned for** 1.5 years

My slightly tatty E-type roadster looks good in a certain light. Of course, as Dudley Moore said in the movie *Arthur*, "the problem is, you can't always depend on that light."

This car is yet another example of me failing to follow my own advice. I'd be hard pressed to call it a "right" car. It's a color change and it has a bit more plastic in the sills and wheel arches than I'd like. Nevertheless, it is at least partially redeemed by the fact that it is mechanically quite good and dammit, I've always wanted an S1 convertible, and this one fit my budget.

The E came into my life as the result of a trade with a local dealer. A Daimler SP250 (an angry catfish-faced V8-powered British sports car, see page 140) I'd restored and was into for about $16,000, plus $12,000 in cash to the dealer. The E sported a 25-year-old paint job replete with dings and scratches, but on the plus side, it had a nice new interior and top, a new exhaust system and a very expensive aluminum radiator. Everything electrical worked and the car ran tremendously well.

My biggest fear on purchasing the car was that my enjoyment of it would be short-lived—spoiled by constant breakdowns and maintenance headaches. No matter, my Plan B was to remove the large window in the front of my house and park the lovely thing on the Oriental rug in my living room.

This would seem the logical point to insert an exciting story about how I saved the car from self-immolation by putting out a dash fire with a spit soaked rag, or that by using sheer skill and quick handbrake reflexes, I narrowly avoided mowing down my neighbor's Shitzapoo after the brakes failed, or boast about being named godfather to my flatbed driver's kid.

Alas, I have none of these bad E-type stories—the car has proven to be as reliable as a Camry (or at least a twenty year-old Camry with 150,000 miles on it). If you simply must have a well-told tale of British car woe, choose your favorite Peter Egan story and insert it here.

Other than the usual oil leaks, suspect hydraulics resulting in alternating flaccid brake and clutch pedals, and one rebuilt alternator, very little has gone wrong with the Jag. It always starts, and has never stranded me. I'm convinced that its reliability is the result of the fact that it's used quite often. Since it's just a tatty driver, I have no qualms about taking it to the local Trader Joe's and Home Depot. It's always fun to see the reaction of people when you use an old sports car as… well… a car. Like the time when I casually stuffed a long fence post into the car with the top down.

Finally, the car does not hibernate for the winter. A happy by-product of global warming is a nearly year-round sports car season in the lower Midwestern United States. It doesn't snow as much as it did years ago, and consequently, there is less road salt around, and an occasional sixty-degree day in the dead of winter isn't uncommon. As long as it's far enough above freezing that the oil isn't coagulating in the pan and there's no salt on the road, I'll probably use the car. And this gets me to a rather important point: There is nothing worse for an old car than sitting. Fuel goes stale, seals dry out, batteries go flat, mice chew wires, etc. Drive your old cars as often as possible. You'll be far better off.

My eventual plans for the car have been rather upset by economic downturn and its affect on the low-end of the collector car market. I had planned to keep the car indefinitely, perhaps sprucing up the body one winter. The idea was to give it fresh paint to last fifteen years or so, by which time, personal finances and the market would support doing the big $100,000 resto, allowing me to return the car to its original color scheme of Golden Sand and red. Now it seems that selling the car for roughly what I have in it and trading up to a nicer car at the early 2009 reduced price might not be a bad idea. By the time this is published, the E will likely have been replaced by a nicer example.

Alfa Romeo

Spider 1991-94		
Parts availability ✪✪✪	Inexpensive to maintain ✪✪✪	Investment potential ✪✪½
Fun to drive ✪✪✪	Price category **$$$**	Nice driver, $15,000; Show winner, $20,000
Performance 0 to 60 in 9.5 seconds; ¼ mile in 16.8 seconds at 84 mph		

Parts Centerline Alfa Parts, www.centerlinealfa.com; AR Ricambi, www.arricambi.com

Club Alfa Romeo Owners Club, www.aroc-usa.org

Last series of classic Alfa Spider with pretty aftermarket Panasport wheels.

History

By 1991, the Alfa Romeo Spider was making Dick Clark look like a newcomer, the Broadway show *Cats* a mere flash in the pan and Joe Montana a green rookie. Introduced as the 1600 cc Duetto in 1966, just in time for Mike Nichols to choose a red one as the graduation present for a callow Benjamin Braddock in *The Graduate*. The last Spiders were sold in the U.S. as 1994 model year "Commemorative Edition" cars. Want to put that into perspective? Just compare Dustin Hoffman in *The Graduate* to Dustin Hoffman in *Outbreak* and it becomes clear.

After 1968, nearly everything that Alfa did to the Spider was wrong (although admittedly, many things were done to satisfy lame-brained U.S. regulations). In 1969, unable to get the dual carb engine to pass U.S. smog regulations, they added a complicated, misunderstood and largely disliked mechanical fuel injection system made by SPICA and derived from a diesel truck injection system. Then, for reasons unknown, in 1971 (there were no U.S.-spec 1970 Alfas), they chopped the lovely boat tail off the car. Bumper regulations dictated an ugly black rubber affair for 1975, and a crude attempt at variable valve timing spoiled the 1981 cars. Things got a bit better in 1982 with a switch back to a normal valve train and Bosch electronic fuel injection. But by 1983, more styling changes in the form of a clumsy front air-dam and ugly rubber rear-spoiler further spoiled the car's appearance.

Final version nearly as lovely as the first

The aging Spider soldiered on until the dawn of the 1990s, when Pininfarina decided to take one final swipe at getting things right again. They nearly succeeded in making the twenty-five year old design look as attractive as it did in 1966. Gone were the awkward front and rear spoilers and the clumsy attempts at integrating huge rubber bumpers onto the 1964 vintage design. Pininfarina reverted to the solution that should have been used in 1975—soft plastic bumpers, front and rear, that harmonized well with the shape of the car. Even the updated 164-style full width tail-lights looked good.

Mechanically, Motronic, Bosch's latest generation of fuel injection, replaced the old L-Jetronic injection and the interior was spruced up with a driver's side airbag, new dash and console, and better seats. An automatic transmission was available for the first time, and air conditioning and leather were standard on the upmarket Veloce. Although the limits of the 1960s vintage chassis were apparent when pushed, and the car couldn't compare dynamically to the cheaper Mazda Miata, in terms of character and cachet, it had the Japanese car beat.

ran when parked...

Potentially a nice daily driver

As a semi-daily driver, the Fourth Series Spider is quite a decent proposition. It's comfortable, and the manual convertible top is one of the best of its type ever designed. It seals well and it can be lowered by a driver at a stoplight.

The usual Alfa issues apply here: Weak synchromesh (especially in second gear) head gasket issues, oil use in tired cars. But since the oldest of these cars is less than twenty years old, and many seem to have lived good lives as occasional drivers, your chances of finding a decent one are better than with any other series of Spiders, especially considering that production numbers were high—nearly 15,000 cars built in three years. Shockingly, even rust seems to be less of an issue with the last Spiders. As always, a thorough check by someone familiar with the marque is essential.

The market

After the Duetto, no Alfa Spider is truly a collectible; I have yet to see a Fourth Series Spider sell for more than its original list price of around $26,000. That said, they no longer seem to be depreciating. Attractive, low mileage examples have no problem selling in the mid to high teens. As usual in a sports car, automatics are a major buzzkill.

Jaguar

XJS 1991-96		❄
Parts availability ✪✪✪✪	**Inexpensive to maintain** ✪✪	**Investment potential** ✪½
Fun to drive ✪✪✪	**Price category** $$$ Nice driver, $13,000;* Show winner, $20,000*	
Performance 0 to 60 in 7.8 seconds; ¼ mile in 5.9 seconds at 90.5 mph (*Road & Track* 5/81)		

*prices are for factory convertibles, coupes are about 40 percent less

Parts Jag Bits, www.jagbits.com

Club Jaguar Club of North America, www.jcna.com

XJS coupe styling considered awkward back in the day has gotten better with age.

History

Pity the poor sod who had to design both the first post-Sir William Lyons Jaguar coupe and the follow-up to the iconic E-type. There was just no way of winning. Anything related to the E-type would be blasted as derivative, and you could lock a hundred stylists in a room for a year with enough clay to build a replica of the Great Pyramid of Giza and they wouldn't come up with anything remotely as lovely as the original E-type. In the case of the XJS, they most certainly didn't.

Left: Attractive interior of Ford-era XJS.
Right: Somewhere under the rubber and cadmium plated spaghetti there's a 6.0 liter V1.2.

As a result of its particularly long gestation period, when the V12 XJS debuted in the fall of 1975, it looked decidedly dated. Journalists at the time couldn't get a handle on its looks. Most commented that it looked vaguely Italian, with elements of the Dino 246 in the flying buttresses and Lamborghini 400 GT in the front. Few liked it and nobody thought it looked like God (or William Lyons) intended a Jaguar should look. But ironically, it was more aerodynamic than the E-type—which was styled by an aerodynamicist.

Body styles

Almost from the beginning, pundits commented that the car would look better as a convertible. Jaguar made a half-hearted attempt at satisfying this market in 1983 with the XJ-SC—a sort of semi-open car, much like what Baur of Germany was doing with 3-Series BMWs. The roof was a rigid targa-style lift-off piece, and there was a folding fabric back window. The body style didn't prove particularly popular, although it did introduce Jaguar's new 3.6 liter AJ6 engine and its first manual transmission since the end of the E-type.

It took a U.S. coachbuilder, Hess & Eisenhardt to do a full XJS convertible. Those that they converted were of particularly high quality and some feel that the top design was more attractive than the factory convertibles introduced for the 1989 model year.

Early cars developed an appalling reputation for reliability. Most experts advise considering only the 1991 and later cars, built after a partial redesign that benefitted from the input of Ford (who by then owned Jaguar).

At over 4000 pounds, an XJS is no sports car. It is, however, an exceedingly pleasant open GT. The ride is supple and well controlled, and the 6.0 liter version of the V12 which put out over 300 hp is simply sublime. 0-60 times were under seven seconds. Brakes are more than up to the task of hauling down the heavy XJS from the obscene speeds that it was capable of reaching. Rear brakes were sensibly moved outboard for 1992, with the difference in unsprung weight not perceptible.

Ford era cars: the only ones to consider

Although it was ironic that it took Ford to iron out Jaguar's reliability problems, the newest of these cars are now nearly fifteen years old. A poor example will rip at your wallet the way an actual Jaguar will rip out the throat of a deer. Again, the key to a happy life with an XJS is to be very picky about the example you purchase. Since dealers at this point will be of little help, an XJS specialist like Fred Garcia of Garcia's Restorations near St. Louis, Missouri is the key to a happy life with one of these complex cars.

According to Garcia, the powertrains are quite robust. "The 6.0 liter V12s were over-engineered, and I've torn down several high-mileage examples for modifications that have had little or no wear." GM THM transmissions generally give no trouble either. It's generally the little things that wear out and are costly— climate control modules, power windows and the like. A thorough pre-purchase inspection is a must for any XJS. Finally, a 6.0 liter XJS is capable of making real horsepower reliably. In addition to his regular service and restoration business, Garcia has created a cottage industry building affordable V12 supercars.

ran when parked...

The market

Many collectors subscribe to the notion that the surest indicator of whether a car has reached collectability is when its value exceeds that of its original price. By that measure, the XJS has a long way to go. Most are still depreciating used cars. This situation is unlikely to change any time soon, in light of the fact that the car's successor was generally viewed to be much more desirable. The XK8 did everything better—and looked like a Jaguar to boot, although it lacked the V12 cachet. As of this writing, there is a more than ample supply of cheap XK8 convertibles on the market. This bodes well for you if you are among the minority who prefer the looks of the XJS. Just don't expect to make any money when you sell.

Mercedes-Benz

R107 (350SL/450SL/380SL/560SL) 1991-89		❄
Parts availability ✪✪✪✪	Inexpensive to maintain ✪✪	Investment potential ✪✪
Fun to drive ✪✪✪	Price category $$$$ Nice driver, $15,000; Show winner, $28,000	
Performance 0 to 60 in 10.2 seconds; ¼ mile in 17.7 seconds at 81.5 mph (*Road & Track* 2/74)		

Parts Miller's, Inc., www.millermbz.com; K&K Manufacturing, www.kkmfg.com

Club Mercedes-Benz Club of America, www.mbca.org

Charlie Kuhn

History

The Mercedes-Benz R107 (Daimler Benz's internal nomenclature for the cars sold in the U.S. as the 350/450/380/560SL) was one of *the* aspirational cars of the 1970s-1980s. As the generic rich dude's car, they were everywhere on television, from *Hart to Hart* to *Dynasty* and *Dallas*. Today, they're close to making the transition from used car to minor collectible.

1987 560SL sits well in this color.

Charlie Kuhn

The first car to bear the SL name was the very sporting 300SL Gullwing which was followed by the 300SL roadster. The roadster was replaced in 1963 by the very pretty but rather softer 230SL. The R107 was part of a trend toward heavier, softer and more feature-laden Mercedes two-seaters which paradoxically retained the suffix "SL" for "sports leicht" (sports light), even though internally the R107 was sarcastically referred to as "die panzer wagen" (the tank).

The 350SL was introduced in 1971. It was the first SL with a V8—and the first to abandon its complex mechanical fuel injection system (actually a development of the system that gave the Messerschmitt Bf109 fighter plane an advantage in the Battle of Britain). A simpler and more mundane Bosch electronic system was used in the 350SL. While the European version of the car was powered by a 3.5 liter V8 (hence the name), the U.S. version needed a 4.5 liter to keep up with emission laws and after several model years, Mercedes changed the name to the one best remembered—"450SL."

The first two model years were among the most desirable. With 190 hp (rated at 240 hp gross), they would be the highest horsepower R107s available until 1986 and they would be the only ones available in the U.S. with the very pretty small Euro-style bumpers.

At nearly two tons, the 350SL was too heavy to be either particularly fast or nimble, yet it was quite benign. *Road & Track* found the compromise between ride and handling to be excellent, stating that "the best thing we can say about the SL's handling is that we have absolutely no complaint."

Unfortunately, U.S. regulations did what they did best to performance cars in the 1970s, and the SL became progressively uglier and slower. The first insult was a set of 5 mph bumpers in late 1973. The next year, emissions regs stole ten real (net) horsepower—but the worst insult occurred in 1981 with the introduction of a new smaller 3.8 liter aluminum V8 that made a miserable 155 hp. As a small consolation, the car got ABS brakes in 1980.

350SL and 450SL bulletproof; 380SL anemic and troublesome

Still, few of the trophy wives who made up the target market for SLs in those days noticed. What they did notice was the premature engine failures brought on by the infamous single-row timing chain design of the 3.8 liter aluminum V8. This design persisted until 1984, when a more robust double-row chain design was introduced. Mercedes retrofitted numerous pre-84 380SLs with the improved design, but unless records are present, there's no way of telling without removing one of the valve covers. In any event, because of the lack of power and questionable timing chain issues, 380SLs are best avoided.

By 1986, performance returned to the SL in a way that hadn't been seen since the 300SL Gullwing of the 1950s. A new 5.6 liter alloy V8 with 227 hp and a modern 4-speed automatic transmission were the hallmarks of the 560SL. In nearly all departments, it was a far superior car to the 350SL of 1971—that is, with the exception of longevity.

Few powerplants are more durable than a cast iron Mercedes-Benz engine. 350 and 450SLs can do as many as a half million miles between overhauls. The alloy engine cars can't come close to that. So a high mileage iron block car is nothing to fear, assuming documented regular maintenance.

R107 build quality was also excellent. Factory paint, brightwork and upholstery will wear about as well as the Coliseum. Mercedes had even made some strides in rust prevention with the R107. That isn't to say that the *Panzerwagen* can't roll over your bank account the way its namesake squashed France, Poland, Belgium and The Netherlands. Water pumps, alternators, fan clutches, starters, catalytic converters and climate control modules fail with regularity. When it does finally wear out, the leather or MB-Tex (high-quality vinyl) and horse-hair stuffed seats are quite expensive to redo—as are convertible tops. But an SL with a ratty interior will likely be deficient in other areas that will cause you to disqualify it.

The market

560SLs are the newest and the fastest of the R107s. Consequently, they command the highest prices. The oldest R107, the 350SL is the second-most desirable with its durable cast iron V8, decent power and small bumpers. One the other end of the scale, pre-84 380SLs and 1975-76 450 SLs are best avoided—the former for the timing chain reasons discussed above, and the latter because of the location of the catalytic converters near the engine compartment which cooked wiring and caused vapor lock.

While there are simply too many around to see appreciation on the scale of the earlier 230/250/280SL, good examples of desirable years are no longer depreciating. Nearly every large auction has at least one. Doggy cars still sell as low as $4,000, but as I mentioned in the Introduction, the cars that are initially the cheapest often turn out to be the most expensive in the long run. High teens should get a very nice SL with books and records. At that price, you should be able to enjoy the car for as long as you want, and maybe even see some modest appreciation.

Jaguar

XJ6 1969-87		❄
Parts availability ✪✪✪	**Inexpensive to maintain** ✪✪	**Investment potential** ✪
Fun to drive ✪✪½	**Price category** $$ Nice driver, $8,500; Show winner, $14,000	
Performance 0 to 60 in 10.6 seconds; ¼ mile in 18.2 seconds at 78.5 mph (*Road & Track* 9/80)		

Parts Jag Bits, www.jagbits.com; Moss Motors, www.mossmotors.com

Club Jaguar Club of North America, www.jcna.com

History

In the opinion of many, the Series I E-type of 1961 was the high water mark for Jaguar. Thereafter, they jumped the shark in 1968 with the Series II E-type before sinking to utter irrelevance under British Leyland

Series III XJ6 with "pepperpot" alloys.

Chip Lamb

XJ6 interiors consist of leather, walnut and wool carpet and a refreshing absence of vacuum-formed plastic.

Chip Lamb

and then Ford ownership. Those who adhere to this view forget that founder Sir William Lyons had one last brilliant car in him with the XJ6. When it was introduced in 1969, the dean of U.S. car magazines *Road & Track* called it "uncannily silent, gloriously swift and safe as a house."

Post-war Jaguar sedans had alternated between ravishing and attractive, but a bit large. The XJ6's immediate predecessor, the 420G, was an example of the latter. While clearly sharing the same parentage, the XJ6 was Ashley Judd to the 420G's Wynonna. Like the E-type, the XJ6—the original car, not including the "AJ40" redesign of 1988—was built in three series. Unlike the E-type, however, the last series was a substantially improved car.

Series I cars are distinguished by their tall grilles and low, small bumpers. In terms of style, they are uncompromised and exactly the car that Sir William Lyons wanted. In fact, Lyons even appeared in UK market commercials for the introduction of the car, calling it "the finest Jaguar ever." Certainly, a Series I XJ6 is among the prettiest post-war four-door sedans, rivaled seriously only by another Jaguar, the earlier 3.8S, Frua's Maserati Quattroporte or perhaps the XJ6's near-clone, the De Tomaso Deauville.

Mechanically, all was quite familiar with the first U.S. XJs getting virtually the same 245 hp twin Zenith-Stromberg equipped 4.2 liter XJ straight-six as the Series II E-type. Fully independent rear suspension was also E-type derived with the same rather inconvenient inboard disc brakes. Over the years, countless XJ6s have been sacrificed for their rear suspensions—Tupperware Cobra builders covet them.

Early cars were allegedly available with Dunlop 72-spoke chrome knockoff wire wheels, the same as an E-type—but I've never seen one so equipped. Most came with the chrome steel-wheels and hubcaps that were the base-wheel on the Series II and Series III E-type. Another option I've never seen is the four-speed manual gearbox with overdrive. The vast majority were equipped with a Borg-Warner automatic.

Series I cars the prettiest, Series III the most usable

Series I cars were handicapped with complex and ineffective HVAC systems, and by this time, Jaguar's legendary reputation for unreliability was being built in earnest. It brings to mind David Niven's famous quote about boozy, swashbuckling Errol Flynn: "You can count on Errol Flynn; he'll always let you down."

Things were to get worse… much worse. The Series II cars were introduced in 1974, primarily to comply with the American five-mph bumper regulations. The bumper size increased dramatically; it was raised,

Chip Lamb

Chip Lamb

necessitating a smaller and less attractive grille and supplemental air intake below the bumper. British Leyland was now firmly in control, and in terms of reliability and build quality, the Series II made the already somewhat dodgy Series I look like a Lexus.

Other than the appalling build quality, the only thing noteworthy about the Series II was the availability of the gorgeous pillarless XJ Coupe. All came with rather distinctive black vinyl roofs which some cynics believe were used simply covered inferior welds. In terms of style, the Coupe was the equal of the BMW 3.0Cs although unlike the BMW, it was available only with an automatic and also unlike the BMW, parts began to fall of long before the warranty expired.

As the cars couldn't possibly get any worse, any Series III cars (from 1980 on) must be considered an improvement. Pininfarina successfully freshened the styling and fuel injection (Bosch electronic built under license by Lucas) at last replaced the ancient Strombergs. Niceties like a sunroof and cruise control became available for the first time. Also offered for the first time were the very attractive "pepperpot" alloy wheels that stayed with the Series III until the end in 1987.

The heart of the XJ6 is the brilliant double-overhead cam XK six. True, it did date back to 1948 and at 4.2 liters, it was stroked to within an inch of its life, but this mattered less in a sedan than a sports car. Most importantly, it was proven technology that even the collection of boobs and Marxists assembling cars for British Leyland in the 1970s couldn't screw up. I therefore find it amazing how many V8 conversions took place in XJ6s over the years. While all of the Lucas ancillaries like alternators, starters, distributors and such may have been highly suspect, the Le Mans-winning engine was not. The absence of funny noises or smoke and oil pressure greater than about 40 psi warm at 3000 rpm usually means that things are fine with the big six.

Rust is problematic in nearly any old car; in an XJ6, it can easily put the car beyond reasonable repair. Rust in the floors, inner sills and the rear radius arm mounting points is a deal breaker. But really, given the values of the cars, one would do well to walk away from any car exhibiting any signs of rust. There are plenty of low-mileage, rust-free examples around.

Another deal-breaker is any XJ6 with a ratty interior. Nearly every surface is covered in leather or wood; none of this is cheap to replace. Sagging headliners are also common, and replacement is the only cure.

Unlike some earlier Jaguar sedans, the XJ6 has yet make the jump from used car to even minor collectible, still turning up on local "buy here, pay here" lots ready to bite the unwary. To make even a low five-figure price, it would take a bit of luck and a really great Series I car in a desirable color like Regency Red. As frequent drivers, the Series III cars are probably the best bets. Be particularly choosey, the best likely won't break $7,000, the worst, however, will break you.

It is highly unlikely that the XJ6 has a future as a collectible; but as a distinctive daily driver, it has some appeal. Unlike a 1980s 7-Series BMW, a vintage XJ6 makes more of statement than "I couldn't afford a newer one." They're always in good taste and will always be remembered as one of the prettier four-door sedans—a fitting legacy for the last car that Sir William Lyons had a hand in.

Left: Forty years later, that's still the same basic XK six from the XK120 shown here with electronic fuel injection. Right: No sedan has better haunches than the XJ6.

credit card cars

Fun cars that can be yours

with just a VISA swipe

or a few trips to the ATM

CREDIT CARD CARS" OR "ATM AUTOS" are so named because the price is within the cash advance limit of many credit cards, or in some cases, with three or four trips to an ATM. To qualify as a credit card car, the car in question must also be dirt cheap to fix. For example, a $2,500 MG Midget is certainly a credit card car while a $5,000 Porsche 928 is certainly not. Around $6,000 is the practical limit of a credit card car.

Several things make credit card cars irresistible. Foremost is the fact that they often tend to be impulse purchases—cars found at swap meets and in driveways with for sale signs.

There's no financing to worry about or pesky paperwork. In fact, I know of at least one person who, in lieu of renting car, bought a $3,000 car before the Scottsdale auctions, used it for the week and before leaving, ran it through the last auction of the weekend for a profit of $500 (not including the avoided expense of renting a car).

The possibility of life-altering or marriage-threatening consequence is also more remote with the purchase of a credit card car. If the worst happens, chances are, you're not staring at a five-figure bill to a mechanic. And if things are really dire, you'll be smart enough to cut your losses and donate the car to the local chapter of the Kidney Fund. That said, I've never actually had anything dire happen to a credit card car that I've owned. After all, we're not talking about 24 Hours of LeMons-style $500 clunkers—$5,000 buys a *very* nice Triumph Spitfire or Fiat Spider that should give little in the way of serious trouble.

The best way to keep your credit card car purchase from becoming either a parts car or a donation to the Kidney Fund is to buy the best example out there. There is little or no sense in buying an $800 '78 MGB when a very nice one will only set you back $5,000. Even doing most of the work yourself, you can't possibly restore any car for just $4,200. If you take away nothing else from this book, learn to keep your inner cheapskate at bay.

1980 Triumph Spitfire—and yes, it fits on the sidewalk.

Triumph

Spitfire 1962-80		
Parts availability ✪✪✪✪✪	**Inexpensive to maintain** ✪✪✪✪✪	**Investment potential** ✪
Fun to drive ✪✪✪✪	**Price category** $	Nice driver, $5,000; Show winner, $11,000
Performance 0 to 60 in 15.3 seconds; ¼ mile in 20.3 seconds at 67.5 mph (*Road & Track* 4/76)		

Parts Moss Motors, www.mossmotors.com; The Little British Car Company, www.lbcco.com;
Victoria British, www.victoriabritish.com

Club Vintage Triumph Register, www.vtr.org

History

In the 1950s and 60s, British sports cars came in two sizes "big" (Austin-Healey 3000, Jaguar E-type, etc.) and "small" (Austin-Healey Sprite and MG Midget). In reality, "small" and "Lilliputian" (respectively) were more accurate. And the Spitfire (named after the WWII fighter plane that saved Britain) was among the tiniest.

Left: From left to right, wiper motor, oil filter and twin charcoal canisters each probably displaced more than all four cylinders combined. This '79 1500 has a dual-throat Weber DGV carburetor replacing the pathetic Zenith-Stromberg.
Right: Minimalist cockpit of a Spitfire 1500.

It weighed just 1,555 lbs, was only 145 inches long and 47-inches high. Even people of non-simian arm length could reach out and get a pavement manicure.

Yet this class of car was quite popular in the 1960s, when Triumph and British Motor Corporation (BMC) were still independent competitors, going head-to-head against each other for the all-important North American market. BMC fired the first shots with the Austin-Healey Sprite and the MG Midget. Standard Triumph was under increasing pressure to respond, but it lacked the money to further develop their Triumph Herald-based prototype, code-named "Bomb" (the notion of naming a British car after an incendiary device still brings chuckles).

After getting a cash infusion from Leyland Motors, Triumph was able to dust off the Bomb prototype and develop it for production. Italian Giovanni Michelotti—who would serve Triumph well over the years—styled the car. It remains to this day one of the prettiest small sports cars ever.

The underpinnings were straight from the Herald, a small sedan introduced in the late 1950s. The little 1147 cc four-cylinder was mildly uprated with twin SU carbs and made 63 hp. 0-60 came up in about 15 seconds at a time when a VW Beetle took well over twenty.

Early cars have diabolical rear suspension

Unfortunately, the Spitfire inherited the Herald's swing axle independent rear suspension. In this setup, there is no flexible link between the axle shaft and the wheel hub, just one on each side of the differential. Consequently, under hard cornering, the extreme rear-wheel camber changes made the Spitfire want to curl up in a fetal position and wet itself. Far more Spitfires probably left the road facing backwards than Corvairs, but GM made a more tempting target for Ralph Nader than Standard -Triumph.

Interiors were very basic with non-adjustable seats, and lots of rubber covering the floors, just four gauges and a few knobs clustered around the center of the dash. The two-spoke, speedboat-like plastic steering wheel was an especially utilitarian touch.

The first major round of changes came in 1967 with the Mark III. In response to new U.S. uniform bumper height laws, Triumph simply raised the existing front bumper up, on top of the grille instead of below. These cars became known as "bone in the mouth" cars because of the resemblance to a puppy gnawing a bone. Perhaps the most significant change was the introduction of an actual folding convertible top, replacing the canvas pup tent which had previously passed for weather protection.

The Mark IV of 1970 brought the most extensive and useful changes the Spitfire would see during its production run. The rear axle was finally tamed, Michelotti freshened the exterior styling, and a new 1296 cc engine replaced the old 1147 cc unit. It was the second of three engine displacement increases for the Spitfire. This was necessary simply to maintain the performance levels of the previous car in the face of increasingly stringent U.S. emissions laws. In the rest of the world, the Spitfire kept getting progressively quicker as a result of the displacement increases.

Spitfire 1500—a Triumph with an MG engine

When the 1296 engine could no longer be kept at respectable performance levels in the States, British Leyland began to search for a replacement. Since MG and Triumph now shared common ownership, in 1973 British Leyland decided to use the MG Midget's 1500 cc powerplant in the Spitfire. With a single Zenith-Stromberg carburetor, in U.S. tune, the Spitfire 1500 made a paltry 53 hp. Adding insult to injury, the MG 1500 was nowhere near as robust an engine as the Triumph units had been, and by 1979, the poor Spitfire was saddled with enormous rubber bumpers that came close to spoiling its very pretty shape.

Like the MGB, the last one rolled off the line in 1980, and like the MG plant in Abingdon, Leyland closed the famous Triumph plant in Canley after the last Spit rolled off the line. The move to turn the British auto industry—a once powerful export engine—into a historic preservation trust was in full swing.

Few options available, but fun standard equipment

During the Spitfire's long run, there were few options available. A very pretty removable hard top, overdrive and wire wheels on the early cars, and that was about it. Any Spitfire can make a cheap fun occasional driver if you steer clear of the herds of SUVs being driven by individuals with cell phones shoved up their ear canals. These are, after all, tiny cars—their height makes them even less visible to these sensory-deprived freeway menaces than a Smart car.

Cheap parts and easy to maintain

Spitfires make ideal first collector cars for several reasons, not the least of which is the fact that anyone with average reading comprehension, a floor jack, a set of sockets and a repair manual can perform significant repair and maintenance tasks. The lifting bonnet makes everything accessible.

Spitfire parts are plentiful and cheap—so cheap that Spitfire parts are always the loss leader or teaser in any British parts supplier's ad—"brake rotors from just $19.95!" Ditto with even the tire ads you see in the Sunday paper—"tires as low as $25.95 each!" Read the tiny print next to the asterisk and you'll find that the insanely low price refers to 155/80/SR13, the Spitfire size.

Because of its three main bearing design, the 1500 engine isn't the most durable engine on the planet, so it's a good idea to give everything a very good listen, have a leak-down test done and check the oil pressure (there is no gauge) before parting with any money. You should also get any car you're interested in up in the air. Spitfires are separate body and chassis cars and frames do rust. Both maintenance and inspection of the front suspension is made easy by the giant forward tilting bonnet.

It's also a good idea to make sure that all of the switches and electrical components are working, particularly the relatively expensive combo switch that controls the horn and lights and the heater blower-switch (a pull-out knob located on the vent slider-control) which never seems to work. Overdrive, a very nice option should function from a switch on the shift knob and should engage smoothly in third and fourth gears. Clunks from the rear end generally mean u-joint issues or other problems with the independent rear suspension.

There is no reason to stay away from an otherwise sound car simply because it has a poor interior. Any number of specialists sell interior kits for Spits. Door panels, seat covers and carpets are all easy to install and not particularly expensive. Do yourself a favor if installing seat covers and buy the original style ones with cloth hound's-tooth inserts. They're much cooler in the summer.

Every Spitfire that I've driven feels basically the same. Climbing in is a chore, the starters all engage with an odd clatter and the seats are thin and uncomfortable. Because of the size and proximity to the pavement, Spitfires, which are really quite slow, feel much livelier than they really are.

But even if you've never driven one before, there is an instant feeling of nostalgia, not necessarily for the Spitfire, but for whatever the first self-propelled vehicle you ever drove was—a bumper car, the little cars on the track at Disneyland's Autopia, a go-cart, whatever. The steering is quick and sensitive, gearbox is notchy and oddly offset to the diagonal plane and the brakes feel reasonably effective when given a good shove.

The market

Spitfires are bought mainly on condition and nearly any year or Mark is capable of bringing up to about $7,000 in top shape. But the early (pre-1967) cars are quite uncommon, rather special, and can bring slightly more because many feel that Michelotti's first attempt was the prettiest (low bumper, full grille). While a bit smaller than an MGA and with slightly more modest performance, at less than half the price of an MGA, an early Spitfire can be a great alternative if you're priced out of that market. Few people at British car shows have even seen an early Spitfire—the survival rate must be miniscule.

While there is no reasonable expectation of serious appreciation for Spitfires, it must be accepted that they have increased in value over the last several years. Good $2,500 cars are now virtually non-existent; around $3,500 to $4,500 is now the starting point for a car you'd want to own.

Case study

1978 Triumph Spitfire 1500		
Purchase Price: $2,800 (2001)	**Sale Price:** $3,500	**Owned for:** 1.0 years

Left: Inca Yellow Spitfire; another solid ex-California car.
Right: Few stylists have updated one of their own designs better than Michelotti's 1971 cleanup of the Spitfire.

I had just bought a large house, had a child, and sold my 911SC. But the thought of not having a collector car around was giving me a rare case of male post-partum depression. Running through the short list of sports cars for the newly impoverished, it boiled down to an Alfa Spider, Fiat Spider or Triumph Spitfire—I may have been poor, but I was still too proud to drive a rubber bumper MGB. It was a relatively simple mission— find the best pre-1979 Spitfire within a 500 mile radius of St. Louis, Missouri.

As luck would have it, I didn't have to go nearly that far, finding an ex-California '78 in Kansas City. Promising a smoked brisket sandwich from the famous Arthur Bryant's as payment, I enlisted my dad to drive me the 230 miles to KC and follow me back. We met the owner and his wife—both sincerely sad to see the car go—at the mechanic's shop where I was having a pre-purchase inspection performed.

I got a look at the car when it was up on the rack. It was typical of cars that have been on a lifetime salt-free diet—not even any surface rust on the frame. Just dirty and oily, they way you like to see an old British car. Compression was excellent, gearbox and brakes strong, body straight as a pin. Feeling obligated to find something, the mechanic mentioned that one wheel bearing could stand repacking, the valve cover gasket was leaking and the one of the steering rack boots was cracking. Frankly, the car probably had more defects when it was delivered new.

The sellers had owned the car in San Diego for fifteen years but found they just didn't use the car in the freezing winters and hot and humid summers of Kansas City. The records went back to the car's delivery in 1977. After settling on a price of $2,800, I was headed back east to St. Louis with my dad following in the emergency breakdown car. The drive home was uneventful, but I was prepared. I had packed a duffle bag full of flares, a flashlight, temporary fan belt, a tow rope, duct tape and cheap Chinese tools. To this day, I still have the duffle bag in my garage packed with the same stuff. It goes with me on every old car road trip.

The trip did point out the Spitball's general unsuitability for Interstate use. It is truly unsettling to be eyeball to lug nut with every 18 wheeler, and the lack of overdrive meant that 70 mph translated to over 4000 rpm, an engine speed that made me feel like I was sitting in one of those Sharper Image vibrating massage chairs for three hours.

Nevertheless, there was a lot to like about my poverty sports car. Inca Yellow was in my opinion one of the better colors available. And it had chrome bumpers and a lovely real wood dash, complete with a little chrome map light on a stalk, and a tiny plaque proclaiming the Spitfire's numerous victories dating back to the Battle of Britain.

Never able to leave well enough alone, I added a set of period UK-made Cosmic alloy wheels and an ANSA exhaust. Ideally, I would have liked the very pretty Michelotti-designed hardtop and I wish that the previous owner had replaced the seat covers with the correct ones with hounds tooth cloth inserts—the solid black vinyl ones the car had were hot and slippery.

I hate to leave the impression that I lead a charmed life with old cars (I don't), but in my experience, when I choose wisely and follow my friend Paul's advice and buy a "right" car, few things seem to go wrong. And this was certainly the case with the Inca Yellow Spitfire. My year with it was trouble-free and quite fun. I even used it as a golf cart during a bar association golf tournament. I could have sold three more that day if I had them.

Like the couple from Kansas City who sold me the car, I hated to sell it but after a year, it was time. I had made partner at my law firm and my financial situation became considerably less strained. When I found a TR4 in Portland, Oregon, the little Spit became expendable. I wound up selling it on eBay to a very nice woman from Laramie, Wyoming for $3,800. She drove it home 900 miles without incident. I wouldn't be surprised if she was still enjoying the car.

As entry-level British sports cars, Spitfires are quite enjoyable. The only area they lose to a rubber bumper MGB is sheer lack of size and roominess. Also, today, in the world of $3,000 used Mazda Miatas, it gets harder to make a case for the Spitfire, which in every category (besides character) is light years behind the Miata.

MGB

Roadster 1974½-80		
Parts availability ✪✪✪✪✪	**Inexpensive to maintain** ✪✪✪✪✪	**Investment potential** ✪
Fun to drive ✪✪	**Price category** $$	Nice driver, $5,000; Show winner, $10,000
Performance 0 to 60 in 18.3 seconds; ¼ mile in 21.5 seconds at 64.5 mph (*Road & Track* 6/76)		

Parts Moss Motors, www.mossmotors.com; The Little British Car Company, www.lbcarco.com; Victoria British, www.victoriabritish.com; British Parts Northwest, www.bpnorthwest.com

Club North American MGB Register, www.mgcars.org.uk/namgbr/index.html

Left: The emission controlled MGB motor—a single carburetor and more hoses than your local lawn and garden center.
Right: Gross seat cover patterns and cheap embossed door panels—the hallmark of a late MGB.

Charlie Kuhn

Chip Lamb

History

Those who think the American auto industry is in trouble from a product standpoint clearly have no recollection of the British industry of the 1970s. Although nearly bankrupt, Ford and GM are at last finally
producing some decent product. In the Britain of the 1970s, what little money there was for R&D went into
miserable and justifiably forgotten little rat holes like the Morris Ital, and Austin Allegro. Older cars like the
MG Midget and MGB were forced to soldier on with some of the most comical and amateurish modifications
ever seen outside of the third world.

The MGB started out as a perfectly pleasant sports car back in 1962. Road testers praised its tight
structure, build quality and nimble handling. Never a powerhouse, its 96 hp gave it a top speed of around 100
mph and a 0-60 time of about 12 seconds. What happened to it as a result of emission and safety legislation
and British Leyland's dim-witted and penny-pinching response to same was just criminal.

Rubber bumpers, raised suspension and just 68 hp

The first atrocity to occur on the 1974 ½ model was the application of the infamous "rubber bumper" for
which this series is known. Not content with designing something black, and massive, designers gave it a
snaggle-tooth split to the grill. MG's solution to uniform bumper height laws was even more ham-fisted—
they simply placed shims in the springs to jack the car up several inches. There was worse to follow.

1975 brought even more stringent emission regulations. And while non-cash and engineering
starved car companies were looking at real solutions like electronic fuel injection, MG simply subtracted

one of the ancient Zenith-Stromberg carburetors leaving the poor tipsy, wheezing MGB with just 68 hp. Performance was utterly disgraceful—a diesel VW Rabbit from the 1970s would leave a rubber bumper B in the dust.

Other offenses had been inflicted on the MGB by British Leyland in previous years: In 1970, cost cutters excised everything that had been charming about MG interiors, including leather seats with contrasting piping. Rubber bumper Bs have vinyl seats with odd embossed patterns. To make matters worse, the interior materials were so cheap, that even the caring and skilled workforce at the Abingdon plant couldn't make things fit particularly well. At least panel fit and paint finish on the bodies remained good until the end.

The options list on rubber bumper MGBs was as sparse as ever—overdrive and wire wheels were the majors. Standard wheels were the attractive styled steel Rostyle wheels that had been around since 1969. 14" wire wheels were optional. The black and silver "anniversary" edition of 1980 sported the same five spoke alloy wheels that were standard on the Triumph Stag.

As one might expect with just 63 hp, 0-60 times were in the region of a week to ten days—handling also felt far less secure because of the greater body roll that was a byproduct of the SUV-like ride height. At least the rack-and-pinion steering remained quick and the disc/drum brake setup was effective.

At least the top goes down

Perhaps the only reason to own a rubber bumper MGB is the fact that the top goes down. Truth be told, there are far better choices for the money in the top-down department—even in the simple task of providing a little sunshine, the poor MGB falls flat. Folding top design was never an MG strong point, and the B's is not particularly good in terms of sealing and user-friendliness with numerous snaps and pinch hazards confronting the driver.

One positive thing about any MGB—parts are easier to find than a fake Rolex in Times Square. They're about as inexpensive too. MGBs are also relatively bullet proof—gearboxes and the cast iron B-Series I.8 liter fours seldom need attention. Ancient lever shocks tend to leak, and kingpins wear out on any MGB. Loss of self-centering action and a sort of sticky feeling in the steering are a sign of the latter.

Rust is also an issue. The same comments apply as to MGB GTs—they rust from the inside out, so the bubbling you see on the outside of the fender bottoms and rockers is often just the tip of the iceberg. Roadsters also suffer from the infamous "MGB crack"—roadster door skins are inherently weak and many crack just below the vent window. The only fix is to reinforce it from behind and weld and refinish the door skin.

The market

The rubber bumper MGB occupies the bottom rung of desirability for British sports cars along with the rubber bumper MG Midget, Triumph Spitfire and the quite underrated Jensen-Healey. In truth, I can think of only three compelling reasons to own one—they're cheap to buy, cheap to maintain and the top goes down. While they may not be going down in value, their appreciation curve roughly matches their acceleration curve—more or less imperceptible. If you simply must have a vintage sports car rather than, say, a $4,000 Miata, knock yourself out. But even at this price point, there are far better choices.

Alfa Romeo

Spider 1971-82		
Parts availability ✪✪✪	Inexpensive to maintain ✪✪✪	Investment potential ✪
Fun to drive ✪✪✪½	Price category $$	Nice driver, $6,500; Show winner, $12,000
Performance 0 to 60 in 9.9 seconds; ¼ mile in 17.5 seconds at 81 mph (Road & Track 3/71)		

Parts Centerline Alfa Parts, www.centerlinealfa.com; AR Ricambi, www.arricambi.com
Club Alfa Romeo Owners Club, www.aroc-usa.org

1973-74 Spiders still had pretty exposed grille and stainless steel bumpers. This one sports non-standard Fly Yellow paint and attractive Panasport alloy wheels. Ordinarily, a color change (especially to one never offered that year by the manufacturer) is a deal breaker for me, but this one was so well done—without a trace of the original color anywhere—and in such an iconic Italian sports car color, I'd own it in a heartbeat.

History

Universally regarded as two of the best open sports cars of all time, Alfa Romeo's 750-series Giulietta Spider and 101-series Giulia Spider of the late 1950s and early '60s were a tough act to follow. To remain the perennial darling of the enthusiast press, Alfa's new convertible would need to be nothing short of an improvement on perfection. Of course, Alfa failed at such an impossible task—or at least it seemed so when the 105-series Duetto debuted in 1966.

Whereas the Giulietta was regarded as a stylistic tour de force, critics panned the Duetto as contrived, heaping scorn upon its boat-tail rear and pronounced side scallop. That the car disappointed many onlookers when new may be hard to believe today, as the Duetto has since been elevated to iconic status, partly as a result of its appearance in "The Graduate," but more because its lines have simply aged well. That hadn't yet happened in 1970, so Alfa tried to remedy things by lopping off about six inches from the rear of the "Spider 1750," as the car was called at its U.S. introduction in 1971.

This new body style, whether you describe it as a "Kamm-tail," "square-tail" or by its least flattering appellation, the "chop-tail," soldiered on little changed until 1991.

Critics were unmoved by the new styling. *Road & Track*, in a startling about-face to its usual adoration of anything adorned with the cross and snake, stated testily that it "didn't care much for the original design and we don't consider this change to be much improvement, if any". Aside from the styling controversy, for the first time, a mechanical issue dogged U.S. Alfas.

In 1969, displacement of Alfa's venerable twin-cam four-cylinder had been increased to 1779 cc, and a second displacement increase in 1972 bumped the engine up to a full two liters. Every Spider built for the U.S. market from 1969 through 1981 also came equipped with, quite possibly, the most controversial device ever fitted to a post-war European sports car, the dreaded SPICA mechanical fuel injection system.

Stung by its inability to emission-certify cars for the 1968 (and subsequently the 1970) model years, Alfa adapted this system, which had been developed by a subsidiary for use in diesel engines. The precise workings (or non-workings) of the inezione SPICA are beyond the scope of this missive; however, opinions as to its merits—or lack thereof—have been known to spark fisticuffs among *Alfisti*. No less an authority than Keith Martin, whose publication *Sports Car Market* magazine started out as *The Alfa Romeo Market Letter*, has called the SPICA system "diabolical," and characterized it as difficult to set up and maintain. Others, however, view it as simply "misunderstood."

Given the fact that I was once stranded by a broken injection pump belt in remote Nederland, Colorado while driving a college girlfriend's Spider, I'm inclined to agree with Mr. Martin; a set of Webers is an enhancement. Whatever your opinion of the SPICA system, you must accept the fact that if good

health is critical to enjoying the car (and it is), sheer complexity probably removes these 1971-81 cars from the pool of suitable collector cars for novice owners. A better choice might be a car converted to Webers or a 1982 Spider, which was the only year that the traditional body style was available with reliable Bosch electronic injection.

The rest of the Spider is refreshingly straightforward. Rear suspension consists of coil springs and a live axle located by a Panhard rod. It works well enough under most conditions that you'd swear it was independent. Relatively soft springs combined with an anti-roll bar strike a nice balance between a comfortable ride and sharp handling and help make the Spider a fairly neutral car. The worm and sector steering is light and precise, especially when tires close to the original 165-14 size are used. Vacuum-assisted four-wheel disc brakes provide decent stopping power.

I personally think the styling of the square-tail Spider has aged well, especially the pre-1975 cars with the smaller chrome bumpers. They have an exotic look from the front, especially when retrofitted with Plexiglas Carello headlight-covers that were standard on earlier Duettos. Ditch the steel wheels in favor or a set of five-spoke Cromodoras, BWAs or Panasports and the Spider really comes into its own. Cars built after 1975 with rubber bumpers are less attractive, but still not as aesthetically compromised as others of the era (think rubber-bumper MGBs).

The best part of the Spider is its cockpit. The main Veglia instruments are found in two "impale-o-matic" pointed binnacles; a full complement of secondary gauges is located on the console in beefy, chromed-metal bezels. The oddest thing about the interior is the shifter that sprouts almost horizontally out of the console. The most common steering wheel is a great looking and feeling three-spoke wheel in real wood.

Alfa's convertible-top design on the Spider is nothing short of sublime. You can actually raise it or lower it from inside the car. Much has been written about the driving position of the Spider. If your build is of the long-armed and short-legged type (more like that of Java Man than modern homo sapiens), you won't have any problems. Otherwise, you may be forced into an extended arm, splayed-knee position, unpleasant at best, an invitation to a visit to the chiropractor at worst. Try on a Spider before you buy one.

Beware worn synchros, rust and blown head gaskets

Things to watch out for are pretty obvious: Rust is your paramount concern and you must be sure the injection system is functioning correctly. The car should start easily from cold, idle should be even, and the engine should pull cleanly from low revs, without surging or backfiring. Be wary of bad second gear synchros, the ever-common coolant in the oil or white smoke. Rather than the selection of a new pontiff, the latter indicates a bad head gasket.

The market

Compared to the Duetto and the mechanically identical 1750 and 2000 GTV coupes, Spiders are grossly undervalued, though the market is wising up. With 0-60 mph times under ten seconds and engineering superior to a TR6, an Alfa Spider clobbers its more expensive British competition in every department save one: sheer machismo. Yet Alfa Spiders trade for roughly half the price of a TR6. While dramatic appreciation is probably not in the cards for a chop-tail Spider, they will see modest appreciation. So there you have it: Now is clearly the time to track down a good chop-tail, a car that may truly claim to be one of the last really worthwhile convertible sports cars to be had for less than ten grand.

Fiat

Spider 2000 1979-85		
Parts availability ✪✪✪½	Inexpensive to maintain ✪✪✪	Investment potential ✪½
Fun to drive ✪✪✪	Price category **$$**	Nice driver, $5,000; Show winner, $11,000
Performance 0-60—10.6 sec, ¼ mile—18.1 sec @ 77 mph (*Road & Track* 7/79)		

Parts Fiat Parts Warehouse, www.spiderroadster.com; C. Obert Co., www.fiatplus.com; Bayless Fiat Lancia World, www.baylessfiat.com

History

Left: A very pretty Spider 2000 in great colors and pretty accessory Cromodora alloy wheels. Right: Lovely interior of the Fiat Spider 2000 is reason enough to own one.

"Baby Ferrari" is a widely abused term in the collector car world, but in the case of the Fiat Spider it's not quite as absurd as it sounds. Pininfarina—which was responsible for the design of the Fiat 124 Spider—also styled the Ferrari 275GTS which is conversely referred to by some as "a big Fiat 124 Spider" because of the great similarity of the two shapes. In another Ferrari connection, the Fiat's twin-cam engine was designed by the great Aurelio Lampredi, who also designed some of Ferrari's most successful V12s.

Introduced at the 1966 Turin auto show with a 1438 cc engine, the very pretty Spider was an immediate hit in the U.S. Unfortunately, it arrived just as emissions regulations were getting serious—Fiat always seemed one step behind despite two displacement increases from 1600 ccs to 1756 ccs. Along the way, in 1975, the Spider gained a pair of truly unfortunate bumpers that looked just like a football helmet facemask. You just want to grab it, yank it off and take the fifteen-yard penalty (and automatic first down).

Near the end of the run, two interesting things happened: With factory approval, Legend Industries developed a turbocharged Spider. These are quite rare today and offer a modest but noticeable gain in performance over the normally aspirated cars. Boost was set at a relatively modest level, and although turbos fail, engines don't seem any more failure-prone.

Second, the car got a reprieve when Fiat quit the U.S. market in 1983 and discontinued the Spider. Pininfarina, not having any other large contracts at the time, actually took over production of the Spider

ran when parked...

calling it the Pininfarina Azzurra after an Italian racing yacht of the same name. Malcolm Bricklin handled the importation along with the Bertone version of the X1/9.

Two-liter injected Spiders: the ones to have

Early small-bumper cars are quite rare today, and the carbureted big bumper 1756 cc cars are hardly worth messing with, their performance is so compromised by emission controls. The introduction of Bosch L-Jetronic fuel injection in 1980 combined with the 2.0 liter engine transformed the car. 0-60 times fell below ten seconds for the first time, and driveability was excellent.

Alloy wheels were available for the first time, the most common being the "iron cross" style made by Speedline. Standard wheels were two different types of styled-steel wheels, with one decidedly more attractive than the other.

The interiors were spruced up with blue, red and tan upholstery choices joining the ubiquitous black. Dashboard surround and trim nicely complimented the upholstery colors. Leather and automatic transmission were available for the first time. The wood dash and numerous Veglia gauges from the earlier cars were retained, giving the Spider 2000 one of the richer looking interiors seen in an inexpensive sports car—so much nicer than an MGB of the era.

The world's best convertible top

Also nicer than any British car was the convertible top. Not only did it seal well, it was dead simple to put up or down in seconds. Fiat engineers developed the best solution ever to the problem of blind quarters in a convertible—the car had glass quarter windows that folded down with the convertible top. Quite clever… and quite elegant.

There was no comparison in the driving experience between the Fiat and its chief competition, the MGB. The Fiat, with over 100 hp, would simply run rings around the MGB. Since the suspension and ride height hadn't been fiddled with in the Fiat as it had on the MGB (to comply with bumper height laws), the Fiat retained its excellent handling characteristics.

Best of all, the Fiat came standard with an excellent 5-speed gearbox, something never offered in the States by MG. Four-wheel disc brakes were quite effective and just added to the Fiat's already class-leading features. On the liability side, steering at low speed is quite heavy, and the Spider suffers from the typical long arms and short legs driving position that seems common in Italian cars. The steering wheel is also angled more toward the horizontal plane than many American prefer.

You do pay a price for the double overhead cams, four-wheel disc brakes and fuel injection in the form of higher maintenance costs than a simpler British sports car. While British cars make do with stout timing chains, the Fiat requires periodic replacement of its rubber timing belt, something that is often neglected by typically cash-strapped Fiat owners, with dire consequences in the early cars—Spider 2000s were thankfully non-interference engines.

Fiats don't tolerate fools with tools

It also pays to be more careful in evaluating a Fiat mechanically than a British sports car—they're more fragile, less tolerant of ham-fisted repairs and certainly more expensive to put right. After you've determined that you're looking at a promising example, always spend the $100-$150 to do a pre-purchase inspection on a Fiat that includes a leak-down test (for compression issues) and a thorough road test to flush out any gearbox, cooling or electrical issues.

Most of these potential trouble areas should be fairly obvious: blue smoke indicates an oil burner, white smoke, a head gasket issue, neither exactly unheard of with a Fiat. Worn synchromesh will be readily apparent—the last two Spiders I test drove had essentially non-existent synchromesh up and down in second and third gears.

In addition to the usual whites, blacks and reds, Spider 2000s were available in a wide variety of very rich, very attractive metallic colors. Unfortunately, the metallics age quite badly, so nearly any Spider that you look at today will have had a respray at some point in its life. My preference is to look at a car with paint that's

1981 Spider 2000 fitted with factory 13 inch "Iron Cross" alloys made by Speedline.

at least five or ten years old. If it's not demonstrating any problems or evidence of old filler at that point, there probably aren't any hidden problems. On the lighter side, some of the most attractive color combinations to be found on any sports car were available on 2000 Spiders. Even the metallic brown looks quite nice with a tan interior.

Fiats being Italian, rust is certainly a problem, although seemingly less so than earlier cars. Whether this is simply a function of the cars being newer or some advance in Fiat's rustproofing skill is unknown. In any event, wheel arches, rockers fender bottoms and doors are the major spots to look at. In any event, the structure of the car itself is quite solid. Cowl-shake is minor and the doors shut with a reassuring thunk. Panel gaps from the factory were quite good, and the cars had the appearance of being well assembled.

The market

Fiat Spiders are still dirt cheap, and if I'm fortunate enough for there to be an 11th edition of this book, they'll still be dirt cheap. For the most part, they bring rubber-bumper MGB money. Between $4,500 and $7,000 buys a nice driver. This makes little sense as the Fiat is a vastly superior car. But that's just the way it is—the market, not the opinion of writers, determines value. This isn't necessarily a bad thing. It means that for the informed, the fuel-injected Fiat Spider 2000 is one of the great remaining vintage sports car bargains.

Lancia

Beta 1975-82		❄
Parts availability ✪✪½	Inexpensive to maintain ✪✪✪	Investment potential
Fun to drive ✪✪✪½	Price category $	Nice driver, $3,000; Show winner, $7,000
Performance 0 to 60 in 12.5 seconds; ¼ mile in 19.0 seconds at 70.5 mph (*Road & Track* 10/79)		

History

To paraphrase Monty Python, the Lancia Beta left a legacy in the U.S. so immeasurable that nobody has bothered to measure it. In fact, is has been largely forgotten by all but those like me who spent way too much time sneaking peaks at the oddball cars advertised in *Road & Track* in the 1970s instead of paying attention

Fiat SpA

Bill Woodard

Above left: 1976 Lancia
Beta coupe.
Right: Lancia Fulvia—Rare
example of an Italian car
engineered and assembled
like a German one.
Left: Beta coupe styling…a
bit odd from the rear.

in Algebra. Today, Betas hide in plain sight on Craigslist and eBay and for an investment of almost nothing, you can have a stylish, entry level Italian GT.

Founded in 1906, Lancia is actually one of the world's oldest surviving car makes. In those hundred and three years, they probably sold as many cars in the U.S. as Toyota builds in a day. Prior to their purchase in 1969 by Fiat, Lancia was known for building very attractive and elegantly engineered cars with excellent build quality—a near perfect combination of Italian passion and almost Germanic precision.

Unfortunately, Japanese-like business acumen wasn't part of the equation, and Lancia was rumored to have lost money on nearly every car they built (and there was no making it up on volume). These pre-Fiat Lancias are quite scarce in the U.S. with the last official imports ceasing around 1967. The jewel-like Fulvia is the one most often encountered. With a unique V4 engine and rally-bred handling, they are delightful cars whose scarcity and challenging in the U.S. parts situation probably places them out of the scope of a novice collector. Nevertheless, at around $10,000 for a good one, they are wonderful bargains.

The last series of cars that Lancia's brilliant engineers had a hand in was the Beta series. Introduced in the U.S. in 1975, they were powered by an emissions-choked Fiat 1756 cc twin-cam 4-cylinder engine. The range eventually grew to include a four-door sedan or Berlina, a coupe, a mid-engine sports car called the Scorpion (the Montecarlo in Europe) and the Zagato Spider (a sort of semi-open version of the coupe) and the HPE, a very handsome two-door wagon.

Road & Track said: so lovely, so agile . . . so slow

All except the Scorpion were front-drivers; and while understeer was the defining handling characteristic at the limit, Betas were entertaining to drive and quite comfortable. The injected cars are smooth with excellent drivability—the carbureted cars are another story. In the 1970s, the Italian solution to limiting hydrocarbon emissions was to make sure that as little of the filthy stuff as possible reached the combustion chamber. Early U.S. Betas used the same tiny Weber carburetor as an early Fiat X1/9. The ultra-lean condition made the car feel like someone applied an LAPD choke hold to the intake system—simply trying to keep the car from surging and bucking while applying partial throttle was difficult. U.S. cars had a pathetic 86 hp.

All the cars built before 1980 suffered from basically the same issues—non-existent rust protection and lack of power due to emission controls. Once again, the Robert Bosch company came to the rescue. Bosch L-Jetronic injection coupled with an enlarged 2.0 liter engine meant that the Beta at last had enough performance to show a clean pair of heels to a BMW 320i. But by then, the Lancia line in the U.S. had shrunk to just the coupe and Zagato Spider. Lancia quit the U.S. after the 1982 model year, but the rest of the world continued to get better and better Betas, culminating with the supercharged Volumex model.

While not particularly fast, Betas embody all that is enjoyable about Italian GTs—sharp handling, revvy twin-cam motors and a modicum of style. This combined with the fact that they were positioned in the U.S. as upmarket cars, means that luxury niceties like leather, alloy wheels and A/C were common.

Although luxurious and well-finished, Lancia Betas were paradoxically constructed out of some of the most sub-standard steel ever to find its way into a Western-built automobile (Fiat had gotten a screaming deal on some Soviet-made steel). To make matters worse, Italians aren't far behind the British in the department of electrical maladies—Marelli is simply Italian for "Lucas."

By far the biggest problem with Betas today is Beta owners. Values plunged when Lancia and Fiat quit the U.S. market in the early 1980s and never recovered. Consequently, few cars received anything resembling regular maintenance let alone loving care. Most Betas that turn up on the market today look like they were rediscovered after the owner mowed his lawn for the first time since the Carter administration. There is no sense in buying a Beta with needs (unless you want a parts car) when less than $5,000 buys the best of the best.

The market

Even nice Betas are dirt cheap. There are several reasons for this. They're orphans in the Unite States, few people know what they are; those who do either couldn't care less or dismiss them as excessively troublesome rotboxes with impossible to find parts. While the former is certainly true—they do fly way under the radar—as a fun weekend driver, they aren't any more troublesome than most other thirty-year-old European cars, and they are actually pretty well supported by several parts specialists. This isn't to say that every last trim item or body panel is a mouse-click away, they aren't. Zagato tail–lights, for example, are notoriously unavailable, but the vitals that you need to keep you on the road are easily sourced.

What struck me about my experience with a pair of Betas is fact that they are almost surely among the cheapest interesting cars left on the scene. At $3,000 for a nice Zagato Spider, they represent the absolute entry-level for a vintage open-top European car. Occasionally, one sees asking prices of close to $7,000, but as my very nice driver struggled to make $3,000 in two tries on eBay, I would be reluctant to pay more than $5,000 for the nicest one on the planet.

Case studies

1976 Lancia Beta Coupe		
Purchase Price $1,900	**Sale Price** $5,000	**Owned for** 0.5 years

1981 Lancia Beta Zagato Spider		
Purchase Price $1,000	**Sale Price** $3,000	**Owned for** 0.5 years

Parts C. Obert Co., www.fiatplus.com; Bayless Fiat Lancia World, www.baylessfiat.com
Club Fiat Lancia Unlimited, www.flu.org

I'm actually old enough to remember the flurry of ads that announced Lancia's return to the U.S. market in 1975. Lancia Betas always struck me as reasonably attractive little cars with nice leather interiors. With Alfa GTVs selling for well into the twenties and good Fiat 124 coupes virtually extinct, the Beta became the default choice for experiencing the fun of a real Italian GT on a Spumante budget.

Left: Immaculate 1976 Lancia Beta coupe with original paint and interior. Right: 1981 Beta Zagato Spider—not a bad looker for a $2,200 investment.

For some strange reason, Portland and Seattle were originally big markets for Fiat and Lancia, consequently, the detritus would turn up on Craigslist with regularity. Most were parts cars or Kidney Fund donations waiting to happen. A picture-less Craigslist posting for a Beta coupe in Portland that I came across in the fall of 2007 looked like it might be different—low miles, original paint, no rust, it all sounded promising.

Nevertheless, I was truly amazed when I saw the car in person. The light metallic blue paint was all original and shiny with just a bit of checking on the upper surfaces. No dents and no rust, a full tool kit and books and records. Hell, the saddle colored leather seats looked like they had never been sat in. I figured if the car blew up tomorrow, I'd have a great set of matching Italian leather office chairs to remember it by.

The seller was determined to get at least $2,000 for the car and I was determined to pay less than $2,000. At $1,900, we could both declare a moral victory. There were many jokes when I brought my prize back to the magazine office, including the infamous photo taken by magazine publisher Keith Martin of the car parked next to a Portland hemorrhoid clinic (insert your pithy caption here; the readers of *Sports Car Market* did).

There was a bit of sorting out to do, as the car had a nasty habit of dying on the freeway—it turns out that the car had sat for over a year and the fuel filters became clogged with debris from the bottom of the tank. After changing the filters and boiling out the tank and replacing the carb with an NOS one I found on eBay, the car ran as well as could be expected with its original emission controls still hooked up, including the tiny stock Weber (this was the People's Republic of Oregon where the poor thing still had to pass smog).

While anything but fast, the car was an absolute blast on the roads that wound around the Columbia River Gorge. Flogged like the underpowered but rev-happy Italian car that it was, the joys of driving a slow car fast were immediately apparent. It had a wonderful snarly exhaust note, the shift linkage was quite decent for a front-driver and the ratios were all appropriately close. Ride quality and four-wheel disc brakes were also first rate.

I enjoyed it for a little while with little trouble, but the car sat outside at my Portland commuter apartment; the drama of cold starts in the morning got old (a manual choke may have helped). I'd had my fun. It was time to send it down the road after picking up a Porsche 912E in Tacoma. I did wind up getting the last laugh on the magazine staff (and the hemorrhoid clinic, whose owner who turned out to be a subscriber) when the pristine little coupe sold for $5,000 on eBay. There was one final bit of drama, however: I was out of town when the transporter came to pick up the car for delivery to its new owner. I left it to Bryan, the magazine's notoriously fragile Web manager to release the car to the truck driver.

According to Bryan, he received a barely coherent and heavily accented message one morning: "My name Sergei, I come today to get Lan-cee-ya, okay?" When Sergei arrived, the Beta displayed its usual stubborn cold starting nature. Sergei—having to be in Novosibersk or some such place with the truck by that Wednesday—needed to get it started in a hurry and proceeded to spray starter fluid all over the outside of the air cleaner. Predictably, the car backfired and ignited the starter fluid. Sergei, at the first sign of fire, ran away like an Iraqi Republican Guardsman, leaving Bryan to find a fire extinguisher and put the thing out before the paint blistered on the air cleaner—or worse, the conflagration spread to my boss's very nice Alfa Romeo Giulia Spider. Bryan's quick thinking saved the car. But to this day, he still suffers from post-traumatic stress syndrome, and I'm still paying for his therapy.

Left: Zagato tail-lights—don't bust one of these. Shared by only a Bristol 412, they're made of genuine "unobtainium". Right: Perfect original interior that sold me on the Beta Coupe. I figured if it blew up, I'd have some cool office chairs.

Thinking that lightening could strike twice and that I could actually be the only person in history to make money selling Lancias, I kept looking at Craigslist for nice Betas. About six months later, I came across one for what seemed like a sound Zagato Spider with the "wife wants it out of here this weekend" admonition. By this time, I had looked at several Zagatos and all fell into the category of being a ding, a seat rip or a starter motor away from a parts car.

This one was different. The paint was original and shiny, it was totally rust-free, the leather, while not as pristine as my blue car was, the A/C and power windows worked, and nothing seemed amiss on the test drive. The only liability was a huge crease on the passenger front fender that a graduate of the Moe Howard school of body work tried to pound out, evidently with a bag of ball bearings. Consequently, the fender was junk, and new Lancia body panels don't exactly come free in a box of Cracker Jack.

Gambling that I could find a fender at a reasonable price, I offered to get the car out the sight of the seller's wife that afternoon if he'd take $1,000. After a trip to the ATM, the car was mine. It was a far nicer driver than the blue carbureted car. More torque, more power and flawless cold starts courtesy of the additional 200 cc and fuel injection. The Spider body style was curious but actually quite handy. The fiberglass center section of the roof lifted off after pulling two latches. The soft rear window could either remain in place or it could be folded down. Although I have to admit, that with the rear window folded down, in profile, the car bore more than a passing resemblance to a Subaru Brat pickup.

The matter of the crunched fender was solved with a phone call to an Italian car salvage yard in California where a clean front fender was found. I had it installed and painted for $1,000. After replacing a clogged catalytic converter and a rusty muffler, I had a very attractive open Italian GT for a total investment of about $2,200.

Unfortunately, right around this time, I decided to leave my position in Portland. Not wishing to spend $1,500 to ship it back home to St. Louis or roll the dice on a 2,000 mile drive in a twenty-five year old Italian car, I threw it up on eBay hoping to get close to what the coupe brought. It didn't happen—the car defied the old adage, "when the top goes down, the price goes up." My friend Donald Osborne (who happens to be the editor of the magazine of the American Lancia Club) opined that Spiders are relatively common while good coupes are nearly extinct. In hindsight, I wish I'd kept it and sent it home. Sporting convertibles with a semi-usable back seat for under $3,000 are pretty thin on the ground.

MG

Midget 1961-79		
Parts availability ✪✪✪✪✪	Inexpensive to maintain ✪✪✪✪✪	Investment potential ✪ ✪✪✪✪
Fun to drive ✪✪✪✪	Price category **$**	Nice driver, $3,000; Show winner, $9,000 (Rubber bumper)
Performance 0 to 60 in 15.3 seconds; ¼ mile in 20.3 seconds at 67.5 mph (*Road & Track* 4/76)		

Parts Moss Motors, www.mossmotors.com; The Little British Car Company, www.lbcarco.com; Victoria British, www.victoriabritish.com; British Parts Northwest, www.bpnorthwest.com

Club The Midget and Sprite Club, www.mgcars.org.uk/midgetspriteclub/index.html

ran when parked...

Above left: It's difficult to comprehend just how small a Midget is with nothing close enough to provide a sense of scale. Right: Midget cockpit contains a full complement of chrome-ringed Smiths gauges.
Left: Tonneau cover—a charming period accessory. Of course, if you hit anything in a Midget, they might as well just zip up the other side and screw some more handles on the side of the car and save a pine tree or two.

History

The MG Midget is a wonderful example of a class of car that simply doesn't exist anymore—the under 2000 lb. under 2.0 liter sports car of modest performance and even more modest price. It's a shame really, as I believe that there is still a large market for a 25-plus mpg convertible sports car based on, perhaps, a Kia Rio or Chevy Aveo platform, selling for around $12,000.

When BMC restyled the iconic Austin-Healey "Bugeye" Sprite, they decided that it would make sense for MG dealers to have a Sprite twin to sell at a lower price than the new MGB. An MG grille was hastily made up for the Sprite, along with some other minor trim differences, and the pre-war Midget name was revived.

As in the Sprite, the 948 cc A-series engine developed a meager 46 hp; performance was predictably modest. Nevertheless, like the Sprite, handling was quite entertaining and the car was eminently tunable. A year into the production run, the displacement was increased to 1098 ccs and BMC added front disc brakes. The 10 hp gain was significant, although the previous drum brakes had been more than adequate. Weather protection was still largely theoretical—side curtains and a pup tent with a removable frame masquerading as a top.

By the early 1960s, even hardcore masochists were beginning to look at side curtains as an unnecessary inconvenience. Rollup windows and a proper folding top finally came to the Midget in 1964—outside of Morgan, it was one of the last side curtain hold outs. An additional 3 hp was also found in the A-series engine.

Perhaps the most desirable Midget was the 1966-67, which had a slightly detuned version of the Mini Cooper S 1275 cc engine that put out a healthy 65 hp and still had the pretty pre-safety steel dash and seats with contrasting piping. 1968 saw an ugly new dash and 1969 brought British Leyland's maladroit cost-cutting measures to the interior and a homely new grille. Wire wheels became a fairly rare option around this time but it matters little as the very pretty Rostyle-styled steel wheels became the standard. They're both attractive and easy to maintain.

1972-74 cars are particularly desirable because in spite of ever-tightening emission controls, the flat-topped wheel arches were rounded off. The Midget finally looked the way it should have all along—nearly as pretty as the Spitfire. Unfortunately, it wasn't to last. Apparently, nobody told the new people at BL that the car was designed with flat-topped arches on purpose. They actually lent structural strength to the rear fenders. Rear fenders on the round-arch cars folded up like a paper airplane.

In late 1974, the Midget suffered an even greater injustice than the MGB—at least the B was allowed to wheeze off to its grave in 1980 with an MG engine. The 1975 Midget got a 1500 cc Triumph engine in place of the no longer smoggable 1275. At least as part of the deal, the Midget got a fully synchronized gearbox for the first time in its life. Worse followed with the grafting on of the infamous rubber bumpers and the lifting of the suspension, the same as the MGB.

Somehow, the Midget's cheeky character managed to survive, and unlike the MGB, performance of the late rubber-bumper cars at least matched that of the early 46 hp cars. For this reason, rubber-bumper Midgets are slightly better regarded than rubber-bumper Bs.

As the name implies, these are tiny cars both inside and out. Anyone much over five feet six simply won't fit. Even for those of the right stature, ingress and egress is tough. Midget doors are tiny, seat travel is limited. With the top up, a Midget could induce claustrophobia in a three year-old.

Tiny Midget feels quicker than it is

Still, a Midget can be quite enjoyable, especially the 1966-74 cars. Because of their size, they feel much quicker than they actually are. Brakes are more than adequate for the car and steering and handling are actually quite entertaining. There's a reason why so many Midgets and Sprites wind up as entry-level vintage racers.

Mechanically, things are straightforward and inexpensive. A-series motors are more durable than Triumph units (another reason to stay away from the rubber bumper cars). Absence of strange noises, smoke and the presence of oil pressure of at least 40 psi are good signs. Gearboxes with a crash first will invariably have a noisy first gear. As long as the gear can be selected and doesn't pop out, assuming the noise isn't ear-splitting, it should be okay.

Nearly every part is still available and along with the Spitfire and the Sprite, Midget parts are always the loss-leader. Nobody who wants to get most of their money out of a car should ever consider restoring a Midget, although doing something like freshening an interior shouldn't cause too much harm. And if you think you've gone crazy because your round arch Midget has navy blue seats and black carpets, you haven't. BL evidently got a screaming deal on blue vinyl in the early 1970s.

Rusty Midgets are best left as parts cars. Main floors, trunk floors and front fenders are the usual rot spots. Even though sheet metal is available, you'll be instantly underwater trying to fix a rusty Midget.

The market

Rubber bumper Midgets along with Lancia Betas are about the absolute entry level into the collector car hobby. They have compromised looks and nearly no performance. And again, when $3,500 buys a decent 1990 Miata, it gets hard to justify owning a rubber bumper Midget. Spend a few more dollars and buy an earlier car. Either way, unless you steal the car, don't expect to do more than get your money back when you sell.

Case study

1978 MG Midget		
Purchase Price $2,100	**Sale Price** $2,900	**Owned for** 0.5 years

This was a car that I didn't need that I bought simply because it was cheap, and my buddy Paul Duchene and I were bored. It came from a friend of Paul's in Eastern Washington State, rust-free and quite lovely. The

previous owner was a very candid woman in her fifties who stated that she was selling the car because in her words, "it had done its job—it found me a husband."

Paul and I figured at the very least, there had to be a few hundred dollars of profit in a very pretty red convertible sports car and it turns out, that's about all there was. While the car had surprisingly excellent paint (I've seen worse on cars costing a hundred times as much), it was a color change that didn't extend to the engine compartment which had been shot flat black.

Even in a cheap car, a color change is a "story"—it's off-putting. But we figured at this price point, the great paint would make up for it. We figured wrong—it took two runs on eBay to make it to just $2,900. And while not making the equivalent of "Shaft's Big Score" on the Midget, both of us admitted that the anemic little sports car was somehow rather amusing to drive.

The steering was quick, the brakes more than good enough to haul down its 1,500 lb. bulk from the car's terminal velocity of around 85 mph. At the time, regular gas in Portland, Oregon was selling for around $3.75 per gallon. The MG never returned less than about 28 mpg. As a cut-rate, considerably-less-safe alternative to a Smart For Two, in an urban setting, the Midget actually made a perverse kind of sense.

 **chapter four**

american icons

Not all great American cars
sell for six figures on the
SPEED Channel.

AMERICANS CAN CREDIBLY LAY CLAIM to starting the old car hobby when hot rodders and hobbyists started restoring, tinkering with and modifying Model Ts and Model As. And we certainly turned classic car auctions into a contact sport with Barrett-Jackson becoming the first auction to be recognized as a brand with considerable equity.

And if you've noticed that this book tends to be a bit Euro-centric, it isn't because of a lack of patriotism or a dislike of American cars. Rather, the simple fact is that many of the really great collectible American cars have been discovered and accordingly, values have skyrocketed beyond what is generally considered affordable.

But when you look past the hyped-up muscle car market, there remain some true affordable gems. Absolute style landmarks like the '66 Toronado and '67 Cadillac Eldorado, not to mention the sublime 1963 Buick Riviera can still be bought for absurdly little money.

The beauty of American cars is the fact that they have the home field advantage—parts will be easier to find and far cheaper than those for most imports. And even though many mechanics today are lost without a laptop or OBD II diagnostic equipment, it's still far easier to find competent help in sorting out your 1970 Pontiac Grand Prix than it is to replace the thermostatic actuator in your Alfa Romeo Spider. For this reason alone, I often recommend one of the cars profiled below as an ideal first collector car.

Buick

Riviera 1963-65 (First-Generation) 1966-67 (Second-Generation)		❄
Parts availability ✪✪✪½	Inexpensive to maintain ✪✪✪✪✪	Investment potential ✪✪✪
Fun to drive ✪✪	Price category **$$$** $18,000 ($12,000); Show winner, $40,000 ($20,000)*	
Performance 0 to 60 in 8.1 seconds; ¼ mile in 16.7 seconds at 86.7 mph (*Road & Track* 2/66)		

*Second Generation in parenthesese

Parts Classic Buick Parts, www.classicbuicks.com

Club Riviera Owner's Association, www.rivowners.org

Bill Mitchell's idea of an American Ferrari, the 1963 Buick Riviera.

Left: Nailhead V8 came
with plenty of power
and a long life.
Right: Handsome
Buick with clear European
styling influence.

History

The 1963 Buick Riviera was the product of a bygone era at GM (before the tyranny of accountants, analysis paralysis and shopping mall focus groups) when the force of will of single individuals like Harley Earl, Zora Duntov and Bill Mitchell really could have an effect on product. As legend has it, Bill Mitchell, then the head of GM design, was in London and got a look at a custom bodied Rolls-Royce and a Ferrari 250 PF coupe. And although nobody at GM had asked for such a car, Mitchell decided that a combination of the two would be the ideal American luxury grand tourer.

The only question was, which division would build it? Mitchell thought that Cadillac would be ideal—the car could be the revival of the LaSalle brand. Cadillac had other thoughts; they were selling everything they could build and they had no interest in reviving a nameplate they perceived as down-market. So the car was thrown up for grabs to the other GM divisions. Buick hired a slick New York ad agency to make their case as to why they should get the car.

Predictably, the hired madmen carried the day, and Buick was awarded the car they dubbed the Riviera. It was a shame that Buick engineers didn't specify a bit more Corvette and a bit less Electra in the final mix; the usual soft suspension, numb steering and marginal drum brakes were part of the package. But at least the styling was fantastic, as good as anything GM had done post-war. The sharp edges, minimal chrome and handsome interior were remarkably tasteful.

Buick's dependable 401 and 425 "nailhead" V8s provided plenty of power, and with the exception of a backup camera, MP3 player and a nav system, most of the luxury items we're accustomed to today were available. Air conditioning, power windows, cruise control and power seats were common options.

The 1965 was the car Mitchell wanted to build all along. Headlights were hidden behind an ingenious clamshell design; there were none of the compromises or obvious headlamp doors of other designs. The GS option was also available for 1965, which gave the car more of a performance edge. But even the GS's forte was digesting large portions of interstate miles rather than making short work of the serpentines.

The first generation lasted just three model years, when the bean-counters realized that it shared its platform with no other GM car. Thereafter, starting in 1966, the Riviera would be built on the E-platform that would also support the 1966 Oldsmobile Toronado and the 1967 Cadillac Eldorado. Strangely, the Riv was the only conventional rear-driver of the three.

The restyled 1966 Riviera was also quite attractive in a massive sort of way. Some have called it one of the more extreme examples of the "long hood, short rear deck" style—not entirely accurate, as there's nothing particularly short about a rear ¾ as long as a BMC Mini. The rear deck could only be considered short when compared to the hood, which was truly a steam catapult and arrestor wire away from being a flight deck.

In GS form, it came closer to a GT in the European sense; but it was just too large and heavy to consider any back road activity. When pushed, the steering was just too imprecise to place the car in a corner, and the nose-heavy Riv would plow to the outside, bias-ply tires howling.

Of the second-generation cars, the 1966-67 cars are the most pure. By 1970, the car had been completely spoiled with a new front and rear skirts. Only the lowrider crowd seems to care about the 1970 Riv.

Rusty examples abound, restoration parts do not

As with any car of the era, factory rust proofing was virtually non-existent. Over the years, most Rivieras out there have suffered from some form of rust damage. Those expecting to find readily available NOS or quality reproduction sheet metal will be sorely disappointed. Rivieras are quite rare compared to Chevelles and Mustangs, and while they've been recognized as milestone cars for quite some time, they haven't really had a following until quite recently. Consequently, there hasn't been much of a demand to reproduce things.

What this means is that while finding mechanical parts—which were common to other Buicks—won't be much of a problem, trim, especially interior items and body panels, will be difficult and time-consuming to source. Badly rusted or incomplete cars are likely to wind up never completed projects. It's imperative to choose wisely. As usual, West Coast cars seem to fare the best.

The market

The 1963-65 Riviera has been recognized as a stylistic milestone for many years. It's as fine a piece of Mitchell work as the 1963 split-window Corvette. Until the last several years, few collectors seemed to care. This all seemed to change when a savvy collector brought a nicely restored car to RM's Amelia Island sale. The $30,000-plus paid for the car was more than anyone could remember at a public sale. Several years later in 2004, a 1965 GS broke $60,000 at a sale in North Carolina and suddenly, the Riviera was on collectors' radar. Since then, there have been other high-dollar sales, but in general, it has taken a very well-restored GS to bring more than $40,000. Very acceptable cars are still available in the $20,000 range. Second generation cars bring about half as much.

Left: The interior of the '63 Riviera—a rare moment of restrained elegance in 1960s Detroit.
Right: Second generation 1967 Riviera displaying a rear fender nearly as long as a Mini Cooper.

Case study

1963 Buick Riviera		
Purchase Price $14,000 (2006)	**Sale Price** N/A	**Owned for** 1.5 years

I'd always been an admirer of the first generation Riviera; I wondered why the market seemed to ignore them for so long. After the Amelia Island sale, I resolved to find one, even though I'd be chasing a rising market. As luck would have it, my good friend, classic car dealer Charlie Kuhn had just bought one out of an estate sale in St. Louis. I saved him the freight of sending it back to Chicago and bought it on the spot.

It was a two-owner little-old-man car that had been well-maintained by someone who'd clearly loved the car. Never rusted, never hit and most importantly, never painted or re-upholstered. In addition to being a desirable first-generation Riviera, as a well-preserved unrestored car, it was incredibly appealing—and potentially, even more collectible, as the stock in original cars continues to rise in the marketplace.

As an investment, it's probably going to perform reasonably well and I do love looking at it; but it's not a car that I live to drive. My preferred way to enjoy an old car is to find a challenging road, clip a few apexes and generally try to at least double the posted speed on the yellow sign advertising a curve ahead. Hitting a

Unrestored '63 Riv—
unchanged since the
Kennedy administration.

straight interstate and cruising in comfort for a few hundred miles isn't high on my list of fun things to do in a recreational car. Yet that's precisely the Riviera's forte.

If I were a traveling salesman in the early 1960s, this would have been my car, but as a 21st century collector, I much preferred the BMW 2800CS I owned—which was what I imagine the Riviera would have been if the Germans designed and built it; more sensibly sized but still comfortable. Handsome, pillarless coupe styling like the Riv, but with real brakes, handling and a manual transmission.

One advantage the Riv clearly has over the BMW is the fact that it has cost me nearly nothing to own. A change of fluids, a new battery and a generator rebuild and that's about it. One thing about buying nicely preserved unrestored car is the fact that the purchase price is not just the entry fee. Because the originality is the attraction, other than mechanical maintenance, you're not tempted to alter things or even freshen them up.

So, if you're a fan of really fine design, like the rumble and torque of a big Detroit V8 and don't mind fade-prone drum brakes, pinky light power steering devoid of road feel and nimble handling, a classic Riv can give you much of what is appealing about a muscle car without the volatility of that market.

Oldsmobile

Toronado 1966-67		❄
Parts availability ✪✪✪½	**Inexpensive to maintain** ✪✪✪✪✪	**Investment potential** ✪✪½
Fun to drive ✪✪½	**Price category** $$$	Nice driver, $15,000; Show winner, $35,000
Performance 0 to 60 in 9.9 seconds; ¼ mile in 17.8 seconds at 83 mph (*Road & Track* 1/66)		

Parts Fusick Automotive Parts, www.fusick.com

Club Toronado Owners Association, www.toronado.org

History

The 1966 Toronado was America's first front-wheel drive car since the Cord 810 thirty years earlier. It was certainly Oldsmobile's (and possibly GM's) last stylistic tour de force. The post-1967 years became increasingly unfriendly to this type of individuality, as committees, legislators, and shopping mall focus groups took over American automotive design.

The project that eventually became the Toronado had a long gestation period and was cloaked in all the secrecy of a Cold War spy plane. The original designation, "XP-784," even sounds like a black ops project.

Bob Lichty

Bob Lichty

Far left: 1967 Toronado shows its brawny profile. Right: Roomy flat-floored interior of 1966 Toronado. Below: Toronado front inspired by coffin-nosed Cord 812.

The name Toronado was chosen to further throw-off inquiring minds, as it was also the name of an unrelated 1963 Chevrolet concept car. Although it sounds like a cross between a beef entrée and a mobile-home-marauding twister, it actually has no meaning in any language—perhaps that's where the Japanese got the idea for car names that mean nothing.

The reason for the car's long gestation period was its unique drive train. Europeans had been mass-producing FWD successfully since Citroën's Traction Avant of 1934, and Sir Alec Issigonis's brilliant Mini was already a micro-sensation. But there was strong doubt whether the concept was transferable to a full-sized American car with a large, high-torque engine. The Cord L-29 had shown a tendency to crack its frame and eventually abandon its front wheels, and the later 810 had greasily illustrated the limitations of constant velocity joints.

Olds aimed to make FWD work with a 425-ci V8 pounding out 385 hp and a pavement-rippling 475 ft-lbs of torque. It seems a near impossible task even today; a recipe for an ill-handling, badly balanced, massive torque-steering beast that disintegrates its driveline in short order. In fact, the Toro is none of these things.

Olds engineers realized that the success of all future FWD vehicles at GM rode on the outcome of Project XP-784. Unlike the bean-counter GM of the 80s, the project fell to a cadre of talented, crew-cut, skinny-tie-wearing, slide-rule-carrying engineers (think Ed Harris in Apollo 13). And if they didn't actually utter the phrase "failure is not an option," they certainly lived it. They delivered a unique and bullet-proof solution to power the new Toronado.

Unlike most front drivers, the power pack in a Toro is not mounted transversely but rather longitudinally. The standard GM 400 Turbo Hydramatic transmission is situated on the driver's side of the engine, with the flywheel and torque converter mounted conventionally on the tail of the engine. The tricky part is the chain linking the engine and the transmission. While a chain doesn't inspire thoughts of longevity with this amount of power and torque, the Morris Company engineered a pre-stretched rubber-isolated steel chain—quiet, with an almost limitless life span. Suspension was by torsion bars in front and a beam axle in the rear.

While the Toronado was a conventional, assembly-line, serial-production car designed to make a profit rather than a statement (unlike, say, a '56 Continental), there were some special touches. Olds junkies maintain that Toronado engines are the best of the best—every bit as good as the 442 and W-30 engines. They were machined to closer tolerances, had aluminized valves set in big valve heads, high-compression pistons, and deeper oil pans that held an extra quart.

The stylists, led by the legendary Bill Mitchell, created an envelope befitting the engineers' accomplishments; a clean, flowing, pillarless fastback with little unnecessary adornment (except when fitted with an obnoxious vinyl top). The unique wheels, hidden headlights, and horizontal slatted grille were an homage to the Cord of three decades earlier.

Jay Leno commissioned a fabulous resto-mod '66 Toronado, and wisely honored the appearance of the car, right down to the 17-inch replicas of the original Cord-like chrome wheels (though he did commit heresy by adding a Chevy engine and rear-wheel drive). Leno has correctly pointed out that some styling cues, such as the muscular and prominent fender arches, still look contemporary.

Although the sheer size of the Toro earned what may have been the first printed reference to a "land yacht," I don't think that *Road & Track* intended the negative connotation that we associate with the term today. In fact, they commented favorably on the car's handling, stating that it was among the best-handling big cars that they had ever driven, and that it could be "driven through winding mountain roads almost as if it were a sports car."

Proving that point, Bobby Unser won the 1967 Pike's Peak Hill Climb in a Toronado as part of a stunning 1-2-3 Olds finish. Only the typically numb Saginaw power steering and drum brakes let things down, although discs became available in '67. The big Olds also had a prodigious appetite for its specially-designed Firestone front tires and the thirst of an Aussie drover for fuel.

Interiors exceptionally roomy and comfortable

The interior of the Toronado has both flat seats and floor, with seats covered in good cloth or leather. The floor is missing a drive shaft hump to allow a more spacious feeling. The dash, while unmistakably American, has full instrumentation, including a unique revolving drum-type speedometer, which works fine until the cable wears—then it becomes as unreadable as the Edsel compass-type.

Toronado sales started with a bang in 1966, with 40,963 out the door, but plunged like the car's gas gauge from then on as the smooth design was progressively mangled. Sales dropped 50 percent in 1967; the '67 is visually very similar with only an egg-crate grille to differentiate it.

The next models lost the purity and therefore the desirability of the 1966-67 cars. The 1968, for example, appeared to have crashed into a six-foot harmonica; but 26,454 were sold in 1968 and 28,494 in 1969, probably thanks to the new 455-ci engine. The hidden headlights were abandoned in 1970 in the alarmingly overdone redesign, but 25,433 cars were sold, including 5,341 GTs. By 1971, the grand experiment was over and a literally square redesign turned Cinderella into her ugly sister.

The market

Truly fine '66–67 Toronados are a rare sight at auctions. Occasionally, one sees well-preserved originals at shows and club events. These must surely be the ones to own, as I would hate to guess what a restoration would cost. The plating bill for the wheels and bumpers will send you reeling, and many trim items are, to use a term coined by frustrated restorers, made out of genuine "unobtainium".

A Toronado is a hard car to pigeon-hole, which may contribute to the market's lack of interest in this arresting and original design. Some fans correctly maintain that it is the world's only FWD muscle car, which is supported by its massive power, roadability and 130-mph top speed. But, the Toronado's personal luxury overtones, and the common belief that "FWD" and "muscle car" are diametrically opposed, count against

ran when parked...

this assertion. Regardless of how one categorizes it, the field of interesting cars that have a potential upside—and can be had at a price of $15,000 or less—continues to shrink. The early Toronado must rank as one of today's best remaining sleepers.

Chevrolet

Soft rear bumper evident on this 1977 Corvette.

MidAmerica Motorworks

History

The 1970s have been called the decade that quality control forgot. It wasn't simply that we forgot how to screw together cars, or that the bean counters cost-cut the quality out of our products. No, it was the perfect storm of an energy shortage, higher insurance rates and pollution regulations—combined with the aforementioned cost-cutting—that ensured that most foreign and domestic product of the time was, to put it simply, bland, slow crap. Even the Corvette wasn't immune from the malaise. Pollution regulations started to attack the performance after 1972. The 454 big-block option and real dual exhaust both went away after 1974. It hardly mattered; by then, the 454 had been emasculated to just 270 hp. Even taking into account the gross vs. net horsepower measurement switch, by 1974, the big block was making less power than a base small-block was making just three years before. There was far worse to come.

The convertible disappeared after the 1975 model year and by then, the base motor was down to just 165 hp—the lowest since the Blue Flame Six disappeared in 1955. Even the "hot" L-82 motor made just 205 hp. All was not lost, as the car at least still looked quite good. GM had pioneered urethane covered bumpers—that was their solution to the 5 mph bumper regulations. 1973 was the first year of the soft bumpers, which showed up only on the front. 1974 was the first year for front and rear urethane bumpers, and the back end lost its distinctive "ducktail."

Still handsome and not as slow as you think

You can quibble about chrome bumper versus urethane cars from a looks standpoint, but the only significant drawback the plastic bumper cars had, from an appearance standpoint, was GM's inability to get the different materials to match. The urethane bumpers almost never matched the fiberglass body; as paint aged and faded, it only became worse.

Left: Handsome
Saddle leather interior
of a 1974 Corvette.
Right: 1977 Corvette
with factory
aluminum wheels.

As if to compensate for the lost performance, former options like power steering, power brakes, and leather upholstery were made standard. And shameful as these 'Vettes may be to those who think that no Corvette should have less than 396 cubic inches or 350 hp, they really aren't bad to live with, nor are they pitifully slow either.

Most road tests reported 0–60 times in the mid-sevens to the mid-eights, as fast as a contemporary Porsche 911 or a Ferrari 308GT4, and considerably quicker than its main Japanese rival, the Datsun 280Z. Handling was respectable—when the box for the Gymkhana suspension option was checked.

Like the 1968–72 cars, the 1974–77 Corvettes are starting to look better as the years go by, especially with the slotted alloy wheels that became available after 1973. And although many would question the wisdom of buying an emasculated C3 over a C4 at the same money, the C4 was a much more complex, and potentially a more expensive car to maintain than the C3.

Accident damage and frame rust are the primary issues to look for. Feel behind panels for factory bonding strips and rough or poorly finished areas; these are indicative of repairs. Headlights should go up and down in unison and fit well when retracted. Another quick way to check for accident damage is to open the fuel-filler lid. The gas cap should be centered (roughly). If the frame has been bent at some point, the tank and the filler-neck will have shifted, moving the cap well off-center.

Panel fit on Corvettes should be reasonably good. Doors and hoods were often ground or trimmed to fit when the cars were assembled, and a certain amount of waviness is acceptable on the sides of the car. They are, after all, plastic rather than steel. Corvette bodies don't rust—but the chassis certainly do. The most likely places are just in front of the rear wheels, and where the frame curves up over the rear suspension. The "birdcage" is another rust area. This is the supporting structure for the cowl and windshield. An expert is essential for checking the condition of these areas.

Corvette interiors are cheap and easy to restore. A complete interior can be purchased inexpensively, and an advanced do-it-yourselfer can do the install. For a crash course in interior installation, make a point of attending MidAmerica Motorworks' Corvette FunFest which is held every September in Effingham, Illinois. Crews install interiors in customer cars all weekend.

Corvettes are notoriously robust mechanically, and the cast-iron pushrod engines are tough as nails. If the C-3 Corvette has an Achilles heel, it is the rear suspension. Hubs, half-shafts, wheel bearings, and differential mounts should be looked at carefully, especially in 454-ci cars, although with less horsepower and torque to deal with, this is not a huge problem in the later cars.

The market

Aside from a convertible, the car to have would probably be an L82 four-speed with air and alloys, in a good period color like orange. But these cars will always lag far behind the chrome bumper C-3 cars with real horsepower—convertibles and L82 engine cars bring a bit more money.

In general, 1974–77 Corvettes have been appreciating modestly. A few years back, they were plentiful in the $7,000–$8,000 range for a standard coupe. Now, $10,000 is more like it. For that money, they represent a tremendous bargain. While an underachiever for a Corvette, you still get a V8 rumble, handsome looks, and decent performance.

ran when parked...

Ford

Thunderbird 1961-63		❄
Parts availability ✪✪✪✪	Inexpensive to maintain ✪✪✪✪✪	Investment potential ✪✪✪
Fun to drive ✪✪✪	Price category **$$$**	Nice driver, $14,000; Show winner, $22,000 (coupe)
Performance 0 to 60 in 8.8 seconds; ¼ mile in 16.9 seconds at 89 mph		

Parts Bird Nest, www.tbirdparts.com; The Vintage T-Bird Sanctuary, www.tbirdsanctuary.com

Club Vintage Thunderbird Club International, www.vintagethunderbirdclub.com

Charlie Kuhn

Bulletbird's styling the best T-Bird look since 1955.

History

Pity the Ford stylists of the late 1950s-1960s. Product cycles were shorter in those days, and so every three years or so, the design team had to come up with a new look for an iconic model like the T-Bird. Sometimes, they did better than others. While the "Squarebird" of 1958-60 was s strong seller, few could argue that it possessed any of the grace of the 1955-57 car.

From a style standpoint, the "Bulletbird" of 1961-63 was arguably the most successful of the post 1957 T-Birds. Even though it has its fair share of clichés from the "supersonic" school of design (the jet-pipe inspired tail-lights and fins come to mind here), the whole thing manages to come off quite well. While often not the case, the convertible is more attractive than the coupe, the formal roof of which seems out of character with the rest of the flowing lines of the car. Those who saw the Vince Gardner designed Thunderbird "Italien" concept car at Barrett-Jackson in 2008 nearly wept for what might have been.

Today's Ford marketers would surely stand in awe of the product placement achieved by Ford for the new T-Bird. It was the pace car for the 1961 Indy 500, Elvis used one in the otherwise eminently forgettable movie *Follow That Dream, and* so did Dean Martin in the much cooler campy spy classic *Murderer's Row*. And if that wasn't enough, former Ford exec turned Kennedy Secretary of Defense, Robert McNamara, engineered a supporting role for the T-bird in the inauguration parade—a nice parting gift to his buddies at Ford.

The only engine available was the new 390 cubic-inch V8 with a Cruise-O-Matic three-speed slushbox. A hi-performance option, the M-Code was offered until mid-1963. M-Code cars came with higher compression-heads and three two-barrel carburetors—it was good for 345 hp, at the expense of anything resembling reasonable fuel economy. Although there was but a single engine option, a plethora of convenience features were optional, such as power windows, A/C and power seats. Power brakes and power steering were standard. Kelsey Hayes wire wheels were a rare and desirable option.

Left: Highly stylized interior actually not as much an ergonomic nightmare as it appears.
Right: Those are tail-lights, not jet exhausts. Classic early '60s kitsch.

On the subject of rare and desirable, for 1962, Ford built just 1,427 Sports Roadster models which harkened back to the two-seater cars of 1955-57. All were fitted with wire wheels and a fiberglass tonneau that covered the otherwise useful rear seating area. Just 120 were ordered with the M-Code engine option—at least twice that many "survive"—so beware of fakes. The Landau model was introduced in 1962 with a vinyl top and gaudy phony landau bars on the C-pillar. The Principality of Monaco Landau edition in Corinthian White was an amusing curiosity. Not surprisingly, there have been no reported Monaco Landau fakes and regrettably, no Martin Landau edition.

Sporty looks, soft drivers

As drivers, Bulletbirds are pretty much standard American early '60s fare—comfortably numb (although reasonably quick) power steering, Fade-O-Matic drum brakes and suspension settings by the Pillsbury Doughboy—stomp on the throttle and watch the front end rise up like a Chris-Craft. A Studebaker Hawk GT is a bit less stylish but a better handling car. Still, if effortless cruising is your style, you could do far worse than a 1961-63 T-Bird.

Tough mechanicals surrounded by dissolving bodywork

Mechanically, all T-Birds are straightforward with basic service items still easily found at the average well-stocked auto parts store. Few things will ever go wrong with a 390 V8. Clearances will gradually increase over time, along with oil consumption, and that's about it. Occasionally, smoking and oil consumption can be caused by a stuck piston ring in a car that hasn't been used much—use will take care of this.

Noisy hydraulic lifters are also not uncommon, and unless accompanied by a miss, are probably nothing to worry about. Like most American V8s, rebuild costs are comical compared to foreign cars. Ford automatic transmissions of the era were about as durable as it gets. When a rebuild is signaled by slow or interrupted shifts, take solace in the fact that tranny rebuilds are also dirt cheap.

Not particularly durable is the bodywork. Semi-unit construction means that extensive rust repairs will be a genuine pain in the neck. Floors, sills, rear-quarters and the convertible top package tray are particularly vulnerable, as is the roof of Landau cars if moisture gets under the vinyl covering. At least some sheet metal is available, as are interior kits, some lenses and plastic parts.

The market

Excluding rare items like the '62 M-Code Sports Roadster, the 1955-57 cars will always be the most collectible T-Birds. And that market has been rather flat for quite some time. What this means for the Bulletbird is unclear, however, as a stylish, and very usable minor classic car, it has a lot going for it. Expect rather modest but steady appreciation, especially in the convertibles and non-Landau coupes.

ran when parked...

Cadillac

Eldorado 1967-68		❄
Parts availability ✪✪✪½	**Inexpensive to maintain** ✪✪✪✪	**Investment potential** ✪✪
Fun to drive ✪✪½	**Price category** $$	Nice driver, $11,000; Show winner, $20,000
Performance 0 to 60 in 9.9 seconds; ¼ mile in 17.8 seconds at 83 mph		

Parts Cadillac International, www.cadillacinternational.com
Club Cadillac and LaSalle Club, www.cadillaclasalleclub.org

History

1967 was a watershed year for GM. It was the last year before the U.S. government got into the car design business, and many of their products and divisions were at the top of their game. Cadillac had just marked its third year in a row of record sales, and was about to introduce its most technologically advanced car ever.

In typical conservative Cadillac fashion, they let Oldsmobile grab the fanfare with the Toronado, but they benefitted from the extra year of experience that Oldsmobile got with the Eldorado's E-body twin. Mechanically, the Eldorado and the Toronado were quite similar. Both employed front wheel-drive with massive V8 engines placed longitudinally rather than transversely, providing power through a chain-driven THM425 transmission.

Suspension was an impressive display of engineering, consisting of torsion bars, A-arms, telescopic shocks up front, a beam-axle on semi-elliptic leaf springs in back, and four shock absorbers—two horizontal and two vertical, with self-leveling control. Although no European GT, ride and handling were excellent for a large American car. Initially, power came from Cadillac's 429 ci V8, which made about 340 hp. Standard brakes were the same barely adequate eleven-inch drums from the Toronado. Optional four-piston disc brakes made a significant difference in stopping power.

But to hell with the mechanical mumbo jumbo, the real story of the '67 Eldorado was the styling. The GM styling department under William Mitchell was like the 1972 Miami Dolphins. They were perfect. The '66 Toronado was one for the ages, but to follow it up with the '67 Eldo was simply amazing. The knife-edged styling continues to influence Cadillac today.

It was a classic long hood, short rear deck affair with some great touches—like the sharp creased fenders and hidden headlights. It was extraordinarily well-received. *Automobile Quarterly* gave it a design excellence award and *Motor Trend* extolled its build quality—which it rated on par with BMW and Mercedes-Benz—and its performance, which included a 0-60 time of under 10 seconds and a 125 mph top speed.

Single digit fuel economy and a dearth of good examples

Other than its abysmal fuel economy, there are few impediments to owning a 1967-68 Eldorado. Finding a good one is likely to be the biggest issue. Values have been low for so long that properly restored cars are

Left: 1967 Eldorado is pure William Mitchell with hidden headlights and no vinyl top.
Right: Current Cadillac CTS still carries the influence of this knife-edge styling theme.

thin on the ground. But fine originals are out there, likely the best route. Restoration costs are daunting indeed—there are few NOS parts left out there, and the original materials used were and of high quality and expensive. Mechanically, the cars have proven quite tough—even the unique chain-driven front-wheel drive arrangement.

The market

In terms of the swagger to cost ratio, the 1967 Cadillac Eldorado may be one of the greatest bargains on the collector car market. The '67 Eldo's sister, the Oldsmobile Toronado, has officially been "discovered" over the last few years, but the 1967-68 Eldo still languishes firmly in the sleeper category. Don't expect this to change any time soon. But it's an inexpensive way to buy a Bill Mitchell classic and a reminder of a time when the General could design cars with the best of them.

Studebaker

Gran Turismo Hawk 1962-64			❄
Parts availability ✪✪✪		**Inexpensive to maintain** ✪✪✪✪✪	**Investment potential** ✪✪
Fun to drive ✪✪✪	**Price category** $$$	Nice driver, $17,300; Show winner, $31,000	
Performance 0 to 60 in 10.2 seconds; ¼ mile in 17.3 seconds at 76 mph (*Road & Track* 3/61)			

Parts Studebaker Parts, www.studebakerparts.com; Lionel Stone Studebaker, http://www.studebakervendors.com/lstone.htm; Studebaker International, Inc., http://www.steudebaker-intl.com

Club Studebaker Drivers Club, www.studebakerdriversclub.com

1962 GT Hawk was as elegant a coupe as anything coming from Stuttgart at the time.

Shawn Dougan/Hyman, Ltd.

History

Studebaker built some of the most interesting American cars of the 1950s and '60s. But to most Big Three-obsessed American car collectors, their orphan status makes them seem virtually invisible. That's a shame, as GT Hawks are elegant cars that are credible handlers and performers.

The Hawk line was introduced in 1956 as basically an extension of the Raymond Loewy-designed Starlight coupes of 1953. Drastically smaller than, say, a Chrysler 300C of the era, they sported tailfins as large as anything else built at the time. Everything was conventional—American cars with separate body and chassis, live axle, leaf springs and drum brakes.

Above left: The rear three-quarters on the GT Hawk is as elegant as the front.
Right: Venerable Studebaker 289 V8 is heavy but virtually unbreakable.
Left: As nice an interior as any made in the U.S. at the time. Bucket seats, floor shift and full instruments put a 1962 Corvette to shame.

By the early 1960s, the fin craze had passed. Brooks Stevens was called in to do a cheapo freshening job for the terminally cash-strapped Studebaker. Originally called the Hawk Monaco, Stevens did a masterful job in cropping the earlier car's fins, giving it a more formal roof line and a Mercedes inspired grille. The latter theft was understandable; Studebaker had a distribution agreement with Mercedes at the time.

Studebaker's venerable, heavy 289 ci V8 was carried over in the new car in a mild state of tune for 1962. Things got far more exciting in 1963 when the same V8 in Avanti tune became available in the GT Hawk; the R1 put out 240 hp, and the supercharged R2 nearly one horsepower per cubic inch. R3s with over 300 hp are quite rare. Front disc brakes became an option at this time as well. Three-speed manual plus overdrive, four-speed manual or Flight-O-Matic automatic transmissions were available.

Performance was quite good, especially in supercharged form with 0-60 in around 8 seconds and quarter mile times of around 16 seconds. Handling was a cut above the usual American car of the era; *Road & Track* remarked that the Hawk was a decent compromise for a sporting driver with a growing family, but advised, "just don't follow a well driven Alfa Romeo Giulia into a decreasing radius corner".

Like the Avanti, Andy Granatelli took the Hawk to Bonneville and posted some impressive speeds, primarily with the hot R3 version. Hawks even competed in a few NASCAR races in 1964.

Studebakers also had about the best equipped and nicest looking dash boards of any American car of the time, including the Corvette. GT Hawks could be ordered with a full complement of Stewart-Warner gauges on a wood grain dash—a very European look.

Like most other cars produced by the independents, non-mechanical parts are problematic. Most NOS body panels are gone at this point; minor trim items are rare as well. Few things beyond glass, rubber, interiors and lenses are being reproduced. It's imperative to buy a complete car with as little rust as possible. Again, with Hawk values what they are, restoring a car as anything but an irrational labor of love is fiscal insanity.

The market

Studebakers have received considerably more attention in the collector car market over the last five years or so; values have increased somewhat. But because of the herd mentality that exists in some sectors of the collector car market, something as pedestrian as a '64 Chevy Malibu SS might still sell for twice as much as an elegant supercharged Hawk GT. It's confounding, but there's no use in arguing; that's just the way it is. Bad news for those who have been sitting on Studebakers since 1966 waiting for an explosion in values, but good news for collectors looking for something different, elegant, easy to maintain and quite nice to drive—almost like an American alternative to a Mercedes 220SE.

Chevrolet

Corvair 1965-69		
Parts availability ✪✪✪✪	Inexpensive to maintain ✪✪✪✪	Investment potential ✪✪
Fun to drive ✪✪✪	Price category $$	Nice driver, $9,000; Show winner, $20,000 (Corsa coupe)
Performance 0 to 60 in 11.9 seconds; ¼ mile in 18.4 seconds at 74.5 mph (*Road & Track* 7/64)		

Parts Clark's Corvair Parts, www.corvair.com; Larry's Corvair Parts, www.larryscorvair.com

Club Corvair Society of America (CORSA), www.corvair.org

As pretty a Corvair as you are likely to see. Great colors, a convertible and the best looking wheel covers ever offered on the car. I want it.

Charlie Kuhn

History

There's an episode of *The Simpsons* where Homer finds out that he has a long lost brother who happens to be the CEO of a major car company. The CEO, enamored with his newfound sibling—but blissfully unaware that he's a halfwit—inexplicably lets Homer design a new car (named "The Homer" of course), with predictable results. While the Corvair was no Homer, it illustrates in a slightly less comical fashion what can happen when a single individual pushes forward with a car that is clearly the answer to a question that nobody asked.

ran when parked...

Roomy Corvair
interior uninhibited by
anything resembling a
transmission tunnel.

Ed Cole was the chief proponent of the idea of an air-cooled rear engine GM compact. Curious, since the limitations of the air-cooled rear engine design were already quite clear by the late 1950s. Most manufacturers were already looking at the front-wheel drive BMC Mini as the future rather than the rear engine Beetle.

Only Porsche, Tatra and VW had made the air-cooled rear engine work successfully—others, including Tucker and Mercedes-Benz hadn't. In the case of Tatra, the Czech-built cars had a well-known reputation of being dangerously unsafe handlers. So much so that the German general staff put out a directive prohibiting their officers from driving captured examples.

Why Cole insisted that GM go down this particularly expensive blind alley is anyone's guess. But for vastly different reasons, both Ralph Nader and the collector car world are clearly better off for him having done so. To clarify the Nader issue, Ralph the Opportunist didn't kill the Corvair, it was on its way out anyway (along with Ed Cole). In spite of its Nader-bestowed reputation—from which it has never recovered—the Corvair is a damned interesting and potentially very entertaining collector car.

While introduced in 1960, the Corvair saga really gets interesting in 1965 when a brilliant restyled version with a real independent rear suspension was introduced. *Car and Driver's* David E. Davis, Jr. called it "the most important new car of 1965" and "the most beautiful American car introduced since the end of WWII". The staff of *C and D* was also pretty taken with the way the car drove: "The new rear suspension, the new softer spring rates in front, the bigger brakes, the addition of some more power, all these factors had us driving around like idiots…We loved it." High praise indeed when coming from a magazine that was more famous for hatchet jobs than Lizzie Borden.

All Covairs were powered by an air-cooled flat-six in varying states of tune. The base engine from 1965 on made 95 hp, a step up brought 110 hp, exactly what a 1969 Porsche 911T made. The Corsa model came with a 140 hp normally aspirated engine with bigger valves and four single-barrel carburetors. The Corsa came only with a four-speed manual transmission, but the engine itself could be ordered in other models with a Powerglide automatic. The 911S of the Corvair line was the 180 hp Turbo, which was incidentally the first use of an exhaust driven turbocharger in a regular production car. No wonder *Car and Driver* was giddy; this was damned interesting stuff.

Although there have been numerous attempts over the years by the Big Three to do import-inspired small cars, the Corvair was the only one to hit the mark. In terms of style, handling and performance, it really has the feel of a European GT. Even people weaned on BMWs, VWs and Porsches will enjoy and respect the way a well-sorted Corvair drives. But the American car crowd (particularly bow-tie fans), welcome them with all the affection that greeted Toyota in NASCAR.

Predictably, Corvairs present a few obstacles to owners, some unique and some not. Body rust clearly falls under the not unique heading. Most Corvairs were given a well-intended but misguided heavy under-

As attractive a shape as GM has done since 1945.

Charlie Kuhn

coating from the factory. In no time at all, the undercoating cracked providing thousands of small moisture-catching pockets on the underside of the car. The A-pillar and cowl are also infamous Corvair rot spots. It's a notoriously difficult area to repair correctly, so it's always a good idea to carry a magnet to make sure that you're not looking at a car with a cowl made largely of plastic.

Corsa engine cars are also rather prone to dropping valves. Getting on the car hard and then getting off the gas suddenly can sometimes induce this. The four carbs can be a bear to synchronize, but the good news is that once they're set up properly, they tend to stay that way. The contortionist fan belts in Corvairs also have notoriously short life spans.

Exhaust leaks, oil leaks and fan belt breaks

Although Ralph Nader made much of the allegedly deadly handling of the first-generation swing-axle equipped Corvairs, in truth, asphyxiation was a greater mortality risk for the average Corvair driver. Like any air-cooled car, cabin heat is supplied by exhaust-heated air. In the Corvair's case, the heating system isn't as well isolated from the exhaust system as it could be; when things rust or seals dry out, carbon monoxide can get into the passenger compartment. Always test out a Corvair's heating system before buying.

Corvairs are chronic oil leakers. Pushrod tube-seals are generally the culprit. Like a Porsche 911 with leaking oil-return tube-seals, the smell can make turning on the heat rather unpleasant.

While technically interesting and potentially powerful, the turbocharged cars aren't terribly practical. The system is primitive, lacking refinements such as an intercooler or even a wastegate. Turbo lag is excruciating—it's either on or off.

The market

Convertible Turbos and Corsas clearly occupy the top of the pecking order as well coupes equipped with the 140 hp Corsa engine. Some Corvair nuts also profess an affinity for one of the 6,000 1969 model year, as these last cars were virtually hand-built in a corner of GM's Willow Run assembly plant. Cars with GM's excellent all-weather air conditioning are also quite desirable. Because of emission control and heat issues, this option was discontinued in 1968. Conversely, sedans and base motor coupes are rather uninteresting to collectors. Like most of the cars outlined in this book, there is little likelihood of sudden or dramatic appreciation with any Corvair. They'll continue to appreciate along with the collector car market, while returning a great deal of enjoyment for little outlay in either purchase or maintenance.

Lincoln

Parts Lincoln Land, Inc., www.lincolnlandinc.com; Lincoln Old Parts Store, www.lincolnoldparts.com; Baker's Auto, www.bakersauto.com

Club The Lincoln & Continental Owners Club, www.lcoc.org

Original Elwood Engle design with "electric shaver" grille.

Shawn Dougan/Hyman, Ltd.

History

Of the big post-war American ragtops, the 1961-67 Continental stands out for a number of reasons. Because it's the only four-door convertible to be produced after 1942 to date, there is a considerable upside from a collectibility standpoint. And, it's an icon of style and good taste from an era when both were rapidly diminishing.

It's a little known fact that Lincoln was on the ropes by the late 1950s. Its reliance on faddish and often bizarre body styles dictated short model-cycles—expensive and labor intensive to keep up with. Ford had toyed with killing Lincoln, but decided to give the marque one last shot for the 1961 model year. Numerous competing proposals were trotted out, none of which gained the support of Henry Ford II.

Elwood Engle was the team leader of a styling group working on the 1961 Thunderbird. His proposal had slab sides, a "Schick shaver" front grill and quad headlights. Nearly everyone in attendance at the presentation including Henry Ford II agreed that the car was "too nice" to be a T-Bird.

Here, thought everyone, was the next Continental—the car that would save the Lincoln marque. When asked if the design could be turned into a four-door, Engle hastily answered "yes." Not only did Engle rework his original design to work as a four-door sedan and a convertible, but later as a hardtop coupe as well. Engle even designed the interior.

Inside and out, the 1961 Continental was a stunning piece of work that continues to influence the designers at Lincoln to this day—once again, on the ropes. The Continental's slab sides and relatively subtle details stood in stark contrast to typically flashy 1950s Americana (and most notably, to its immediate predecessor). The twin outward-opening "suicide" doors were a unique feature. As expected, power came from one of two massive V8s of either 430 or 462 cubic-inch displacements.

Left: Massive 462 cubic inch Lincoln V8.

Above right: Continental's knife-edge styling is particularly apparent from this angle.

Right: Continental interior with suicide doors open.

Below: In spite of its name, the Continental was not even slightly European—but it was the size of Antarctica.

The 1961-64 model years are generally regarded as the most attractive. 1965-69 cars had a considerably more conventional front-end treatment that most people feel spoiled Engle's sublime design. No matter; the Continental was a consistent sales success for Ford, and was the longest lived Lincoln design of the time. Engle's Continental was the car that saved Lincoln.

As drivers, there's not much to say. The Continental is cruising vessel that one points, rather than steers, and one would do well to ask little of the brakes. Still, as a very stylish mobile tanning-bed for you and five close friends, the Continental has a great deal to recommend it.

The old adage that large cars cost large dollars to restore is certainly true with the Continental. As one might expect, body panels and trim items are extinct. The massive slab sides of the Continental can swallow up hours of paint and body work, to say nothing of the plating bill. Buying a "ran when parked" project Continental is foolish indeed. If spending the money on a recently done car is out of the question, look for an older restoration that has held up well, or even better, a well-preserved unrestored car.

The market

Continental convertible values had been stagnant for a good while. Until recently, the only big-money sales were cars reputed to be the former property of Jacqueline Kennedy and Lyndon Johnson. Perhaps it was the car's inextricable association with that awful day in Dallas that kept it from being more popular with collectors. Certainly, black is not the color of choice for a Continental convertible. Silver, gray, white or any lighter color with wide whitewall tires is generally very pleasing.

Collectors seem to prefer the pre-1965 cars with the original grille, although not by much. Prices are no longer stagnant, and have been on the upswing lately; the market seems to be struggling to find its new level. A nice convertible purchased for under $40,000 should be considered well bought. Sedans bring about half that.

Ford

Mustang Coupe 1965-66		❄
Parts availability ✪✪✪✪✪	**Inexpensive to maintain** ✪✪✪✪✪	**Investment potential** ✪✪
Fun to drive ✪✪✪✪	**Price category** $$$	Nice driver, $15,000; Show winner, $25,000
Performance (K-code) 0 to 60 in 8.3 seconds; ¼ mile in 15.9 seconds at 85 mph (*Road & Track* 9/64)		

Parts Mustang Depot, www.mustangdepot.com; Classic Mustang, www.cmustang.com

Club Mustang Club of America, www.mustang.org

History

They just don't do product launches like this anymore. Named after the famous WWII fighter plane, the Mustang was launched at the 1964 New York World's Fair before a massive throng of consumers with buying power the likes of which the auto industry had never seen. With the oldest baby boomers now approaching twenty, for the first time, boomers were starting to figure into the car market. Even if few of them were actually buyers, they were certainly influencing choices. It was the perfect time to introduce a youth-oriented car.

Never one to let a subordinate bask in the glow of an accomplishment, devoted self-promoter Lee Iacocca generally takes the credit for "inventing" the Mustang (as well as the minivan). And while he did push the design enthusiastically as Ford Division General Manager, it was actually Ford's Product Manager, Donald N. Frey, who conceived the car. To hold down costs, much of the car was based on existing components. In this case, the compact Ford Falcon.

The Mustang bettered its first-year sales projections by close to tenfold. Nearly everyone, with the exception of the hard core enthusiast press, was thrilled with the car. *Road & Track* was one of the dissenters. They were disappointed that the rather mundane Falcon underpinnings couldn't deliver on the promise of the car's looks.

Left: GT coupe with styled steel wheels, redline tires and fog light bar.
Right: 289 V8 with non-stock Cobra valve covers.

Although some sources refer to the earliest Mustangs as 1964 ½ models, in fact, they were all officially '65s. The early cars (those made before the official August 1964 model year changeover) had generators rather than alternators. Powertrain options consisted of a 260 cubic-inch V8 and a 170 cubic-inch straight-six. Three-speed and four-speed manual transmissions as well as a two-speed automatic were offered.

The 260 went away after the model year changeover in favor of a 289 V8 and the new base-six was 200 cubic inches. The Hi-Po K-code 289 was also introduced after the model year changeover. A convertible was available from the start of production, along with the notchback coupe. A fastback joined the lineup in 1965. Of the three, the notchback coupe is the only body style that falls into the truly affordable category.

Vintage Mustang an ideal first collector car

A vintage Mustang is the O-positive of collector cars. It offers a near ideal first collector car experience for just about anyone. Nearly any size person can fit inside, parts are cheap—many parts are as close as the local NAPA store. What isn't available over the counter is a mouse-click away via numerous resources. Unlike some vintage cars, a Mustang is a practical daily driver with enough power to keep up in modern traffic. The usual caveats for evaluating any forty-something car apply here, but Mustangs are simple Falcon-based cars with few inherent mechanical issues.

On the downside, classic Mustangs were all built during the age of automotive oxidation, long before any form of rust protection became the norm for car makers. Minor fender-rust is not tragic, because repair panels are inexpensive and easy to come by. However, be careful with what you categorize as "minor"—the rust you can see is often just the tip of the iceberg.

Beware of rampant rust and poor rust repairs

Mustangs from the salt belt will often have rust in the floor pans, trunk floor, shock towers, torque boxes and frame rails. Because they're more leak-prone, convertibles are especially vulnerable to rust in the floors, and floor-rust often goes hand in hand with rust in the torque-boxes and frame. Frame and torque-box rust is structural, affecting the integrity of the car. Do your best Carl Lewis impersonation in running away from a car with rust in these places.

Panel fit on any Mustang you look at should be up to the standard of other comparably priced American cars of the day, which is to say, not entirely laughable. Doors, hood, and trunk should fit reasonably flush, but don't expect Mercedes-like precision and uniformity in the panel gaps. Doors that stick out at the bottoms, large uneven gaps between panels and hoods, and deck lids that don't fit flush are often the sign of bad collision-repair or extensive structural-rust repairs.

On the other hand, a toasted interior on an otherwise sound car may represent an opportunity to get a small bargain and put some sweat equity into a car that will pay off. Mustang interior pieces are readily available and generally inexpensive. The quality of reproduction pieces varies considerably, so it is advisable to do your homework before buying an interior.

If you're concerned with originality, consult the build-plate of your Mustang. Compared to the very basic information found on, say, an E-type tag, it's the Library of Alexandria—Ford fit a wealth of information on that small piece of tin. Among other things, it will tell you the factory your car was built in, the powertrain option, whether your car was originally equipped with a standard or deluxe "pony" interior, and what colors were correct. To find out how to decode a Mustang build plate, go to www.vintage-mustang.com.

The market

Fastbacks and convertibles are the darlings of Mustang collectors. Even though they were the most popular, most photographed and most tested of the early 1965 cars, coupes have been largely forgotten by collectors. Six cylinder coupes are still relatively common under $10,000, and base V8 cars are just a bit more. Other than durability, simplicity and slightly better fuel economy, the sixes have little to recommend them. The V8's torque and sweet exhaust note are worth the premium. A four-speed is also worth a bit more.

Few other options (besides working air conditioning) are worth obsessing over unless you're looking at a screaming deal on a real GT K-code car. In any event, it's not uncommon for collectors to restore cars with upgraded optional accessories like a fog-light bar, pony interior or styled steel wheels. In the case of the latter, a set of reproduction styled steel wheels are the first thing I'd buy for a car with hubcaps. They really are quite attractive.

Mustang coupes have always been at the bottom of the pecking order, and that's just not going to change. Even so, they're attractive, stylish and dead simple to maintain. If you can't live happily with one of these, you might consider taking up stamp collecting or Beanie Babies®—Mustangs really are about the least demanding old cars that I can think of.

chapter five

practical classics

Cars that are cheap to acquire,

cheap to run and with a potential

upside at sale time

P RACTICAL CLASSICS" MAY SEEM LIKE an oxymoron to those who have never owned a car beyond the end of a lease or worse, after the expiration of the warranty. When I started using my 202,000 mile 1976 Porsche 912E as my daily driver, I caught my Honda-driving neighbor making the swirling-finger-next-to-the-temple gesture behind my back. Surely, I was inviting disaster—or worse, regular visits to our quiet subdivision from those unsavory tow-truck driver types.

He's convinced that I'm having constant trouble and the flatbed goes in and out under cover of darkness. Yet, in two years of regular use, it has never been on the end of a hook nor has it let me down in any way. I don't lead a charmed life, it's simply a good example of a practical classic, a cheap to maintain and reliable old car that can easily be used as a stylish daily driver like the other cars profiled here.

The key to using an old car as a reliable daily driver is familiar advice to those who have persevered to this point of the book—buy the best example, one that is absolutely turnkey and read to go. If you follow this advice, there really is no reason that you can't use one of the cars in this chapter as a daily driver with a few caveats: The first is rust. With the exception of a post-1975 Porsche 911, there are very few cars in this book that came from the factory with adequate rust protection. And if you're anything like me, you can't bear to see a car you even remotely care about rust. The solution here is to buy a sacrificial lamb or a salt car. An old Accord or Civic that wont' divert maintenance funds from the car you care about is perfect. Use it when there's salt on the road and let it dissolve knowing that it's saving your collector car.

The other impediment to daily use of a classic car is the lack of air conditioning. Your options here are to limit your search to the vintage cars that had good A/C available (those noted throughout with the snowflake symbol). Or, you can buy a salt car with good A/C as I did and use it on the unbearably hot days. Finally, you can go for the permanent solution and install one of the new air conditioning systems made for vintage cars. A company called Vintage Air www.vintageair.com is probably the best known supplier of A/C kits for old cars. They make a wide range of kits to fit most cars.

Datsun

240/260/280Z 1970-78 ❄*		
Parts availability ✪✪✪✪	**Inexpensive to maintain** ✪✪✪✪✪	**Investment potential** ✪✪
Fun to drive ✪✪✪✪✪	**Price category** $$	Nice driver, $8,000; Show winner, $17,000
Performance 0 to 60 in 8.7 seconds; ¼ mile in 17.1 seconds at 84.5 mph (*Road & Track* 4/70)		

*Air conditioning in the 260 & 280Z only

Parts Black Dragon Automotive, www.blackdragonauto.com; Motorsport Auto, www.motorsportauto.com

Club The Internet Z Car Club, www.zhome.com

240Z's Classic long hood, short rear deck proportions look great today. This one sports period aftermarket Shelby wheels and odd but totally original non-metallic gold paint.

$10,000 is no longer a particularly consequential sum of money. It won't build a schoolhouse in Africa, pay for an organ transplant or even make much of a dent in college tuition. And in the great scheme of your retirement—even taking into account the miracle of compound interest—it won't make the difference between gated community and trailer home.

So, you might as well go out and blow it on the Japanese car that made people stop snickering and joking about Japanese cars.

Fully instrumented 240Z interior—shift knob is real wood, wheel is plastic. This one sports an excellent aftermarket dash-cap that effectively repairs the typical cracked dash.

History

In late 1969, the Datsun 240Z was a shock the magnitude of which has seldom been seen in the automotive world. For $3,500, Datsun had produced a car that could hang with a Porsche 911T and a Jaguar E-type for half the money. The only thing I can liken it to is the consternation produced a decade before when an obscure Spanish truck maker came out of nowhere and produced the magnificent Pegaso, a sports car that rivaled Ferraris and Maseratis of the day.

These were the days when the public perception of Japanese products still fell into one of three categories: outright copies of Western products, smaller copies of Western products, and or complete crap. In fact, none of this was true—companies like Sony, Seiko and Nikon had already built enviable reputations for quality, and Japanese cars were, for the most part, well-made and thrifty if uninspired.

Datsun had learned several lessons from Toyota's attempt to build a world-class sports car in the 2000GT. While lovely, the 2000GT cost more than a Jaguar or a Porsche and wasn't as fast. Not a formula for success for an underdog manufacturer. And there was also the problem that anyone over 5' 8" simply wasn't going to fit in it.

With styling inspired by Count Albrecht Goertz's earlier work for Nissan and equal measures of the E-type, Ferrari 275 GTB and Porsche 911, the 240Z certainly looked the part. North American chief Yutaka Katayama made sure that the car was fit for American consumption by insisting that it accommodate six-foot-plus Americans.

With a lusty 150 hp straight-six, independent rear suspension, rack-and-pinion steering and good brakes, the Z was the real replacement for cars like the Austin-Healey 3000 and Triumph TR6 the British couldn't build. Sadly, it came at a time when it looked like convertibles were going to be a thing of the past, so there was no open Z car until the 1990s. There was, however, a slightly more practical but ungainly 2+2 option from 1974 on.

When it hit the market in late 1969, the 240Z acted like the comet that killed the dinosaurs. Within four model years, the Opel GT, Fiat 124 coupe, Triumph GT6 and MGB GT had all been displaced in the automotive ecosystem by the Datsun. All were fairly mediocre cars that cost as much or more than a 240Z and had no place in a GT world ruled by the 240Z.

Other than some front-end wandering that was later cured by either the adoption of a wedge-front attitude or a front-spoiler, the car had few vices—until the onset of 1973 pollution regulations. The drivability

ran when parked...

of these later cars was destroyed by leaning out the carburetion and retarding the ignition timing. In places where these cars are not subject to asinine emissions laws encumbering the few pre-1980 cars still on the road, simply swapping the dreaded flat-top Hitachi carbs for an earlier set of SU copies is a quick fix. If you live where draconian smog regs apply, buy a pre-73 240Z or a 280Z.

240, 260 and 280Z all have merit

Conventional wisdom holds that the original 1970-73 240Z is the only Z worth having. I say this is utter nonsense. The 260Z and 280Z both have their merits. With post 1974 ½ cars, you do lose the lovely small bumpers and the simpler rear tail-lights, and the bigger displacement cars are also less inclined to rev. But there are some worthwhile gains, and in fact, the early 1974 260Z might be the best Z to own, especially if you live in a warm climate where air conditioning is required.

Effective A/C a desirable option in the 260 and 280Z

Alone among foreign manufacturers in the 1970s, the Japanese perfected effective air-conditioning. While a 240 will at best have a crummy dealer-installed (and probably broken) A/C unit, the 260Z was available with fully-integrated GM-style factory A/C. With four fan speeds and a bi-level control that lets you defog your windshield while keeping your toes warm, it's a thing of beauty. Even better, the early '74 260Z retained the small bumpers of the 240Z. If the car doesn't have to pass smog, you simply replace the carbs with a pair from a 1970-72 car, and you've got what might be the best early Z of all.

The 260Z was a one-year-only affair and its successor, the 280Z is a much misunderstood car. Probably owing to confusion with its replacement, the flaccid 280ZX, it is often derided as portly and unsporting. While the larger bumpers did nothing for the looks (for the record, the 1975-76 versions are a bit subtler) they certainly didn't destroy what was still a very pretty car. With the exception of the bumpers, nothing was changed from the pure 1970 Z shape.

Fuel injected 280Zs run flawlessly

The real news was the fact that the drivability problems were solved with the addition of Bosch L-Jetronic fuel injection built under license by Nissan. Cold-starting was no longer a problem, flat spots were gone and power was back up to roughly 1970 levels. A bit of extra weight meant that the 280 was a few tenths of second slower 0-60, but it was a fair trade. The aforementioned excellent A/C was a common option, and a proper 5-speed was even added for 1978.

Aside from the carburetion issues, all early Zs suffer from the same basic issues: They rust worse than an Italian car, and the interiors are fragile and cheap. In the 1970s, the science of rust protection was non-existent. The thinner-gauge sheet metal on the 240Z exacerbated the problem. A few years in a salty environment caused them to melt. Floorboards, hatch surrounds, fender bottoms, and battery boxes suffered the worst. For these reasons, I just wouldn't even bother looking at anything but a western car. A cooked interior is a small price to pay for intact sheet metal.

Interiors are the other weak point of an early Z. The cars were built to a price, and thankfully, the interior rather than the suspension is where Nissan opted to save some coin. It isn't the design (which for the record is tasteful) and the car is fully instrumented, but the seats, carpet, door panels and trim are just plain crappy. Non-carpeted surfaces are covered in a nasty diamond pattern vinyl, seats are thin and have a pronounced and rather tacky grain to the vinyl. There is very little sound deadening which makes the car seem quite tinny; the whole thing resonates at certain speeds. Finally, nearly every Z dash cracks above the minor gauges.

Fortunately, much of this can be cured. There are sources for better seat materials, and adhesive sound-deadeners under the carpet will do wonders. A full dash cap, a nearly undetectable fix, works wonders. For the most part, redoing a Z interior is a cheap and simple weekend project. I've even managed to find good original used seats out of a junked car that saved me hundreds over reupholstering.

Mechanically, the Z is quite rugged. The straight-six—based on a Mercedes-Benz design—will do over 150,000 before attention is required. Low oil pressure and smoke will be the most obvious indicators of

Left: Original Z-car looks great from any angle. Right: 150 hp Nissan straight-six breaths through two Hitachi-built SU carburetors.

a tired Z. Transmissions are also sturdy. I've never driven an old Z with a worn out gearbox or really bad synchros. But parts for autoboxes are getting scarce and really, who wants a two-pedal sports car anyway?

As a daily driver, Z-cars are quite reliable. My good friend and fellow Missourian Lance Young bought at auction what may be the best unrestored 280 on the planet for a paltry $7,500. The car had not been used in the last five years and showed less than 32,000 original miles. Lance paid for the car (on his VISA card no less), we filled it up with fresh gas, and pointed it south to St. Louis, some 250 miles away.

The only problem along the way was some hesitation and a miss, which I took to be clogged injectors from stale gas. As it turns out, a lead to one of the injectors was loose. We pressed it back on, and the car has utterly been trouble-free for the last three years. The cold factory A/C is a big plus in the Bangkok-like summers of St. Louis.

The market

Just as they were when new, the Z is an incredible bargain. Perfectly acceptable cars can still be bought for less than $7,000 and great ones seldom exceed $15,000—the only exceptions being the rare examples that Nissan restored and sold to keep interest in the Z alive (when there were no new Z cars marketed in the U.S.). These remanufactured cars have brought into the $20s.

260s generally bring about 20 percent less with the discount being about 40 percent for a 280Z. The choice is fairly simple, if you must have the original unadulterated experience, a 240 is the car. If you want A/C and a few more creature comforts, it's a 280. The 260 represents a nice compromise between the two.

Case studies

1971 Datsun 240Z		
Purchase Price $2,500	Sale Price	Owned for 1.0 years

1977 Datsun 240Z		
Purchase Price	Sale Price $7,000	Owned for 0.5 years

1977 Datsun 240Z		
Purchase Price $4,500	Sale Price $4,900	Owned for 1.0 years

1974 Datsun 260Z		
Purchase Price $1800	Sale Price $5,800	Owned for 1.0 years

I keep going back to the abundant Z-car well. They're just such an attractive mix of style, performance and practicality that roughly every 4.5 years, I seem to wind up with one. My first was a 1977 280Z with just 45,000 miles, no rust and the original paint and interior. It was sold new by Bankston Datsun in Dallas, TX and had never seen a salty winter. I paid $4,500 for it.

With great A/C, it was a perfectly usable everyday driver. So much so that I sold my everyday driver and had the 280 Zeibarted for winter use. After a year and a child, I decided that a two-seater wasn't ideal and I sent it down the road for $4,900 to a college student. I felt guilty immediately—with visions of my wonderfully preserved Z-car being abused, vomited in and ultimately totaled leaving a Nine Inch Nails concert.

In a year's heavy use, I put in a battery and replaced the cold-start injector. The old Datsun didn't use a single quart of oil between changes, nor did it leak a drop of anything; a first for any old car of mine.

Several years later, the Z-car bug bit me again. This time, I wanted an earlier car to restore. After several weeks of looking, I found an early '74 260 in Rancho Cucamonga, CA. It was a diamond in the rough—no rust, straight sides and original chalkboard flat paint. The mechanicals had all been recently freshened, including a VERY expensive triple Weber carb setup replacing the hated Hitachi flattops—and, it had cold factory A/C. We agreed on a price of $1,900. As I was the head of marketing for an auto transport company at the time, shipping was quite painless.

The cosmetic freshening was pretty easy: I removed the lights, door handles, bumpers and glass in a weekend (with help from the glass company). A flatbed took it to the body shop for a straightforward respray. It was back three weeks later when I had a new rubber kit waiting, re-chromed bumpers, and a pair of very nice seats pulled from a 260 in a local Z-car only wrecking yard. The finishing touch was a set of period American Racing Libre wheels—in my opinion, the definitive set of aftermarket wheels for a 240Z.

It all went back together easily with some help from my high school friend Dave Weber. Sadly, Dave was in town for his dad's funeral. His father Norm was a wonderfully affable guy who never met a speeding ticket he couldn't charm his way out of. Norm and Dave helped me restore my first car, a horribly rusty Triumph TR4 when I was 16. Twenty years later, we were at it again.

A few days after the service, we wandered down to my garage where the Datsun project had stalled about a weekend of work away from completion. Dave mentioned that if his Dad were here, we'd be finishing up the car. I couldn't argue with that. After picking up a twelve-pack, we got to work. It felt like we were in high school again, and by about three in the morning, the car was back together. A fitting tribute to one of the guys who got me started in the hobby.

The 260 was about as trouble-free as the 280 had been, but it was no longer needed as a daily driver. After about a year or so, I decided that my fun car should be a convertible. It was the last car that I sold without the aid of eBay. All totaled, I had about $4,500 in it. It went to a guy in Pennsylvania for $5,800, replaced by a very nice Triumph TR4 that I paid $7,800 for.

Resto project 260Z after completion with help from a high school buddy.

Left: Portland, Oregon Z-car by way of Central Valley of California.
Right: The kinds of things you want to see with any car you buy—tools, books and window sticker.

My most recent Z-car experience came when I was working as the VP of Business Development and General Counsel for *Sports Car Market* magazine in Portland, Oregon. Portland has a special place in my heart as probably the best old car city in the U.S. It was a major port at one time, and as my buddy Paul Duchene was always quick to point out, "a lot of weird stuff rolled off the boat in Portland and stuck around." The city is positively lousy with stuff like early Toyota Crowns, Citroen DSs and Volvo P1800s, most of it rust-free.

Since I was commuting back and forth from St. Louis to Portland, without family around, I had a fair amount of time on my hands, much of it spent trolling Craigslist. One night, a posting for a '71 240Z fresh from California popped up. With a price of $2,750, I was a bit skeptical. Nevertheless, minutes after the call ended, I was off to beautiful Gresham, Oregon (hometown of kneecap-rapper Tonya Harding) to have a look.

The seller had thoughtfully placed the car on jack stands for my inspection. He explained that he bought it as part of a collection of three cars. It was all of them or nothing and the Z was the one he didn't want. The "keepers" were some kind of bad fiberglass street rod and an unfinished Cobra kit so bad that nothing could get Carroll Shelby to sign the dash. And this pristine Z was the castoff? No accounting for taste, I thought.

The paint was faded but all there and the car was remarkably straight and rust free. Courtesy of the Central Valley, CA heat and sun, the interior was cooked far past well done. The owner remarked that although his attempts were limited, he could never get the car to run quite right. Something seemed off in the carburetion.

We agreed to a price of $2,300 and I drove the car back to the spacious, well-lit and toasty garage at the *Sports Car Market* office. The running issue turned out to be a combination of fouled plugs and the lack of a thermostat. The previous owner was apparently not aware of the lack of a thermostat, and since the car never really got up to running temperature in the Oregon winter, he drove the car with the choke out all the time, fouling the plugs. A thermostat and new plugs later, the car ran like a champ.

The Z really did turn out to be a diamond in the rough. A paintless ding removal expert removed the minor dings and dents, and a detailer coaxed a shine out of the 36 year-old acrylic enamel. A carpet kit, good seats pulled from a wreck, and a dash cap made the interior look quite nice. New rubber seals quieted things down a bit.

It came down to a choice between the Z and the really nice MGC GT that I had been using as my Portland car. Conventional wisdom would hold that the Z is a far better car than the C, and in areas like room, ventilation and comfort, it was. But the leather-lined C felt more expensive, was nearly as powerful and had a bit more charm. It stayed and the Z went via eBay—for a few thousand more than I had in it.

Lessons learned from the trio of Z cars? They remain what they were in 1970—a lot of bang for the buck, very little trouble and likely to return most if not all of their purchase price when you move on. The things that were irritating back then are still irritating—cheap interior appointments, and tinny construction. But if you can look past these minor shortcomings, an early Z-car should be at the top of your list.

TR6 factory promo shot. Large rubber bumper overriders and signals below bumper mark this as a 1975 or 76 year car.

British Leyland

Triumph

TR250 1968		
Parts availability ✪✪✪✪✪	**Inexpensive to maintain** ✪✪✪✪✪	**Investment potential** ✪✪✪
Fun to drive ✪✪✪½	**Price category** $$$ Nice driver, $16,000; Show winner; $35,000	
Performance (2500M) 0 to 60 in 10.6 seconds; ¼ mile in 17.8 seconds at 76 mph (*Road & Track* 12/67)		

TR6 1969-76		
Parts availability ✪✪✪✪✪	**Inexpensive to maintain** ✪✪✪✪✪	**Investment potential** ✪✪½
Fun to drive ✪✪✪½	**Price category** $$$ Nice driver, $13,000; Show winner, $25,000	
Performance (2500M) 0 to 60 in 10.7 seconds; ¼ mile in 17.9 seconds at 77 mph (*Road & Track* 2/69)		

Parts Moss Motors, www.mossmotors.com; The Little British Car Company, www.lbcarco.com; Victoria British, www.victoriabritish.com; The Roadster Factory, www.the-roadster-factory.com

Club Vintage Triumph Register, www.vtr.org

History

Among all the great stories of British car industry ineptitude, the genesis of the Triumph TR250 must rank among the best. Triumph had planned to replace the TR4A in the summer of 1967 with the car that eventu-

ally became known as the TR6. But as legend has it, the Germans at Karmann who handled the development of the new model supplied all the tooling specifications in metric units. Unfortunately, the Brits were still employing the English system, and the resultant conversion not only taxed Triumph's slide rules, but also delayed the TR6 launch.

The hastily designed TR250 was pushed out the door in its place, destined to live for just a single model year. It was based on the same Giovanni Michelotti-styled TR4 body with the addition of a silver transverse hood stripe, a different grille and a slightly wider chrome side molding. In place of the TR4A's agricultural 2.2-liter four-cylinder, the TR250 got a smooth-revving inline six, essentially a stroked version of the motor found in the Triumph 2000 sedans.

Calling this new powerplant "under-stressed" is just a kind way of calling it underachieving. In a feat seldom matched by modern engine designers, Triumph engineers nearly attained an anemic output of fifty hp per liter. With an additional 300 cc of displacement and two more cylinders than the four-cylinder unit it replaced, the inline six managed only six more horsepower (111 hp vs. 105). At least torque was improved, from 128 to 152 lb-ft.

Officially, Triumph blamed U.S. emission regulations for not importing the potent Lucas fuel-injected TR5, essentially the same car as the Stromberg-carbureted TR250 but with about 45 additional horses. (Curiously, Porsche, Mercedes-Benz and BMW all managed to certify mechanically fuel-injected engines during the same era.) Many suspect that Triumph just didn't have enough faith in its U.S. dealer network to service what was a rather finicky fuel-injection system.

But the TR250 wasn't all bad. Even in carbureted form, the new six was a pleasant engine. Creamy smooth and with abundant torque, it could propel the TR250 to 60 mph in about ten seconds, pretty much on par with a Healey 3000. The exhaust note is also up there with the all-time British greats.

TR6 lacks some vintage charm

Still, it wasn't to last. Karmann and Triumph finally got their measuring systems coordinated in late 1968 when the TR6 bowed as a 1969 model. Given the fact that Triumph's development budget for the new model was pitifully meager—dictating that Karmann keep the inner structure, cowl, windshield and doors the same—Karmann did an amazing job of freshening the looks of Triumph's sports car. Perhaps almost too good; the TR6 looks relatively modern even today.

Flat black Kamm tail of the TR6 roots it firmly in the 1970s.

TR6s offer above average driver comfort

Behind the wheel, the TR250 and the TR6 are quite nice as British sports cars go. The seats (low backs with no headrests in the TR250, high backs with integrated headrests in early TR6s and low backs with removable head rests in the late TR6) are comfortable and offer decent support, and the cockpit, although narrow, is reasonably accommodating for two average-sized people. Happily, little engine heat invades the interior. The full complement of Smiths gauges, although minus the chrome rings of earlier cars, is still handsome.

Face-level ventilation in the form of two "eyeball" vents on the dash provides scant relief on warm days. The dash itself, while changed to a matte finish for "safety" reasons, is still a real plank of wood. No tacky rubber-and-vinyl injustice suffered here, unlike the post-1967 MGB.

While the TR250 and TR6 inherited as standard the optional independent rear-suspension from the TR4A, don't expect it to perform like a modern multi-link setup. The cars still point their nose skyward under acceleration, dive on braking, and the ride is fairly bouncy. On the positive side, the servo-assisted front-disc and rear drum brakes are more than adequate. The car is a great around-town driver, though overdrive is a nice option to have for higher-speed cruising.

Other desirable options include 72-spoke painted wire-wheels (the standard setup for the TR250 and 1969 TR6 was steel-wheels with nasty fake Rostyle hubcaps), a tonneau cover and Michelin X redline tires. The most fully-kitted car I've seen had all of the above, plus dealer-installed A/C, dealer-option magnesium wheels, and factory hardtop. In the case of the TR250, the hardtop option was the rare "surrey top" which consisted of a handsome, wrap-around fixed backlight with a removable center section in either steel or fabric. No convertible top was fitted to these cars. The TR6 hardtop was the handsome Michelotti-designed unit that looked similar to the Spitfire top. Convertible tops came with hardtop equipped TR6s.

Frame rust all too common

The usual considerations in approaching any old car apply to the TR250 and TR6 as well. Rust is the number one enemy, but not only in the floors and body panels—in the frames as well. This is especially true in the vital rear trailing-arm mounting points. Front-lower wishbone attachment points are notoriously weak too. Look for body rust on both cars in the lower fender and rocker areas and all over the rear deck, especially in the panel seams. TR6s also like to rust just behind the headlights in the front fenders and at the tips of the rear fenders above the tail-lights.

Left: 2.5 liter straight-six is smooth and torque. Green hoses as per original in this example.

Right: Factory hard top is attractive and desirable.

Drivetrains are generally robust, with the weakest point being the clutch. The Roadster Factory (www.the-roadster-factory.com) offers a heavy-duty clutch package—the best fix in this area, and runs $319. It also operates a rebuilding business for, among other things, the rear-hubs and half-shafts that always seem to be in need of attention. These will set you back $269 (minus a $150 refund if you send back the cores).

Parts support is second to none

For parts support to be any better, Girl Scouts would have to give away TR6 distributor caps with cookie orders. Nearly everything is available, and committed suppliers even reproduce items such as the unique green radiator hoses that the cars came with when new.

The future collectibility of the TR250 and TR6 are interesting questions. Most attention in naming the heir apparent to the Big Healeys has been focused on the TR6 as the obvious next British sports car that should see serious appreciation. I'm not sure I agree—and the reason is the TR250. British Leyland built 92,000 TR6s in a production run that ended a little over 30 years ago. Furthermore, Karmann did such a competent job designing the TR6 that it barely looks dated today. This means it lacks much of the vintage charm of a Healey or MGA.

The TR250, however, is another story. The safety regulations of 1967 didn't hurt it badly, and the six-cylinder makes it an infinitely better car than its well-regarded older sister, the TR4A. The short tailfins, vestigial hood bulge, and full-wheel cutouts give it a tough look that's firmly rooted in the early sixties. Combine this with its single-year-only status and I think the TR250 is a real sleeper—the best alternative to spending forty or fifty large on a Healey 3000.

Case study

1968 Triumph TR250		
Purchase Price $21,000	**Sale Price** $26,000	**Owned for** 1.0 years

The red Triumph TR250 was one of the rare occasions where I followed my own advice to the letter. It was a professionally restored car; I let someone else spend the big bucks and essentially bought the restoration and got the car for free. Everything was meticulously documented with photos and receipts.

The body had been removed from the frame, which was sandblasted and painted, the drivetrain and suspension had been completely rebuilt; the paint, interior and bodywork were all expertly done. It was completed with a correct reflector top, Michelin redline tires and original style green radiator hoses and wire clamps. The receipts for the work done totaled over $30,000 and it was a screaming bargain at that.

In short, my Signal Red TR250 drove like a new car, with none of the squeaks, creaks and rattles that a poorly restored or worn out Triumph would have. The only trouble I had with the car was with the clutch. Pedal effort was tremendous and it was stubborn on the release.

Clutches are a sore spot for TR6s and TR250s; they've been plagued by low-quality replacement parts for many years. The Roadster Factory in Pennsylvania now sells a high-quality replacement clutch kit with

ran when parked...

Buying the best TR250 example I could find was money well spent.

an up-rated release fork and throw-out bearing. Had it been available at the time, I would have certainly replaced the clutch in the car.

Other than a leaky clutch master cylinder, I had no trouble with the car. I toyed with the idea of installing vintage air in the car and using it as a daily driver, however, something else came up and I reluctantly put the TR250 up for sale. I had no trouble finding a buyer at $5,000 more than I had paid a year before, illustrating the wisdom of buying the best example available.

Pontiac

Grand Prix 1969-72		
Parts availability ✪✪✪½	Inexpensive to maintain ✪✪✪✪✪	Investment potential ✪✪
Fun to drive ✪✪½	Price category $$ Nice driver, $15,000; Show winner, $30,000	
Performance (428) 0 to 60 in 6.8 seconds; ¼ mile in 15.3 seconds at 89 mph		

Parts California Pontiac Restoration, www.pontiacparts.net

Club Pontiac-Oakland Club International, www.poci.org

Charlie Kuhn

No shortage of chrome on '71 Grand Prix.

Left: Coke bottle flanks of Grand Prix apparent here.
Above right: Hurst Grand Prix interior.
Right: Distinctive gold and white color scheme of '71 Hurst Grand Prix.

History

The 1969 Pontiac Grand Prix was a product of the last great period of creativity at GM that brought cars like the 1964 Pontiac GTO, 1966 Oldsmobile Toronado and 1967 Cadillac Eldorado. John Z. DeLorean, hip father of the GTO, decided to do a more luxurious "personal car" with most of the performance of the GTO as his follow up.

Built on a shortened GM A-Platform, DeLorean specified a long hood and short rear-deck with aggressive "Coke bottle" flanks. Viewed as a sort of Cadillac Eldorado for the masses, with more of a performance emphasis, the base 400 cubic-inch V8 put out a respectable 265 hp, but it was the 428 HO that was the pavement ripper. Not particularly easy to find with the 428 HO or a manual transmission, a GP so equipped is worth seeking out. With 370 hp, the 428 HO Grand Prix was capable of 14.1 quarter-mile times. Not too shabby.

Interiors were in keeping with the near luxury theme of the car with leather and thicker pile carpeting available along with real wood trim and bucket seats with a center console.

1970 brought a new grille and the 428 was replaced with a 455, also with 370 hp and an astounding 500 lb. ft. of torque—enough to pull the Washington Monument off its base and drag it down Constitution Avenue.

Parts more difficult than typical Pontiac muscle

At the prices that GPs bring, there's no sense in buying one with needs beyond a quickie respray or new seat covers. NOS parts are rare, and unlike the GTO, the aftermarket doesn't care much about the GP, so

ran when parked...

reproduction parts are hard to come by. Like most American cars of the era, GPs rust with the best of them. Keep in mind that replacement sheetmetal beyond rocker panels is quite difficult to find as well. Again, do yourself a favor and hold out for a good original car.

The market

It's a mystery why the muscle car crowd has largely overlooked the 1969-72 Grand Prix. The '69 GP was a John DeLorean project with handsome styling, decent interior appointments, some serious high horse engine options and an available manual transmission. Even though they have the same father, if it's not a GTO, the Pontiac muscle crowd just doesn't seem to care. No matter, it just means that the Grand Prix is a flat out steal at $15,000-$20,000 for a nice example.

Mazda

RX7 1979-85		
Parts availability ✪✪✪½	**Inexpensive to maintain** ✪✪✪✪	**Investment potential** ✪
Fun to drive ✪✪✪	**Price category** $	Nice driver, $4,500; Show winner, $10,000
Performance 0 to 60 in 9.2 seconds; ¼ mile in 17.0 seconds at 83 mph (*Road & Track* 8/78)		

Parts RX7 World, www.rx7world.com; Mazdatrix, www.mazdatrix.com

Club Mazda RX7 Club, www.rx7club.com

Toyo Kogyo, Inc.

Original factory promo shot of 1979 Mazda RX7.

History

By the late 1970s, the sports car world was looking bleak indeed. A 1975 *Road & Track* comparison test of the Maserati Merak, Lamborghini Urraco, and Ferrari Dino 308 GT4 showed none of these detoxed beasts to be capable of a sub eight-second 0–60 mph run. It was far worse for mainstream sports cars.

The Triumph TR6 was gone, replaced by the trainwreck that was the TR7. The MG B was wheezing along with just 68 hp and comical bumpers. The Datsun 240Z had morphed into the bloated two-tone discomobile that was the 280ZX, and the Porsche of the future—the 924—was an overpriced, underpowered, hard-riding mistake.

In short, the sports car world was ripe for the second coming of the original 240Z—and that's just what Mazda sought to do. In fact, the original ad for the 1979 RX-7 had images of the MG TC and the 240Z in the background.

Mazda introduced the RX-7 in the spring of 1978 as a '79 model. It was an instant hit, and 474,565 first-generation cars would be built by 1985, with 377,878 sold in the U.S. alone. *Road & Track* hailed it as a major breakthrough for the enthusiast—although they were lukewarm about the styling, which they viewed as derivative. In fact, it does resemble a Porsche 924 from the front, with a dash of TVR 2500M in the rear.

Price gouging not seen since the 240Z

At the original price of $6,395, there were waiting lists and price gouging by dealers on a scale not seen since the Datsun 240Z. Early buyers could reckon to get all their money back if they resold the car within the first year or so. From a performance standpoint, the RX-7 and the 240Z were evenly matched. Both would do 0–60 mph in under nine seconds, and both topped out at about 120 mph.

Although a conventional front-engine rear-wheel-drive car, the RX-7's powerplant made it thoroughly unconventional. The twin-rotor 12A rotary engine was built under license to NSU Wankel (by then a Volkswagen subsidiary), and it was massaged to make 100 hp. Unlike NSU, Mazda had been able to actually make the rotary work, largely solving the tip-seal problems that sank the NSU Ro80 (and the company along with it).

First-gen RX-7s are a blast to drive, and sound much like a chainsaw on steroids. They are so rev-happy, Mazda installed a rev-limiter that buzzed when the car reached its 7,000-rpm redline.

Handling was quite good, although the chassis was fairly conventional—unit structure with MacPherson struts up front and a live rear-axle with coil springs and a Watt's linkage not unlike some Alfas. All this made handling benign enough, but at the limit, early cars could be a handful, displaying exuberant oversteer.

Interiors were nothing special, like most Japanese cars of the day, with waxy hard plastic and cloth or vinyl seats being the rule. At least the RX-7 had full instrumentation, with a big centrally located tach on the earliest cars.

Probably the biggest liability the earliest cars suffer is appalling fuel economy. Pre-1981, 12A rotary cars rarely saw the high side of 20 mpg on the highway, and driven hard around town they often saw single digits. Cars built after 1981 were rated at 21 mpg city and 30 mpg on the highway, but most RX-7 owners laugh at these figures.

The one to have is the injected GSL-SE

The first-gen RX-7 to have is the fuel-injected 13B rotary-powered GSL-SE of 1984–85. A 35-hp boost over the 12A engine made this RX-7 competitive with the new Porsche 944. The GSL-SE also came with all of the interior refinements available, including very effective A/C; the Japanese were the only foreign manufacturers who came close to the Americans in that department. Both 4- and 5-speed manuals were available. Each was quite stout, though the second-gear synchro will only withstand limited abuse, and rotaries provide little engine braking, leading to panic downshifts by novices.

A limited number of first-gen RX-7 convertibles were converted in California by a company called Avatar. None has surfaced at auction recently, and the conversion quality is a bit of an unknown, but the car looks great as a convertible. It makes one wonder why it wasn't in the original plans.

The market

As collector cars today, RX-7s are a tough sell; they're not really old enough to be especially collectible and the rotary engine scares people off. It isn't as though they are particularly troublesome (150,000 miles isn't unreasonable, double that is possible on synthetic oil), but the knowledge base for rotary repairs is dwindling. Smoking cars with bad rotor-tip or apex-seals should be avoided like the plague, as should any example with any indication of a less-than-healthy motor.

Although a bit less rust-prone than earlier Japanese cars, RX-7s can and do rust. Those with sunroofs should be checked extra carefully, as they can leak over time, with predictable floorboard consequences. There are few RX-7s around that have been restored in the traditional sense. The values simply don't support it. However, good original cars with under 100,000 miles do surface occasionally. Good cars tend to live in the $3,500 to $5,000 territory.

ran when parked...

First-gen RX-7s are among the last worthwhile credit card cars out there. There's no rush, because this status is unlikely to change any time soon, as the first tier of Japanese collectibles consists of just one car (the Toyota 2000GT), and aside from the 240Z, a second tier of Japanese collector cars has yet to emerge.

MGB

GT 1966-74		
Parts availability ✪✪✪✪✪	Inexpensive to maintain ✪✪✪✪✪	Investment potential ✪✪
Fun to drive ✪✪✪	Price category **$$**	Nice driver, $6,000; Show winner, $12,000
Performance 0 to 60 in 13.6 seconds; ¼ mile in 19.6 seconds at 72 mph (*Road & Track* 5/66)		

MGC

GT 1967-69		
Parts availability ✪✪✪✪	Inexpensive to maintain ✪✪✪✪✪	Investment potential ✪✪½
Fun to drive ✪✪✪½	Price category **$$**	Nice driver, $10,000; Show winner, $19,000
Performance 0 to 60 in 10.1 seconds; ¼ mile in 17.7 seconds at 80 mph (*Road & Track* 5/69)		

Parts Moss Motors, www.mossmotors.com; The Little British Car Company, www.lbcarco.com; Victoria British, www.victoriabritish.com; British Parts Northwest, www.bpnorthwest.com

Club North American MGB Register, www.mgcars.org.uk/namgbr/index.html

1967 MGB GT—lovely sloping roof line courtesy of Pininfarina.

Steve Haas

History

Like the Datsun Z, the MGB GT/MCG GT is a car that I keep finding excuses to own. They're attractive, cheap, well made, entertaining and parts grow on trees. And if there's one going cheap anywhere in the world as you read this, I'm probably on it.

MG has a long history of doing very attractive coupes. The airline coupes of the 1930s were particularly rare and lovely. The MGA coupe of the 1950s is nearly as charming and graceful as a Jaguar XK120 coupe. The only thing surprising about the fact that BMC turned the MGB into a coupe was the fact that it took them four years to do it.

Left: Interior of 1969 MGC GT minus the contrasting piping and pretty steel dash of earlier cars.
Right: Twin brake boosters, an extra six inches of valve-cover: a dead giveaway that this is an MGC, not an MGB.

The result was worth the wait. Pininfarina designed the fastback roof with a nice taper to it, and a very handy hatchback. To appreciate how successful the design was, one need only look at a BMW Z3 coupe. The GT also gained a higher windshield, really useful carrying ability and semi-useless rear seats.

At first glance, there seems little reason to seek out a GT when there are so many MGB roadsters out there. But frankly, the MGB as a convertible has never held much appeal for me. The convertible tops came in several different designs ranging from "pitch it like a tent" to "pinch your fingers, rip the plastic window and force down," all of which were designed by the Marquis de Sade and none of which were remotely water tight. As a roadster, the B just doesn't do anything for me. As a coupe, I find it irresistible the way I like a Porsche 356 or an Alfa Giulietta Sprint coupe.

MGBs are surprisingly well built

Yet the MGB GT costs a fraction of the Porsche or the Alfa. So naturally, you're giving up tons in performance, style and quality, right? Not really, especially in an early "steel dashboard" 1966-67 B GT. It bears pointing out that the infamous British Leyland wasn't in the picture yet and in any event, the workforce at the Abingdon plant was one of the most content in the UK. They generally took pride in what they did, right up until the day BL management rewarded them by unceremoniously shuttering the plant and throwing them out of work without so much as a "by your leave."

British cars are often dismissed as half-baked and casually assembled. In actuality, pre-1969 MGBs were beautifully made cars. Doors shut with a substantial sounding thunk, panel gaps were generally quite good and body seams carefully leaded and smoothed. Even *Road & Track* commented on this in their first test of an MGB: "Our test car was a very early production model and yet, when we went over every square inch, the quality of workmanship and lack of flaws were remarkable."

Interiors were particularly charming as well. 1966-68 B GTs all came with fine English leather upholstery with contrasting piping. Porsches and Alfas of the period on the other hand came with vinyl standard. Wire wheels were all but standard at a time when Porsche and Alfa offered only steel wheels and hubcaps.

What you do clearly miss in a B is the free-revving DOHC motor of the Alfa, but at around 95 hp, you get about the same power as the Veloce and Super versions of the Porsche and Alfa, with considerably more low-end grunt. And of course at rebuild time, you're looking at a fraction of the cost. Finally, with overdrive, a B GT is a more relaxed tour car than most competitors.

Handling is also quite decent. The rigidity of the GT makes everything feel more buttoned down; the steering is quick and precise, making it easy to place the car in a corner. Benign and neutral best describe it overall. The disc/drum setup makes for adequate braking. It's not a car that you're afraid to drive in modern traffic, although without overdrive, things can get a bit tedious on the freeway.

ran when parked...

MGC remedies horsepower deficit

The only thing that the B GT lacks is about fifty more horsepower. And this is precisely the shortcoming the MGC GT was designed to remedy. This unfairly maligned car was essentially an MGB with a 145 hp 2912 cc straight-six and a redesigned torsion bar front suspension. Critics at the time bemoaned its slower steering and strong understeer at the limit when compared to a B. In light of the car's three-second better 0-60 time and real 120 mph top speed, it seems like rather silly quibbling.

Perhaps the only legitimate knock on the MGC is the fact that it's nearly identical to the MGB, aside from a giant hood bulge, 15" wheels and a 140 mph speedometer. An automatic transmission was also available; they turn up from time to time. Not a great thing to have on an already resale-challenged car. The C was around from just 1967-69.

The most desirable years for the MGB GT are the first two, 1966-67. This was the only year that the GT came with the pretty black crackle-finish steel dash and cool toggle switches. 1968 brought the ghastly "Abingdon Pillow" safety dash which was a giant piece of vacuum formed plastic with no glovebox. They crack horribly with age, and none of the aftermarket dash caps seem to fit or look particularly good.

And although emission controls did the MGB no favors, an attractive new dash with face-level vents partially redeemed things in 1972. Wire wheels became less common, but the 14" styled steel Rostyle wheels that were standard looked quite good. Early 1974 cars had chrome bumpers with huge blocky rubber over-riders. Mercifully, most of these have been replaced by chrome overriders from a '72 or '73. Late '74s got the full horrible rubber bumpers that marred the last generation of MGB roadsters through 1980. These 1974 ½ cars would be the last GTs imported, although the model remained popular in the UK until the end.

Overdrive heads a short option list

Other than wire wheels and overdrive, there are few unique GT options. The colors Grampian Gray and Sandy Beige were GT-only colors. 1967 GTs were available in an anniversary Special Edition that added a wood steering wheel, special mirrors and a plaque. Occasionally, you'll see A/C on a B GT, however, this was dealer installed, and virtually guaranteed to be non-functional today.

Air conditioning in a GT is not a bad thing to have as they do get a bit warm; Moss Motors now makes a reasonably priced and effective kit. The other accessory that you see from time to time is a rare and desirable one indeed: Sliding fabric sunroofs were popular in the UK, but rarely seen here. Webasto and Britax made the sunroofs which slide and fold back almost the entire length of the roof. In a way, it's the best of both worlds—the practicality and looks of the coupe with the airiness of the roadster.

Inspecting a prospective B or C GT purchase is pretty straightforward. With their mechanical simplicity and cheap readily available parts, the thing that matters most is the condition of the body. Although you do tend to see less floor rust from leaky tops, and GTs don't suffer from the infamous MG door crack (a structural weakness found in roadsters), it doesn't take much for a B GT to be beyond economical repair.

Floors, rockers and sills are the areas to pay the most attention to. To look at the sills, you may have to peel back some rubber trim or carpeting; the area to look at is just beyond the door threshold where the structure steps down to the floor. Any crunchiness here is an automatic deal breaker. Also, MGBs tend to rust from the inside out. Any bubbles you see in the lower fenders and rockers will be worse on the inside. Finally, check for bubbles on the cowl where the tops of the front fenders and cowl come together. It's a common rot spot.

The ultimate in mechanical simplicity

Mechanically, MGBs are straightforward. Front suspensions are prone to wear to the point where many MG experts advise that if you have nothing better to do on a particular day, your time would be well spent oiling your kingpins. Signs of wear here include a sticky feeling in the steering and loss of self-centering action. A kingpin rebuild is time consuming--and not particularly cheap.

The BMC cast iron 1.8 liter four-cylinder could probably take a 20mm cannon shell and still run on three cylinders. Warm oil-pressure of 25 lbs or more at idle and over 40 under load usually indicates that things are okay. Geaboxes are equally tough. Noisy first-gears are common, particularly in those cars with a non-synchro first-gear. Soft hydraulics are common on cars which have sat for long periods of time. Fortunately, rebuilding clutch and brake master-cylinders and wheel cylinders is relatively simple stuff.

If Bs and Cs have an Achilles Heel, it would be the fuel pump. If your car still has an original SU fuel pump, by all means, change it, even if it seems to be working fine. Eventually, the points will wear out and the pump will just stop pumping with no warning. Sometimes you can limp home by un-sticking the points with a rap from the knockoff hammer…and sometimes not.

The market

MGB GTs generally trade for around a third less than the roadsters, and not surprisingly, it's much harder to find a good one. $10,000 seems to be the top of the market for a well-restored early B GT. Strangely, MGCs tend to bring a surprisingly small premium over Bs. For car performance on par with a Big Healey, they're huge bargains—although with only 4,458 built, they're about as easy to find as an orthodontist in England.

Case studies

1969 MGB GT		
Purchase Price $2,900	**Sale Price** $4,800	**Owned for** 1.5 years

1969 MGC GT		
Purchase Price $7,500	**Sale Price** $10,000	**Owned for** 1.5 years

Left: A late Bar Mitzvah present to myself—a California black plate MGB GT.
Right: British Racing Green MGC—a delightful car in spite of everything you've read to the contrary.

I bought my first MGB GT while in San Diego to attend a bar mitzvah. Blaming too much chopped liver and bad kosher wine, I disappeared for a few hours to scour the local Auto Trader. I returned to the hotel with a yellow MG. A black plate car with shiny primrose yellow paint, a fresh black leather interior, chrome wires and overdrive for less than $3,000. Really, what would you have done? The seller was a navy pilot who had been using the car to commute every day to NAS North Island. He had bought a truck with A/C and the little MG became expendable.

It was a rust-free California car its whole life and drove beautifully had good oil pressure, and recently rebuilt kingpins. At the time, my daughter was about eight, so I installed rear seat belts and we'd stuff our pet greyhound in the hatch area and go for rides. I was amazed at how much you could fit into a B GT. I even used it to bring home an occasional piece of furniture or large car part.

The only drama during the time the car was with me came on the way home from a holiday party. I watched the little square oil pressure gauge drop to zero. Thinking the worst, that my oil pump had failed and hoping I'd caught things in time, I shut it off and called a tow. It turned out to be the gauge sender. But it did illustrate a point from early in the book; pay attention to your gauges. Better safe than sorry.

Although the MGB GT had modest performance, what impressed me the most about the car was its solid structure and build quality. It didn't squeak or rattle, the doors shut with authority and for a car with a very live rear-axle and ancient lever shocks, the ride while a bit bouncy, was not too bad. The yellow B GT was the first car that I sold via eBay; it went to a gentleman in Arkansas for a bit more than I had in it.

My next GT came under rather unhappy circumstances. I had just started working for *Sports Car Market* magazine and was commuting to Portland, Oregon from St. Louis on a regular basis. I clearly needed a car to keep out there, so I decided to ship my Mint Green '76 BMW 2002 to the Pacific Northwest.

Not two weeks after it arrived, some cretin in a pickup truck cut me off on the highway one rainy night. The little 2002, which had survived thirty years without acquiring so much as a scratch, was done for, and under my watch too. I felt miserable. At least there wasn't a fight in store with the insurance company to compound my misery. Illustrating the benefits of agreed value coverage, a check was soon in my hands for $7,500.

Rainy Portland seemed like a good place to own a coupe and my thoughts returned to the primrose B GT that I had sold a few years earlier. As luck would have it, there was a green C GT listed on Craigslist in Seattle just three hours north of Portland. Coincidentally, David Slama, then GM of *SCM*, needed to get his Lotus Esprit turbo up to Seattle to be serviced. He asked if I'd like to take it up there and drive the MG back.

It seemed like a good plan with two exceptions—it lacked a contingency in the event the MGC was a loser, and it also meant I'd first have to spend three hours in his Lotus. The drive up to Seattle illustrated the fact that the Lotus Esprit, while great fun in limited doses, was positively horrifying for a long drive and in I-5 rush hour traffic in Seattle. It's loud, the seats are uncomfortable and you can't see out of the damn thing. Changing lanes involves a leap of faith, a downshift and generous application of the throttle.

In any event, I dropped the Lotus off at the dealer and took public transportation to go see the MG, which was stored in an old brick garage in the Capitol Hill area of Seattle. It was a good sign that the garage was shared with some of the owner's obviously enthusiastic friends—flanking the C was a Ferrari 330GT and a Citroën SM.

Within thirty seconds, it was clear that the C was a right car. A nice older respray, no signs of filler anywhere and the underside was clean and rust free with a generous amount of the Abingdon applied Pepto-Bismol pink primer showing through. It had working overdrive, fresh leather seats and happily, someone had installed three point seat belts on retractors. The only odd thing about the car was its weak fourth gear synchro. In all the years I've been messing with old cars, I've never seen a weak fourth gear synchro and I wondered if perhaps it didn't come that way. I leaned to take the 3-4 shift slowly and it never bothered me.

We agreed on a price of $7,500 which not coincidentally, was the amount of my insurance settlement. I decided to spend the night in Seattle and head back to Portland the next day. I was pleased to see that the car fired right up the next morning even after it spent a cold February night out on the street. I decided to grab a bowl of clam chowder at the Pike Place Market before filling up with gas and heading back to Portland.

As luck would have it, I managed to find a spot at a meter on one of the steep downhill streets that heads down to Elliot Bay and the market—the kind you have to back into at a forty-five degree angle. In hindsight, I might have considered filling up the tank before taking care of lunch.

When I got back and started the car, the C caught once briefly and died and then cranked and cranked. It was getting spark, and I could hear the fuel pump ticking its little guts out but it wouldn't catch. I looked at the gas gauge and it showed the same quarter-tank it had the night before. Because of the extreme angle at which the car was parked, all of it was sloshed into the corner of the tank furthest from the fuel pickup. There was no budging the car out of the spot. It took a tow truck to winch the thing onto level ground where after some cursing and a fair amount of effort, the car finally fired up.

As further luck would have it, Superbowl Sunday, 2006 will probably ring a bell for most Seattleites. The Seahawks were actually playing the Steelers for the NFL championship but a good percentage of Seattleites couldn't see it because they were without power from the brutal windstorm in which I was setting out for a 170 mile drive in a now suspect forty-year-old British sports car.

I expected the little MGC to be blown all over I-5 by the 70 mph wind gusts but surprisingly, it was quite stable. In fourth gear overdrive, at 75 mph, it was turning a relaxed 3,200 rpm. And therein lies the

Note to self: Fill tank before parking at absurd angle on Seattle side streets.

appeal of the MGC GT—I was crossing the I-5 bridge over the Columbia River into Portland in a little over two and one half hours. I had averaged about 73 mph and gotten 25 mpg. After the wind had died down, on a particularly deserted stretch of Interstate past Olympia, I saw an indicated 100 mph for several miles. It wasn't at all scary and I couldn't imagine doing it in a four cylinder MGB, especially one without overdrive.

Immediately after making the trip back from Seattle, the fuel pump died. It was the original SU pump that I would have replaced anyway. Other than that, I had the carbs adjusted, changed the oil, repainted the hood (it was aluminum and there were paint adhesion issues) and replaced a stuck thermostat. That was it, in almost two years and probably 5,000 miles. I took a few trips back and forth to Seattle and drove out to the Oregon Coast several times—it was as faithful and bulletproof as one could ask. Even with gas and insurance figured in, the cost per mile was laughably low, especially in light of the fact that I sold it for $2,500 more than I paid for it. When it was time to head down the road, the buyer drove it back to Salt Lake City—800 miles with no problems.

Instead of a slightly clumsier MGB, the C reminded me more of a very poor man's Aston Martin DB4—a car capable of eating up a lot of miles at high speeds in leather-lined comfort. And as far as the handling issues go, yes, at low speeds (particularly in parking lots), it is quite obvious is that there is an extra turn of the wheel dialed into the steering. This was done to lighten up steering effort. At speed, the steering feels quick enough and a set of modern tires at the right pressure mitigates most of the understeer that auto journalists in 1967 carped about.

There really wasn't anything inherently wrong with the MGC in general. I truly believe that most of the writers who slammed the C back in the day were simply disappointed that the beloved Austin-Healey 3000 had been killed without a real successor and that this car—which looked no different from an MGB—was being positioned as its replacement. But the C's reputation as somewhat of a dog has stuck. No matter, it simply means that you can still pick one up at a reasonable price. I'd have mine back in a heartbeat.

Sunbeam

Alpine 1960-67		
Parts availability ✪✪✪	**Inexpensive to maintain** ✪✪✪✪✪	**Investment potential** ✪✪
Fun to drive ✪✪½	**Price category** **$$**	Nice driver, $9,000; Show winner, $14,000
Performance 0 to 60 in 14.0 seconds; ¼ mile in 19.3 seconds at 70.5 mph (*Road & Track* 3/66)		

Parts Classic Sunbeam Auto Parts, www.classicsunbeam.com; Victoria British, www.victoriabritish.com; Sunbeam Specialties, www.rootes.com

Club Tigers East, Alpines East, www.reae.org

History

Sunbeam's parent company, The Rootes Group, Ltd. were clever marketers indeed. Realizing they were late to the sports car game and that it would be foolish indeed to try to take on BMC and Standard-Triumph directly, they carved out a different niche in the market. Where MGs and Triumphs of the day were uncompromising and lacked creature comforts, Sunbeam's new Alpine was softer and more luxurious—almost like a British Ford Thunderbird.

Left: A lovely Series V Alpine sporting aftermarket Panasport alloy wheels. Below left: Luxurious Alpine interior has full instrumentation, reclining seats and rollup windows. Right: Cropped fins of a Series V Alpine. This example still wears its coveted California black plates.

Built on the Hillman Husky platform, the Alpine was a fairly conventional sports car, but it beat MG to the punch as far as offering unibody construction. Rear suspension was by live rear-axle and leaf springs and all the braking power needed by the Alpine was provided by front discs and rear drums.

Alpines came in five distinct Series with varying degrees of differences between them. Series I Alpine, which went on sale in July of 1959, came with a 1500 cc engine of around 80 hp and very tall sharply angled tail fins. The Series II cars which came out a year later introduced a 1600 cc engine and reclining seats. The Series III of 1963 sported twin fuel tanks located in the fins which gave greater trunk space. A rather curious sub-model, the GT, was introduced at this time. It had nicer interior appointments including a wood dash and steering wheel, but curiously, while the hard top was removable, there was no soft top.

The Series IV cars introduced a year later were the first to have any substantial visual changes. In keeping with the fashion of the times, the tailfins were made considerably more subtle. Opinions are split rather evenly as to which style is more popular. A very nice removable hardtop was available with all five series of the Alpine.

The final Series V cars brought another 100 cc increase in displacement, dual carbs and nearly 100 hp. Face-level vents were finally added as well. Curiously, in spite of the multiple displacement increases and an almost 20 hp boost over the original car, the Alpine remained a slow car with 0-60 times consistently in the 14 second range.

Still, road testers were enthusiastic about the car's comfort and ability to accommodate larger drivers and its quality of assembly. Handling was also considered benign in keeping with the general nature of the car. Puny 13" wire wheels, removable hard top, a clock, leather, overdrive and whitewall tires were the main options.

Parts situation a bit more challenging than an mg

Alpines are a bit more of a challenge to own than an MGB because there simply isn't the wide range of reproduction parts available. That said, the necessities are easily obtained as well as interior kits and some of the badges and lenses. Body panels are not readily available. Chrysler bought Rootes in late 1964 and when the Alpine and Tiger were discontinued after 1967, they had no interest in preserving the tooling and consequently, it was lost.

Alpines are rusters extraordinaire. Because of their unit construction, this can be serious business. With values where they are, it doesn't take much rot before an Alpine is beyond the point of economical repair. The 1725 cc Rootes four cylinder also doesn't enjoy the same reputation for robustness as, say, a BMC B-Series engine, so compression and oil pressure should always be checked on a prospective purchase.

The market

Alpines used to occupy the bottom rung of British sports car values along with Spitfires, Midgets and rubber bumper MGBs. Somewhere along the line, the market realized that these charming and unusual cars can be quite rewarding to own. And although they've roughly doubled in value recently, they still cost about half to 2/3 as much as a Triumph TR4. And while they're likely fully priced for now, they're still quite a bargain, especially for someone who doesn't quite fit in an MG or a Triumph.

Ford

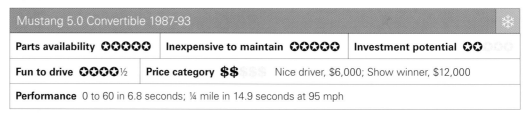

Mustang 5.0 Convertible 1987-93		❄
Parts availability ✪✪✪✪✪	**Inexpensive to maintain** ✪✪✪✪✪	**Investment potential** ✪✪
Fun to drive ✪✪✪✪½	**Price category** $$ Nice driver, $6,000; Show winner, $12,000	
Performance 0 to 60 in 6.8 seconds; ¼ mile in 14.9 seconds at 95 mph		

Parts Mustang Depot, www.mustangdepot.com; Classic Mustang, www.cmustang.com
Club Mustang Club of America, www.mustang.org

History

If American performance fans have any sense of gratitude, they'll take up a collection to commission a statue of the 1987 five liter Mustang. After a good thirteen years in the wilderness, good old fashioned American V8 performance was back. The trauma of the bloated 1971-73 Moose-stang followed by the Pinto-based Mustang II nearly killed the franchise. It seemed highly unlikely that a rather uninspired mid-sized sedan would be its savior, although, come to think of it, isn't that how it all started in 1964 with the Falcon?

Moving the Mustang to the Fox (Fairmont/Zephyr) platform offered an immediate aesthetic and handling improvement. Unfortunately, the engine choices were low-horsepower carryovers from the Mustang II. A second fuel crisis in 1979 gut-punched the new Mustang and as a result, it got a de-bored version of the five-liter that put out only 120 hp. For most of the early history of the Fox platform Mustangs, the real interesting engines were the turbo fours, culminating with the SVO cars of the mid-1980s.

In 1987, the five-liter received well-designed and better breathing cylinder heads and intake manifolds. Power was now rated at over 225 hp measured in the net system, making it roughly comparable to the old solid lifter K-code 289 V8 from 1965-66, which was rated at 271 hp gross.

Also by 1987, the gulf between the performance Mustangs and the secretary Mustangs had widened considerably, with just the 2.3 liter four and the 5.0 liter V8 available. The latter could be had in both the LX and GT trim levels. The GT came with a deep front air-dam, rocker panel extensions, louvered tail-lights and two round front fog-lamps. Although it's a matter of personal preference, I prefer the cleaner LX with the optional five-spoke Pony alloy wheels.

A Change to engine management system in 1989 was a mixed bag. While it reduced the rated horse-power slightly, it made the car much easier to add performance accessories to since the new engine management system would recognize and compensate for changes to the intake and exhaust systems. An airbag steering wheel in 1990 and some special colors was about it as far as changes to the Mustang until the model was replaced in 1994.

Left: 5.0 liter Mustang seen here in LX trim a cleaner and better looking car than the GT.
Right: Mustang top has a blind spot big enough to hide an RV.

Much better drivers than classic 1965-70 Mustangs

While Fox-platform Mustangs lack the charm of the 1965-70 cars, they are light years ahead in virtually every other category. The unibody structure is superior, as are the rack-and-pinion steering and brakes. Only the live rear-axle is a throwback. While better located than in a 1960s Mustang, it still makes itself known on rough winding roads.

Also rather unfortunate is the interior, which is pure 1980s Ford low-grade plastic. If you think the hard, waxy, petrochemical residue inside a 2005 Mustang is insufferably downmarket, you clearly haven't sat in a Fox Mustang lately. The airbag wheel introduced in 1990 is quite possibly the ugliest of its kind ever seen. Finding a Fox Mustang with leather seats at least mitigates some of the Motel 6 atmosphere, but really, it's like putting an Aresline Xten office chair in a frat house.

One of the most endearing things about the Fox Mustang is the huge aftermarket of both replacement and performance parts that's sprung up around it. The only late model car that even comes close is the Mazda Miata.

Left: Happy days were here again in the form of a fuel injected five liter with real horsepower.
Right: White leather interior clashes with cheap black plastic.

As a daily driver a Fox Mustang is an absolute blast. A power top (with a glass rear window and defroster), air conditioning and a slick five-speed are all you need and the exhaust note is a welcome change from the whoopee cushion flatulence common to the slammed Honda Civics that pass for performance cars today.

The market

A funny thing happened here recently. Right around the time I started seriously looking for a V8 LX convertible five-speed in good colors, I noticed that they weren't dirt cheap any more. Not long ago, $4,000 or so bought one. Now, this is hatchback or notchback money. Convertibles that you'd want to own start at around $6,500.

Fox body Mustangs aren't going to be the next Chevelle LS6 convertibles, but there is undeniably a following; unmolested cars are both rare and in demand. But since the following is made up of budget-minded enthusiasts, it isn't as though the speculators are going to jump in and spoil things. Buy one now, enjoy the sweet small block Ford—and room for three friends. When you're ready to move on, it'll be gone within a week, I promise.

Porsche

914 1970-76 1.7/1.8 liter		
Parts availability ✪✪✪½	Inexpensive to maintain ✪✪✪½	Investment potential ✪✪✪
Fun to drive ✪✪✪✪½	Price category **$$** Nice driver, $6,000; Show winner, $11,000	
Performance 0 to 60 in 13.9 seconds; ¼ mile in 19.2 seconds at 70 mph (*Road & Track* 6/70)		

914 1970-76 2.0 liter		
Parts availability ✪✪✪½	Inexpensive to maintain ✪✪✪½	Investment potential ✪✪✪
Fun to drive ✪✪✪✪½	Price category **$$$** Nice driver, $10,000; Show winner, $15,000	
Performance 0 to 60 in 10.3 seconds; ¼ mile in 17.8 seconds at 78 mph (*Road & Track* 2/73)		

Parts Stoddard Porsche, www.stoddard.com; Pelican Parts, www.perlicanparts.com
Club Porsche Club of America, www.pca.org

History

Anyone who has ever worked for a charismatic, entrepreneurial individual who flies largely by the seat of his or her pants and engages in frequent handshake deals will understand perfectly the genesis of the Porsche

ran when parked...

1976 914 with appearance group consisting of black vinyl on targa bar, foglights and alloy wheels.

914 styling has aged quite well and silver is one of the better colors for the car.

914. Heinz Nordhoff, VW's legendary post-war Managing Director and Ferry Porsche, the son of Porsche Founder Ferdinand Porsche saw a jointly developed model occupying the opposite ends of their respective lines as an answer to both of their problems.

VW needed a modern replacement for its top of the line Karmann-Ghia. Porsche, feeling ever more pinched by currency fluctuations, needed a new entry-level model to replace the 912 for 1970. The deal that Nordhoff and Porsche struck involved VW marketing a four-cylinder 914 in Europe as a "VW-Porsche" and Porsche would market the six-cylinder model as the Porsche 914-6. In the U.S. market, both would be marketed by Porsche.

As a result of the Nordhoff/Porsche deal, Porsche would be able to take advantage of VW's purchasing power and buy 914 bodies at a large discount. Unfortunately, nobody bothered to put things in writing and when Nordhoff died suddenly, his successor Kurt Lotz took a dim view of the sweetheart deal of his predecessor.

This revision to the deal doomed the six-cylinder variant from the start. The 914/6 was less practical and not as nicely finished as a Porsche 911T, yet it was only marginally cheaper. As a result, only 3,332 were produced before the model was dropped. The four-cylinder 914, however, was hugely successful, ultimately selling well over 100,000 copies.

Left: Appearance group included a console and extra gauges.
Above right: Spacious rear trunk matched by one in front.
Right: Thin race-car like buckets offer support commensurate with the car's high cornering power.

There is a great deal of controversy over who was actually responsible for the 914's controversial styling. Hans Gugelot, the designer of the famous Braun shaver is generally credited with it. But Gugelot, died early in the development of the car; and while his drawings were likely an influence, a Porsche studio designer named Heinrich Klie more likely penned the final shape of the 914.

914's once controversial styling has aged well

Much has been written and said about the looks of the 914. Initially, its rather similar front- and rear-ends and the "basket handle" rollover bar came in for much derision. Today, the general consensus is that the design has aged extremely well. The gentle curve of the rear fender and the somewhat Bauhaus-like minimalist approach to the whole thing is quite appealing.

As with most collector cars, colors make a big difference; fortunately, the 914 came in far more good shades than bad. Today, red, white, black and silver seem the most common. But many of the unique period colors like Signal Orange and Viper Green are quite wonderful, as are almost all of the blues offered like Gemini Blue, Alaska Blue and Adriatic Blue (an especially nice medium non-metallic blue). Interiors were done in a waffle pattern vinyl in black, brown and tan.

ran when parked...

In its first year, the 914 was available from U.S. Porsche dealers in two distinct flavors; the $3,695 1.7 liter 85 hp four-cylinder 914 and the $6,099 2.0 liter 110 hp six-cylinder, 914/6. for reasons already mentioned, the 914/6 was essentially dead on arrival. It was only $431 (about $2,300 in today's money) cheaper than a base 911T, an altogether more desirable car. The 1.7 liter four made for a disappointing car.

Road & Track perhaps established the 914's second class status by noting that it took the 2.0 liter 911T six to turn the 914 into "a real Porsche." Brilliant chassis aside, *Road & Track* opined that the 1.7 liter four-cylinder version still came off as a VW. Little changed with the 100 cc bump the base engine received in 1973; the 1.8 liter still offered rather anemic performance.

2.0 liter is far superior to 1.7 or 1.8

The transformation that took place in 1973 was the introduction of the 2.0 liter four-cylinder 914. The new engine, a VW Type 4 that made 91 hp cut the 0-60 time to around ten seconds and gave the car a near 120 mph top speed. In essence, the car had much of the performance of the 914/6 without the expense and complication.

1975 brought 5mph impact bumpers, and Porsche did nearly as well integrating them on the 914 as they had on the 911. Although black rubber, the shape gave a less blunt look to the front of the car. Only the rears looked a bit heavy. 1975-76 cars look better in dark colors.

The shift linkage on a 914 is an acquired taste. And while all are five-speeds, they are the early 911-derived five-speed that had the spring-loaded first off the "H" on the bottom left. Once you get used to it, it isn't so bad. Handling is the reason to buy any 914. Front suspension is 911 derived with torsion bars. Steering is sharp and quick; ride and brakes are quite decent as well. It takes a far more ham-fisted driver to get into serious trouble in a 914 than in a 911. The 2.0 liter cars are quite quick, and numerous parts exist to wring even more performance out of them.

Interiors are basic and will be familiar to any 911 driver. The big VDO gauges are similar and the ventilation controls are also the same. 914s of this era, unlike 911s, had large face-level vents at the end of the dash. Materials, switches and hardware, however, were a cut below the 911's level. The lift-off roof was a model of simplicity—it removed in seconds and stowed in the rear trunk. And unlike some sports cars of today, when the top was stowed, there was still plenty of storage space. The 914 you see, had two ample trunks—one in the front and one in the rear.

Regrettably, all 914s were built before Porsche got the hang of rust protection and many 914s have suffered horribly. The infamous "hell hole", otherwise known as the battery box, is the first place to look. Bad corrosion here (from battery acid) can eat into the suspension mounting points with dire results. Both trunk floors rust as do the floors, fenders, doors and even the rollover bars under the vinyl covering. Out-rocker rust, however, is nothing to worry about, as these are bolt-on non-structural decorative pieces that are easily replaced.

VW sourced parts dirt cheap, Porsche ones not

As to expensive versus inexpensive items on a 914, it's rather hit or miss. Chances are, if it's shared with a 911 (like the gearbox, front suspension, gauges and climate controls), it's not cheap. On the other hand, the engine is a cinch. While not a straight swap from a VW 411 or Transporter (the tin, heads and heat exchangers are different) pistons and cylinders are pure VW. Any flavor of 914 four-cylinder is around $2,000 to rebuild. Just beware of inferior parts from Latin America and China.

Like most Porsches, 914 interiors are relatively comfortable. The seats are not as well-padded as those in a 911, but they are good looking and will hold you firmly in place. Most are covered in a basket weave vinyl that also covers the door panels and dash. Appearance group cars will have a console that includes several extra gauges. Correct materials to re-do a 914's interior are still widely available. Minor items like switches and door handle hardware are of distinctly lower quality than their 911 analog. Things like gauges and steering wheels were supplied by the same manufacturers in similar (if not identical) styles. A few 914-only parts are becoming scarce. The U.S.-spec red rear-turn-signal lenses are extinct, as are some early Bosch D-Jetronic fuel injection parts.

Factory wheels ranged from several styles of steel wheels (some with and some without hubcaps) as well as some fine looking alloy wheels from Mahle and Fuchs. The latter looking like four-spoke versions of the famous 911 wheels and will also fit a 914/4 with adapters. Numerous aftermarket wheels are also common on 914s, the better looking are marketed by EMPI and Riviera. Both are still available from MidAmerica Motorworks (www.mamotorworks.com).

The market

The 914 is an excellent example of what can happen when the market re-examines a car after the passage of time. Old school conventional wisdom was that the 914 was a homely wannabe Porsche, rejected by both VW and Porsche fanatics. The popularity of a new mid-engine Porsche, the Boxster, has focused more attention on Porsche's first production middie, the 914. Those who've looked have liked what they've seen and consequently, the surviving good 914s have been in considerable demand. So much so, that a great 2.0 liter car can be expected to bring as much as a 911SC—a curious situation indeed. For now, 914s are looking rather fully priced, so don't expect to see the sort of appreciation that those who got in early did. Nevertheless, a 2.0 liter 914 is easily one of the most entertaining cars in this book and one that should be both reliable and cheap to maintain.

Volvo

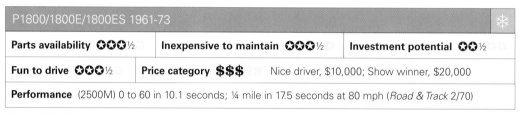

P1800/1800E/1800ES 1961-73		❄
Parts availability ✪✪✪½	**Inexpensive to maintain** ✪✪✪½	**Investment potential** ✪✪½
Fun to drive ✪✪✪½	**Price category** $$$	Nice driver, $10,000; Show winner, $20,000
Performance (2500M) 0 to 60 in 10.1 seconds; ¼ mile in 17.5 seconds at 80 mph (*Road & Track* 2/70)		

Parts P1800.com, www.p1800.com
Club Volvo Sports America, www.vsa.org

1972 1800E with factory alloy wheels.

Shawn Dougan/Hyman, Ltd.

History

Until recently, when Volvo introduced the R-line of cars to ostensibly compete with the likes of BMW's Motorsport cars and Audi's "S" line, the company was known for anything but performance. Volvo's had been the automotive equivalent of a pair of Birkenstocks—sensible and long-lived. Like many foreign manufacturers in the U.S. in the 1950s, Volvo was seduced by the notion of increasing sales of its more pedestrian wares by adding a sports car as a showroom magnet.

There was a little known and abortive first attempt called the P1900, a poorly engineered fiberglass convertible in the late-1950s. It was not particularly attractive and most un-Volvo like in both appearance and execution. Not surprisingly, Volvo went outside the company for their next attempt, the P1800. Initial styling was accomplished in Italy by Pietro Frua. Lacking the capacity to do it themselves, Volvo shopped the assembly work to Karmann in Osnabruck, Germany. Heinz Nordhoff of Volkswagen, however, flipped out when he heard that Karmann was considering producing a car that would be in direct competition to the Karmann-Ghia.

Realizing they no longer occupied Norway next door with several Panzer divisions, the Germans needed other leverage over the Swedes. VW found it when they threatened to pull all of their contracts from Karmann. Karmann immediately broke off negotiations with the Swedes, leaving them without a production source that could meet their quality standards—so they contracted with one that clearly couldn't, rather than let the car die. Jensen Motors of Castle Bromwich, England was a small car company with a big factory. They agreed to do assembly work for Volvo on the project, contracting the actual body building out to Pressed Steel, Inc.

Mechanically, the car was quite conventional, employing Volvo's stout unit construction, a live rear-axle and leaf spring suspension, front disc/rear drum brakes and the brilliant B18 four cylinder engine. It was a slightly hotter version of the Amazon motor that was essentially half of a Volvo truck V8. With five main bearings and engineered for heavy-duty use, to say that it's simply durable would be like calling Howard Hughes merely "eccentric."

Frua's styling reflected the fact that the car was conceived in the 1950s with tailfins and a high beltline. Also clearly a 1950s carryover was the original interior of the car—it's quite charming with lots of bright trim, attractive gauges and steering wheel and very pretty, comfortable upholstery.

No matter, it was quite attractive with a bit of Ferrari Boano coupe in it. Critics gave the car generally positive reviews when it was introduced, but it soon became clear that Jensen was not up to the task of assembling the car. There were serious quality issues and worse, the Jensen-built cars were among the worst rusters of all time.

Volvo terminated the Jensen contract after just 6,000 cars and moved production to Sweden in 1963, going so far as to rename the car the 1800S to denote assembly in Sweden. The few surviving Jensen-built cars can easily be spotted by a set of split/bent bumpers that resemble the moustache of cartoon character Snidely Whiplash.

The S cars were largely the same with the exception of a different grille insert, straight bumpers and an additional 8 hp. In the face of tightening emission controls, 1969 saw the insertion of the 2.0 liter B20 engine,

Left: Late P1800 interior with good–looking, supportive seats and handsome dash.
Right: Fuel injected B20 engine good for around 300,000+ miles.

Rear ¾ view with fins
rooted in the fifties.

longevity freaks needn't have worried, it was hewn from the same solid block of granite as the B18—and it now delivered 120 hp.

The real news came in 1970 with the introduction of the injected 1800E. Horsepower was now up to 130 hp but fuel economy was still over 20 mpg overall. The car also got disc brakes in the rear as well as the front, and a new interior with considerably less charm than the original. Although still sporting a full complement of Smiths gauges, the gauge rims were now black instead of bright, and the "safety" steering wheel looked like something out of a Ford wagon. Worst of all, Volvo finally succumbed to the fake wood trend.

ES wagon is handsome and practical

For 1972, Volvo had one last trick in store for what by now was looking like a pretty dated car. The 1800ES (for "estate" or Brit-speak for wagon) was a two-door sport wagon. And while many have taken a crack at this body-style, to date, only Volvo and Chevy with the Nomad have really gotten it right. The 1800ES was particularly attractive with the small vestigial tail fins left intact and an all-glass tailgate in the rear. An ES can make a very practical daily driver or even an only car.

One other body-style worthy of note; the convertible conversions. Radford coachbuilders of the U.K. and Volvoville, a Long Island, New York Volvo dealer, did conversions that were so attractive that one wonders why Volvo didn't do a factory convertible. Top up or down, there was a bit of Maserati 3500 Spyder in the car. Accurate production numbers are hard to come by, but there were almost certainly under 100 conversions done by both Radford and Voloville combined.

All 1800s are very pleasant drivers. While too heavy to be genuinely quick or particularly sharp handlers, they are wonderful GTs that are delightful on long drives. Overdrive was a common option; it was one of two different Laycock de Normanville types common to British sports cars of the era. It really is a must to enjoy the essential character of the car; that of a long-legged GT. Dealer installed air conditioning was common on later cars as were an automatic transmission; unique to the 1800 were five-spoke alloy wheels.

P1800 engines have no expiration date

The other thing that 1800s certainly are is mechanically durable. B18 or B20 motors really have no set lifespan. 300,000-400,000 miles between overhauls is probably reasonable, a bit less for gearboxes which start to lose their synchromesh eventually. Irv Gordon's 1800 (although it has had some mechanical attention over the years) is still listed as the Guinness Book record holder, closing in on 3 million miles.

Unfortunately, while engines and gearboxes may last forever, the bodies don't. Perhaps it's the curse of Jensen, but even the Swedish-built cars don't seem to be as well rust-proofed as an Amazon or a 544 built at the same time. Rockers, lower fenders, door bottoms and particularly floors, jacking points and outriggers seem to fare the worst. It is essential that you look carefully underneath the carpets of any 1800 and get it up in the air before parting with any money.

Other than rust, any other faults should be fairly obvious. Overdrive units can become schizophrenic, often turning themselves on and off. Usually, it's a simple fault like a switch or a solenoid. Interiors wear and dashes crack, but all of this can be put right by someone with the cash and the commitment.

The market

1800s are bought more on condition than the individual variant. That said, coupes will always be more desirable than the ES and there seems to be a bit of a premium paid for the surviving Jensen-built cars because of their rarity. The better performance of the injected E seems to be an even swap for the more attractive interior found in the earlier S. As usual, automatics are a knock and overdrive is worth paying extra for. Acceptable drivers can be found in the $7,000 to $8,000 range with really great cars priced in the high teens to low twenties. 1800s have been steadily appreciating at a modest rate for some time now, and there is no reason to believe that this won't continue. They're practical, cheap to maintain, decent performers and very pleasant tour or rally cars that are eligible for some very fun events.

Case study

1973 Volvo 1800ES		
Purchase Price $2,800	**Sale Price** $6,000	**Owned for** 0.5 years

1972 1800ES spotted from an airplane and bought at a Volvo swap meet for $2,800.

Left: 1800ES seats had been re-done in a very attractive but incorrect black cloth.
Right: Slick frameless rear glass still a Volvo trademark.

I found the red 1800ES in a fairly unconventional way—aerial reconnaissance. I was on my way back to Portland and looking out the window on final approach to Portland International Airport. Just prior to touchdown, we passed an office park with a lot full of vintage Volvos. I surmised correctly that it was the annual all-Volvo swap meet and car show held by IPD, a Portland-based Volvo institution.

Upon arriving at the swap meet, the ES was literally the first car that I encountered with a for sale sign. It was a four-speed, overdrive car with A/C, minimal rust and a somewhat faded but decent quality respray in the original red. The interior showed signs of care as well, with just a cracked dash top and faded carpets requiring attention. The asking price was $4,200.

Not really needing an 1800ES in Portland, I called my good friend and colleague Paul Duchene and asked him to come by and talk me out of it—fat chance. Paul pronounced it "a right car." Although neither of us needed it, I'm embarrassed to say that we wound up partners in the car for $1,400 each.

Paul's philosophy with these things is quite simple—never buy anything that you wouldn't mind being stuck with for an extended period of time. And neither of us would have minded being stuck with the very attractive Volvo.

A weekend of detailing had a shine back in the paint, and we removed the carpets in the cargo area that had faded to a light orange color, re-dyed them red and bought a dash cap to cover the cracked dash top. While certainly not concours, it was a straight, honest car that drove quite well, didn't smoke and showed good oil pressure. A few bubbles in the bottoms of the front fenders was the extent of the rust.

We figured the car to be a bargain by about half. It was far from the first time that I've seen this sort of thing happen at a swap meet. Although most people think that swap meets are rapidly becoming irrelevant in the digital age—when the part you need can be found on eBay without looking at hundreds that you don't—swap meets are still interesting because they represent an opportunity for a motivated seller to make a car go away in an afternoon. And that's what happened here. The seller promised his wife that the car wasn't coming home and Paul and I were surely the only ones not there just to purchase a set of door panel pockets for a 240 wagon.

We brought our prize back to the magazine and kept it around for a while before deciding to throw it up on eBay. The high bidder turned out to be a Swede who lived in Gothenburg, a stone's throw from the factory. The sale price was $6,000. We doubled our money because we ignored the conventional wisdom that swap meets are a waste of time.

BMW

2002 1968-76		
Parts availability ✪✪✪	Inexpensive to maintain ✪✪✪	Investment potential ✪✪½
Fun to drive ✪✪✪✪	Price category **$$$** Nice driver, $8,000; Show winner, $20,000	
Performance 0 to 60 in 11.3 seconds; ¼ mile in 17.5 seconds at 79 mph (*Road & Track* 5/68)		

Parts Maximillian Imports, www.mbwmobiletradition-online.com; Bimmer Parts, www.bimmerparts.com
Club BMW Car Club of America, www.bmwcca.org

ran when parked...

Left: 1976 BMW 2002 in
Mint Green.
Right: $22,000 Sahara
Beige BMW 2002 sold
at RM's 2008 Amelia
Island sale.

History

The BMW 2002 is perhaps one of the only instances in which U.S. emission control regulations actually had a positive affect on a car. The 2002 was a derivative of the BMW 1600, a two-door version of the BMW *neu klasse* sedan introduced in the early 1960s. At the urging of influential importer Max Hoffman, BMW finally abandoned big, expensive and largely sale-proof cars like the 503 and focused on cars that people actually wanted to buy in volume.

After U.S. emissions equipment was applied, the single carburetor version of the 1600 was deemed to be too anemic to be competitive. The dual carburetor version was powerful enough, but couldn't pass emissions. Max Hoffman's suggestion was to take the 2.0 liter sedan motor with a single carburetor and stuff it into the 1600 two-door body. Thus, the 2002 (two liters, two doors) was born.

The automotive press was instantly smitten. David E. Davis, Jr. called it "the greatest way to get somewhere sitting down." Here was an upright, classy and comfortable two-door sedan that could outperform and outhandle most sports cars of the day. All of the goods were present—German build quality, independent rear suspension, a willing sohc four-cylinder and a fully-sychronized four-speed.

Ventilation primitive and five-speed sorely needed

The 2002 wasn't perfect; the car lacked face-level vents, so cabin ventilation was always poor, and a sorely needed five-speed was never offered in the U.S. But the 2002 is fondly remembered by a generation of enthusiasts as the car that invented the sports sedan category.

2002s can be divided into two different series, each with two different engine options. 1968-73 cars are unofficially referred to as "roundies" for the round shape of the tail-lights. Most collectors seem to prefer the earlier cars. 1974-76 cars are referred to as "square tail-light" cars. The latter also acquired the unpopular large 5 mph bumpers.

Injected tii rare and desirable

The 2002tii model was a available from 1971-74 with an additional 40 hp courtesy of Kugelfischer mechanical fuel injection. They're lovely cars; sort of the 911S of the 2002 range, but like the 911T, there isn't that much of a performance differential and the ordinary 2002 is just fine under most circumstances. Additionally, mechanical fuel injection is at best an oddity today. Few mechanics understand the workings of it regardless of whether it was produced by SPICA, Lucas, Bosch, Kugelfischer or Rochester—and you don't want to know what a set of tii injectors costs.

The 2002 option list was short. Few cars came with alloy wheels although 2002s are often seen with later 320i alloy wheels. Period mags from Minilite, BWA and Cromodora look great as do a set of new Panasports. Air conditioning and a sunroof were available and both are desirable. The sliding crank operated Golde sunroofs are huge and the A/C, while not really effective, compensates somewhat for the dreadful ventilation on a 2002. An automatic by ZF was optional as well, but it really ruins the essential character of the car. Parts for the transmission are becoming scarce, a common theme with almost any vintage ZF transmission.

2002s are yet another car where color can add considerably to the value. In my opinion, while 3.0 coupes look great in light metallics, 2002s look better in cheeky period colors like Inka Orange, Golf Yellow and Colorado Orange. An Inka 2002tii with a set of accessory fog-lights and period alloys is about as cool as vintage BMW gets.

Mechanically, 2002s are robust and simple and present few upkeep issues. Marginal cooling systems can be addressed by using an up-rated 320i radiator. Five-speed conversions also make for more relaxed highway cruising. Like most other old cars, rust issues can rear their heads in a very big way. Major rust in the shock towers may be beyond economical repair. Bottoms of the fenders and doors are also common rust areas. Again, you're way ahead of the game confining your search to the western United States.

The market

A dual market for 2002s seems to have developed. While there have been some relatively strong private sales, 2002s seem to do particularly well at auctions. They're cult cars of the highest magnitude; there always seem to be at least two now wealthy men or women in the crowd who had fond memories of one. Since there generally isn't more than one 2002 even at the largest sales, you often seen several of the aforementioned well-heeled types fighting over the lone 2002. This was the case several years ago when a very nice Sahara Beige roundy went for over $20,000 at the RM Amelia Island sale. I spoke to one of the underbidders after the sale; it turns out his wife had one back in the 70s.

Case study

1976 BMW 2002		
Purchase Price (2006) $5,000	**Sale Price** N/A (totaled)	**Owned for** 1.0 years

Left: Kermit the 2002—large bumpers on post-73 2002s detract a bit from the looks.
Right: 2002 a casualty of a rainy Oregon interstate. It looked like Rocky Balboa after going ten rounds with Apollo Creed.

The ill-fated Mint Green 2002 was among the nicer cars that I've owned, which is why its ultimate fate is still rather upsetting. The car had been a Northern California car its whole life (Concord, just far enough inland to avoid any salt air) and was a beautifully preserved original car with fine original paint and interior, the original tool kit, a huge binder of receipts and no deferred maintenance. The fastidious first owner had even made custom dash and rear-deck covers which ensured that both of these usually sun-baked areas remained in perfect condition.

The original owner sold the car to a gentleman who shipped it back to Chicago, where I found it on Craigslist advertised for $5,500. The $5,000 that we ultimately agreed on seemed light by around $2,000 to me given the condition of the car, but perhaps the color was off-putting to some. I personally like the "Lifesaver" colors from the 1970s, like orange and yellow; lime green evokes the period. Although called Mint Green, it's actually closer to lime and is quite like the popular Porsche color "Viper Green."

Ordinarily, I don't recommend buying a vintage car and then driving it home a large distance. Better, I think, to ship it home and spend some time sorting things out, building a level of "trust" between yourself and the car. I made an exception for the 2002, since not only was it clearly in impeccable condition, but had also been used as a daily driver.

I bought a $29 plane ticket and flew up to Chicago and took the CTA to the seller's house. I threw my bag in the car and started out on the 275 mile trip back to St. Louis. I made it exactly 100 yards from the seller's driveway before shutting off the car in a cloud of coolant smoke. No burst hoses, nothing coming from the water pump and an ice cold radiator could mean one thing—a stuck thermostat. Undaunted, I figured, in September in Chicago, won't need the heat, I'll just remove the stupid thing and be on my way.

Nothing doing. As luck would have it, BMW couldn't just use an ordinary thermostat like you'd find in an MG or a Triumph. The offending part actually formed a sort of "T" junction between two major hoses, so there was no removing it without a replacement—not exactly a NAPA part. I took another plane home and the seller fixed the car, which came home about a week later on a truck.

The 2002 was everything that I expected it to be—adequate power, sharp handling and good brakes. The steering was bit heavier than I expected, but I think that was a function of the oversized tires mounted on BBS alloys that the previous owner had fitted. Although the car didn't have A/C, the sunroof and vent windows provided adequate ventilation under most conditions. The only thing about the car that I really didn't care much for was the dash. In BMW style, it was under-instrumented and the fake wood appliqué used on later 2002s reminded me of the dash of a VW Scirocco.

More than anything else, it was the originality of the car that was the most charming. It was clear that the car had never been painted for several reasons: There was no sign of overspray or masking anywhere, particularly around the windshield and rear window. On high spots, the paint was thin enough to see primer underneath. If you ran the car through an automatic car wash, it would strip the wax and the car would have no gloss whatsoever.

As I said, the previous owner had kept up with all needs so when I got it, there was literally nothing to do except enjoy the car. I put a Blaupunkt stereo in the car, and that was it for expenditures over the year I had the car—which, I am convinced, I would still have but for my decision to send it out to Oregon. One night on my way home from work at *Sports Car Market*, I was cut off by a pickup truck who decided that he needed to exit the highway in front of me; there was nowhere to go but into his trailer hitch.

While I wasn't hurt (and the pickup driver pulled over, then took off) the difference in bumper heights meant that the 2002 was a total loss, with grille and surround, lights, hood and both front fenders affected in varying degrees. If there was a silver lining to the story, it is the fact that I was able to buy the salvage from the insurance company. I sold the car to a body shop owner who amassed a pile of new parts, straightened everything that could be straightened and perfectly matched the aged green paint, leaving as much original as possible. It's back on the road in Portland, looking almost exactly as it did pre-crash.

Triumph

TR4/4A 1962-67		❄
Parts availability ✪✪✪✪✪	**Inexpensive to maintain** ✪✪✪✪✪	**Investment potential** ✪✪✪
Fun to drive ✪✪✪✪	**Price category** $$$	Nice driver, $12,000; Show winner, $30,000
Performance 0 to 60 in 10.5 seconds; ¼ mile in 17.8 seconds at 77.2 mph (*Road & Track* 2/62)		

Parts Moss Motors, www.mossmotors.com; The Little British Car Company, www.lbcarco.com; Victoria British, www.victoriabritish.com; The Roadster Factory, www.the-roadster-factory.com

Club Vintage Triumph Register, www.vtr.org

Michelotti's TR4—a huge improvement in looks over the TR3.

Donald Osborne

History

Before being assimilated into the same corporate conglomerate, MG and Triumph had been bitter rivals competing for the same critical export dollars. Their 1950s mainstays, the TR3 and the MGA, were pretty evenly matched. The TR3 was more rugged and a bit more powerful, but the MGA was undoubtedly much prettier and more nimble. If the TR3 was Winston Churchill in a sensible British cloak, the MGA was Diana Rigg in a PVC catsuit.

Determined to redress the balance in the looks department while maintaining the performance edge (especially with the threat of the new MGB), Triumph once again turned to Giovanni Michelotti to turn the TR3 into something less bulldoggish.

Michelotti had done several sports car prototypes for Triumph, one looking very much like a smaller Ferrari 250PF cabriolet and the other looking like a narrower version of the eventual production TR4. A team of the former was entered at Le Mans with an exotic twin-cam engine, code-named "Sabrina" but in the end, it was the odd eyebrowed design with the old cast iron Standard-Vanguard tractor motor that became the TR4.

This isn't to say that there weren't considerable improvements made over the TR3. The new car had an extra 200ccs of displacement, rollup windows, a bigger trunk, rack-and-pinion steering and an all-synchro gearbox. But the TR4 seemed slightly behind the times from the beginning, because it remained a separate body and frame car after MG had gone to a unibody design with the B. But it was more powerful and quite a bit quicker than its rival from Abingdon, and with its longer hood and tailfins, it looked a lot tougher too.

The interior of early TR4s was quite similar to the TR3. Gauges had the unique convex "globe" glass, the same barrel-backed bucket seats with contrasting piping, and a plain white enamel dash no matter what the exterior color was. Tops were also of a similar design in which you had to unfold the top frame, remove the top itself from the trunk, drape it over the frame, fasten around twenty snaps and then pull a lever to make the whole mess reasonably taught. At least the windows rolled up.

Triumph did have a rather interesting take on the hard top though. The design consisted of a fixed wrap-around rear-window with a steel or aluminum lift-off center section. With the center section on, it has the appearance of a very neat coupe. With it off, it was very similar to Porsche's Targa design some five years later. The rigid center section, would not fit in the trunk, so for weather protection, Triumph designed a rudimentary frame and a canvas center section. The canvas piece was called a "Surrey Top," but this name has been applied retroactively to the whole hard top design. It's rare and quite desirable.

ran when parked...

The original design lasted until 1965 when Triumph introduced the TR4A. Outside, it took an expert to distinguish the 4 from the 4A. There was a rather baroque side-light and chrome spear on the 4A, new seats and a better quality grille stamping plus a top that actually folded on its frame and could be put up or down in around thirty seconds. TR4As also came from the factory with wood dashes. But the real news was a re-designed frame and available independent rear suspension ("IRS").

Left: Factory tool kit—always a nice thing to have and adds value. Right: Standard-Vanguard 2.2 liter—four more durable than The Sphinx.

Collectors prefer the IRS, but it's no better than the solid axle cars

It had been Triumph's intention to make the IRS standard, but a revolt of U.S. dealers who argued that in the land of the billiard table smooth road, Americans weren't going to pay extra for IRS. Thus it became an option in the States, although the majority of TR4As were sold with it. No matter, it's not a particularly good setup with the rear half shafts running below the frame severely limiting their travel. Worse still, the new bell-shaped frame was proving to be less strong than the simple ladder design that it replaced. Anyone buying a 4A, TR250 or TR6 today would do well to have someone competent check out the from lower control arm mounting points.

With the announcement of U.S. emission laws, it became clear that there was little to be done with the Standard Vanguard four which was at the end of the road as far as displacement and development goes. It was replaced by a smoother (albeit no more powerful) six cylinder to make the TR250 and ultimately by a restyled TR6.

TR4 surprisingly quick

Snobs can carp all they want about the "tractor motor" that powers the TR4; although far from silky-smooth or revvy, it's torquey, powerful and completely unbreakable, with a nice exhaust note to boot. It makes the TR4 one of the quicker middle-weight British sports cars. In addition to good power, the TR4 has excellent steering and brakes. The unassisted rack-and-pinion is both light and quick, and the also unassisted front-disc/rear-drum setup, while requiring a decent shove is confidence inspiring. The all-synchro gearbox is a pleasure to use as well. Overdrive is a useful option for relaxed highway cruising.

TR4 driver comfort is decent too. The seats, while never acquiring a reclining mechanism, got more comfortable as the model progressed. All had contrasting piping and optional leather. One of the few areas where the TR4 was truly ahead of its time is in the ventilation department. It was actually one of the first cars anywhere to have face-level vents that could be opened and closed with modern-type knurled knobs. A cowl vent opened via a lever under the dash and the driver could instantly have a blast of fresh air in the face (assuming there was some forward momentum to ram the air through the vent). Heat was marginal, like most British sports cars of the day.

Having had two TR4s and two TR4As, it's a nearly a tossup as to which I prefer. The 4A has a better convertible top and a prettier grille. I actually prefer the simpler live-axle of the 4, and I really dislike the side lights and trim on the 4A. Given my druthers, I think I'd go for an early 4 with a surrey top. Collectors seem to like IRS cars, though.

Right: Early style seats in gorgeous red leather and white enamel dash mark this as a very early TR4. Below: Subtle tail fins and neat two-piece factory hard top pre-dated Porsche's Targa design by five years.

Donald Osborne

Donald Osborne

TR4s, like most old cars are rusters. Tops tend to leak, letting water collect in the stamped ribs in the floorboards where the rust-out process begins. Rocker panels, tops of the rear-fenders, inner-fenders and trunk-floors are also targets. Frighteningly, frame rust is not uncommon either. Perhaps the most serious spot for this is on the 4A frame where the rear trailing arm-brackets mount to the frame.

Mechanically, everything is straightforward and durable—with the exception of the IRS. Clunks from back there generally mean that the axle shafts u-joints or even wheel splines need some attention. Also, there has been on ongoing problem in obtaining replacement clutch parts that are suitably long-lived. Premature clutch failures are not unheard of. The Roadster Factory in Pennsylvania seems to have this problem licked with the clutch kits that they sell.

The market

After Big Healey prices went through the roof, many figured it might be the turn of the TR4 next. And the $97,000 price brought by one at Barrett-Jackson in West Palm Beach in 2006 made it look like that would be the case. But one sale does not a market make. The best follow up sale after that was at Gooding and Company in Phoenix in 2008 for $40,000 for probably the best one on the planet, black and red with a surrey top. It seems safe to say at this point that there are still a number of very good cars that can be bought in the mid- to high-teens. Low-twenties should buy a competently restored example. While it's difficult to imagine a sudden increase in value, a nice TR4 will always appreciate at a modest rate while demanding very little in upkeep.

Case studies

1964 Triumph TR4		
Purchase Price $6,900	**Sale Price** $12,750	**Owned for** 0.5 years

1966 Triumph TR4A		
Purchase Price $7,800	**Sale Price** $16,000	**Owned for** 3.0 years

The first car I ever owned was a 1964 TR4 that tried to kill me in several ways, the first with tetanus (I sliced my hand sawing off the remains of its rusty floorboards. This being the pre-*Web MD* days, I spent an inordinate amount of time with the "T" volume of World Book Encyclopedia, convinced I would develop the worst case of lockjaw since Katherine Hepburn). The brakes also failed on my first post-restoration test drive; but the garage wall succeeded when the brake pedal sunk to the floor.

I've owned several better ones since then, including a white '66 4A with wire wheels, overdrive, and a rare surrey top. It was the car that introduced me to the *Sports Car Market* crowd as it was located in Portland, Oregon, the home of *SCM*. Publisher Keith Martin graciously took a look at it at the Portland All-British field meet where it won the peoples' choice award.

It was a very good amateur restoration; not better than new in any way, but quite authentic. It reminded me of a well-cared for six or seven year-old used car. It was one of the first cars that I had owned that really wanted for nothing. Frustrated, I began to fix and replace things that needed neither fixing nor replacing. I pulled out a perfectly serviceable vinyl interior in favor of a new leather one chock full of bovine-smelling goodness, added chrome wire wheels and a wood Moto-Lita steering wheel. All nice stuff, but I have to admit that the car had the look of a rolling Moss Motors holiday catalog.

In three years, I'm quite sure that I put well over 10,000 miles on the car, replacing just the fuel pump and rebuilding the carbs and generator. I sold it—after buying a rare Daimler SP250 V8—to a dealer who promptly flipped it for a $3,000 profit. So much for my handle on what the market would bear.

I bought the next TR4 (a white '64), in the Summer of 2008 and barely got to know the car. Selling it was an incredibly short-sighted move on my part. Having written articles for *The New York Times* and the *Chicago*

Left: 1966 Triumph TR4A. Right: I've never seen anything like this before. The sun had burned a sepia-toned image of the car's California black plate "DKM 009" into the paint on the trunk. At the risk of blaspheming, it reminded me of The Shroud of Turin.

Unrestored '64 TR4 with Coventry-applied Old English White paint.

Tribune on the charm and inherent value of unrestored cars, of all people, I should have known better. Here was a total virgin California black plate example of a car that I liked well enough to have owned no less than five of over the years, and I threw it up on eBay without a second thought. I chalk it off to the pressure of starting a new business.

It had first crossed my radar, on Craigslist in of all places, St. Louis, Missouri. The owner had purchased it in Lancaster, California from the family of the original owner. It had never been hit, rusted or painted, and showed 78,000 miles which certainly appeared original. It was still wearing its original California black plates and a set of ancient Sears-branded Michelin tires.

Tom Cotter, author of the books *The Cobra in the Barn* and *The Hemi in the Barn* has told me on numerous occasions that original cars drive noticeably different from restored cars. According to Cotter, "restored cars lose their cohesiveness, becoming just a collection of pretty parts. Unrestored cars just drive better, and are often more reliable." Collector/dealer/author Colin Comer feels the same way. "It's almost like the old Native American superstition about being photographed and losing one's soul—to a certain extent, restored cars lose their soul." Cotter also makes the excellent point that unrestored cars are cheaper to own in the long run: "With an unrestored car, there's nothing else to do but conserve and maintain it. There's no temptation to take the body off the frame and do it all."

This car embodied all of Cotter's and Comer's wisdom on the subject. It really did drive better than any TR4 that I'd owned. No creaks, no rattles, and excellent panel fit. The only think jarring about the car was the fact that the owner before me had fitted the car with a very nice new leather interior, but juxtaposed with the ancient white paint, it looked odd. Wisely though, he saved every piece that he removed, having immediately regretted re-doing rather than conserving the interior.

Amazingly, the original leather seat–covers, while heavily patinated, were in good shape except for a few seam splits. The door panels were fine, and even the carpet, while stained, was not beyond reclamation. If I had kept the car, I would have removed and sold the new seats and carpet, bought a set of worn out seats as cores, put the old coverings on and perhaps tried to locate an NOS top. Then the car would have looked really right. Alas, I sold my soul for a quick profit and the car now resides in Germany. I'm still kicking myself, so by all means, e-mail me and pile on.

Left: 1954 Beetle sedan.
Right: 1954 Beetle with
second rear-window
design—a single piece but
still tiny.

Volkswagen

Beetle Sedan 1948-67		
Parts availability ✪✪✪✪✪	**Inexpensive to maintain** ✪✪✪✪✪	**Investment potential** ✪✪
Fun to drive ✪✪½	**Price category** **$$**	Nice driver, $9,000; Show winner, $16,000
Performance (1500) 0 to 60 in 22.5 seconds; ¼ mile in 21.7 seconds at 59 mph (*Road & Track* 2/67)		

Parts MidAmerica Motorworks, www.mamotorworks.com
Club Vintage Volkswagen Club of America, www.vvwca.com

Karmann-Ghia 1955-74		
Parts availability ✪✪✪½	**Inexpensive to maintain** ✪✪✪✪✪	**Investment potential** ✪✪½
Fun to drive ✪✪✪½	**Price category** **$$$**	Nice driver, $10,000; Show winner, $18,000 (coupe)
Performance 0 to 60 in 21.7 seconds; ¼ mile in 21.7 seconds at 60 mph (*Road & Track* 2/63)		

History

Mark Twain famously said that "many a small thing has been made large by the right kind of advertising." And while not talking about the Beetle specifically, he might has well have been referencing both the car and the famous Doyle, Dane and Bernbach "Think Small" advertising campaign of the early 1960s.

While the history of the Beetle and the involvement of personalities such as Adolf Hitler and Ferdinand Porsche is well documented, few people realize that the post-war phenomenon of the Beetle (and perhaps the entire foreign car movement in the U.S.) was just one unexploded bomb away from never happening at all.

At the end of WWII, much of the world's population was understandably weary of Germany's rather prominent involvement in the two most destructive wars the planet had ever seen. There was a great deal of support for the notion of the "pastoralization" of Germany—stripping it of its industrial capacity and turning it into a nation of pacified lederhosen-wearing 17th century farmers. Before it was realized that West Germany would be needed as a bulwark against encroaching communism, several entire factories were shipped off to France and Russia.

The Volkswagen factory, in what had then become known as Wolfsburg, produced a car that not even war-ravaged France was interested in. After taking control of the factory, a British Army major named Ivin Hirst had to first deal with an unexploded bomb that had lodged itself near some valuable tooling for the car. Had it gone off, there would have been no post-war Beetle production. Major Hirst managed to restart production and even convinced the British Army to buy 20,000 cars. Within thirteen three years, one million Beetles had been produced in Wolfsburg.

Changes were both incremental and subtle. The most obvious concerned the size of the windows. In 1953, the two small oval rear windows were replaced with one smallish oval window; a full-rear window did not appear until 1957. The side windows were raised slightly in 1964, and that was about it for cosmetic changes. 1961 brought an all synchromesh four-speed transmission and an effective steering damper—a 1300 cc engine arrived in 1966. Federal safety standards began to remove much of the charm from the car, starting with the glass-covered headlights which became illegal after 1967.

Early VWs were inexpensive—but never cheap

Anyone who is at all unclear about the difference between cheap and inexpensive need only look at a well-preserved original Beetle. Pre-1967 cars especially were finished beautifully, given effective soundproofing, and were exceedingly tight. Interiors were basic but attractive, with good quality carpeting and vinyls (often with contrasting piping) on the seats. Notoriously outspoken *Road & Track* said that "the most convincing item of all is the finish, which can be quite unbelievable. Not a trace of shabbiness can be found anywhere on the car."

Factory options were few indeed. but probably the nicest one on a Beetle sedan is a folding Webasto sunroof. It rolls back to expose nearly the entire roof of the car, making it nearly as open as a cabriolet, without the multi-thousand dollar hassle of replacing the soft top—or the compromised view that comes with a cabriolet.

The aftermarket that grew up around the Beetle could fill volumes. Everything from roof racks to rear-fender skirts were sold. Perhaps the best known aftermarket performance company was EMPI. Period EMPI accessories were generally desirable high-quality items.

The one thing Beetles didn't come with from the factory (aside from the name, which was not officially used until 1967) was performance. With between just 34 and 40 horsepower, 0-60 times were in the high twenties and top speed little more than 70 mph. Still, compared to the other "people's cars" out there like the Morris Minor and Citroën 2CV, it was far superior.

Beetles are ideal first collector cars because everything is available and cheap. Mechanically, Type 1 air cooled engines are reasonably durable with 80,000 to 100,000 miles a normal overhaul interval. Overhauls themselves, which include pistons and cylinders, run between $1,300 and $2,000. Care should be taken to avoid some of the substandard-quality parts that come out of Latin America, where the Beetle lived on long past its retirement in Germany.

Beetles are rusters but again, sheet metal from floorpans to fenders and running boards is all available. Still, with so many Beetles out there, why not hold out for a rust-free car? Interiors are widely available too, but again, skimping here can compromise the essential high-quality character of the car.

Left: No bad angles on the Karmann-Ghia.
Right: 1300 cc VW Type 1 air-cooled engine.

Enter the Karmann-Ghia—a Beetle in an Italian suit

By the mid-1950s, it appeared certain that the West German economic miracle would be sustained. Luxury models from BMW and Mercedes-Benz began to reappear. Even Volkswagen began to consider something more special than the prosaic Beetle sedan.

The Italian coachbuilder Ghia had proposed designs for Studebaker and Chrysler, though they both came to naught. Ghia then suggested a variation on its Studebaker work to Volkswagen, modifying the design to fit on a chassis twelve inches wider than a Beetle sedan. VW accepted, and they showed the car at the 1953 Paris show.

Production began in 1955 for the 1956 model year, with Karmann building the bodies to Ghia's design. The workmanship was exquisite. Unlike the Beetle, fenders were welded, not bolted, and seams were carefully leaded. Interior fittings were done to a higher standard as well.

Unfortunately, nothing was done with the standard 1200-cc VW Type 1 air-cooled motor. With less than 40 hp and a split-case transmission with a crash-first, in spite of advertising copy, the Karmann-Ghia was no sports car. Still, it was a solid hit for VW, selling over 10,000 copies in its first year. Performance was leisurely at best, and *Road & Track* concluded that the Karmann-Ghia was simply "a Beetle in an Italian suit." At least it's a lovely suit. Industrial designer Walter Dorwin Teague named the Karmann-Ghia one of the 100 best-designed products in the world in 1958. Built until 1974, when it was replaced by the Rabbit-based Giugiaro-designed Scirocco, the Karmann-Ghia changed very little over its long production life.

Early cars rarest and most expensive

The earliest cars are identified by headlights mounted lower on the fender than post-1959 Ghias. A cabriolet was added in 1958. Changes were minor until 1967, when 12-volt electricals appeared, along with a 1500-cc engine. Thereafter, the safety police got into high gear; the handsome painted dash went away, and the tail-lights quadrupled in size. Impact bumpers spoiled the last two years of Karmann-Ghia production. As an aside, 1969 at least brought real independent rear-suspension, and 1970 saw the introduction of the 1600-cc motor. The vestigial rear-seats were eliminated in 1973.

Early cars (especially cabriolets) are frightfully expensive to restore, with trim items and original upholstery scarce and expensive. Count on spending several thousand to replace the lined convertible top of a cabriolet.

Mechanically, everything is straightforward Beetle; generally cheap, with the exception of cars equipped with VW's tricky and undesirable "Automatic Stickshift." Similar to Porsche's Sportomatic, it was a clutchless, two-pedal semi-automatic transmission. Parts for it are scarce, and it's hardly worthwhile, making an already

Good luck finding a replacement steering wheel. Items like that for early cars are unobtainable.

slow car even slower. A perfect, orange, autostick-equipped, 14,000-mile, 1971 cabriolet sold at Silver's Reno auction in August 2007 for a modest $25,380, thanks to the gearbox.

You can go faster, but not fast

But at least slow can be remedied. Most of the early Type 1 speed equipment from EMPI and other manufacturers is still available in one form or another. Doubling the original horsepower and making significant chassis upgrades is not too difficult if that's your thing. Most of the period alloy wheels that were such nice upgrades over the steel wheel and dog-dish hubcaps are also still available, along with most mechanical parts from Mid America Motorworks, www.mamotorworks.com.

The real bug with any Karmann-Ghia is rust. It's claimed nearly all of the early low-headlight cars, and it can appear nearly anywhere on the body. Floors, rockers, and fenders behind the headlights are all fair game.

And in any Karmann-Ghia, the protruding nose is particularly vulnerable. A K-G that hasn't been popped in the nose is as rare as a sunny day in January in Portland. And it doesn't help that a badly rusted or hard-hit Ghia can require a complete front clip... and you'll get that where?

In any case, a stock Karmann-Ghia is really no more than an attractive ice cream-getter. With 0–60 mph times in the 20-second-range and 80 mph flat out, a K-G has no place in modern freeway traffic. At least the ride is relatively comfortable, and the styling is attractive enough to provoke backward glances when you leave it in a parking lot.

ran when parked...

Left: 1963 Beetle with folding Webasto sunroof. Right: Beautifully simple, completely original '63 Beetle interior.

As one would expect, collectors seem to prefer the earliest cars, which are the rarest, purest, and highest quality Ghias—any pre-1967 steel-dash car is desirable. Also reasonably well-liked are the 1969s, with small tail-lights and fully independent suspension.

Nice Karmann-Ghias (especially cabriolets) have long since risen above the ranks of credit card cars. Perhaps it's the law of substitution coming into play. As Porsche 356 prices have soared, K-Gs have become more desirable, and prices have gone up. No, they're not going to set any quarter-mile records, but K-Gs are well made, comfortable, easy to maintain, and very pretty. Sort of like a VW 190SL.

Case study

1963 Volkswagen Beetle 1300		
Purchase Price (2006) $8,500	**Sale Price** (2008) $9,500	**Owned for** 1.5 years

I'm almost ashamed to admit it, but I had never even driven—much less owned—a VW Beetle, one of the most iconic cars of the 20th century until about two years ago. In the great scheme of things, the notion of owning a car with less than 10 hp per seat just never rose to the top of my priorities. An affinity for unrestored cars finally pushed me into Beetle ownership.

A friend of mine, a local collector bought a collection of pre-war classic cars that for some reason included a Beetle that was a dead ringer for Max, the car then starring in VW's rather uninspired ad campaign. This car was unlike the Beetles that generally show up at auctions; rather than being over-restored and festooned with every silly accessory that could be hung anywhere on the car's 160-inches, it was utterly original down to the Firestone "Gum Dipped" wide whites. The paint and the interior were untouched, and the car was positively rust-free. It showed about 70,000 miles and had every piece of paperwork from new.

I got the impression while driving the car that I really was having the same experience that *Road & Track*'s testers had in the early 1960s. It's a cliché, but if Einstein is right, then old cars really are the closest thing that we'll ever have to a time machine. Everything that *R&T* had written about the car when new applied in 2006. The build quality and finish was astonishingly good, doors sealed well and shut with a reassuring sound. The materials from seat coverings to door panels to the German square-weave carpeting were all top-notch.

The car always started right up and settled down to a smooth idle. The all-synchromesh four-speed was a bit of a row, but in all, it was a pleasure to shift, and of course, the sound is like nothing else. True, the Beetle is tediously slow, really not suitable for modern freeways. They're around town cars, fun ice cream getters really. That's pretty much how I used this one. The folding Webasto sunroof was an especially nice feature. It slid back with ease and opened up a generous portion of the roof over the front and back seats. As expected, the Beetle was dead reliable. Other than oil changes, nothing needed even the slightest attention.

The best part of owning any Beetle is the fact that literally everyone over a certain age has a story involving one. They generate no envy or hostility in anyone. Just good humor, nice stories and a lot of fun. I enjoyed every minute I owned the car.

Porsche

912 1965-69		
Parts availability ✪✪✪✪	**Inexpensive to maintain** ✪✪	**Investment potential** ✪✪✪
Fun to drive ✪✪✪	**Price category** $$$ Nice driver, $13,000; Show winner, $28,000	
Performance 0 to 60 in 11.6 seconds; ¼ mile in 18.1 seconds at 78 mph (*Road & Track* 2/66)		

912E 1976		
Parts availability ✪✪✪½	**Inexpensive to maintain** ✪✪✪	**Investment potential** ✪½
Fun to drive ✪✪✪	**Price category** $$ Nice driver, $8,000; Show winner, $14,000	
Performance 0 to 60 in 11.3 seconds; ¼ mile in 18.2 seconds at 75 mph (*Road & Track* 1/76)		

Parts Stoddard Porsche, www.stoddard.com; Pelican Parts, www.pelicanparts.com
Club Porsche Club of America, www.pca.org

History

The Porsche 356 lineup had always been relatively diverse with several body styles and engine choices available. With the discontinuation of the 356 in 1965, Porsche was left with a single expensive product, the 911. The 912—a de-contented 911 with a slightly detuned version of the 356SC four-cylinder engine—was designed to remedy this oversight and give Porsche an entry-level product.

Early 912s, although beautifully made, were quite sparse; a four-speed gearbox and three-gauge dash was standard, rather than the 911's five-dial setup and five-speed box. The development of the 912 more or less followed the 911, with a soft rear-window targa body style added in 1967, followed by a wheelbase stretch and flared fenders in 1969.

Most 911 options were available on the 912, including a gasoline-powered auxiliary heater, sunroof and five-spoke Fuchs alloy wheels. As the 911 lineup started to resemble the old 356 lineup (911T, E and S mimicking 356 Normal, Super and Carrera), the 912 was seen as an anachronism—essentially a 356D. After 1969, the 912 was discontinued in favor of the mid-engine Porsche 914.

Left: 912 shares the same Butzi Porsche shape as the 911. This 1967 wears added Fuchs alloy wheels. Shorter wheelbase of the pre-69 cars evident here. Right: Those with a sharp eye can tell a 912E from this angle by the badge and small tail pipe.

Strangely, the 912 returned the favor six years later, after the 914 was axed. The revived 912E replaced it as a one-year entry level car designed to anchor the low-end of the Porsche lineup, until the dreadful 924 became available.

912 potentially as expensive to maintain as a 911

Today, the appeal of the original 912 is a bit hard to grasp, especially at the prices they're now bringing. Although conventional wisdom holds that the four-cylinder car is easier and cheaper to maintain than a 911, this really isn't the case. These are not VW-based cars; the engine is pure Porsche and can cost about two-thirds the price of a 911 engine to rebuild or up to $10,000. What's more, 912 crankshafts have been known to break; because of the lack of a full-flow oil filtration system, engine life is generally shorter than that of a 911.

The only explanation for the recent popularity of the car is the fact that as the 356 has gotten more expensive, the appeal of the early 912s has become stronger. The 1965-67 cars share some of the vintage touches of a 356 such as chrome ringed green typeface gauges, plenty of bright trim and lightweight simplicity.

Another issue with the 1965-69 912 is the fact that it was built during the dark ages of Porsche rust-proofing. A badly rusted 912 is a frightening and unfortunately common thing. Suspension pans, battery boxes, main pans, torsion tubes, fenders, rockers, even roofs were all fair game. Even on the West Coast, it is rare indeed to find a 912 that has never had any rust repairs.

912E more durable and cheaper to maintain

Contrast this to the 1976 912E, built on the "G-Series" short hood/ big bumper 911 platform. Bodies are fully galvanized, and the 2.0 liter VW Type IV engine (from the 914) provided performance similar to the 1965-69 912, with the added benefit that when it's time to rebuild it, the cost is about $2,000.

Unfortunately, the fact that 912E production was limited to just under 2,100 units means that the few things that are unique to the car are very tough to find. Probably the most significant piece that falls into this category is the heat exchanger. They're unique to the car; 914 or VW 412 items will not work. I've seen used ones go for over $1,000 a set. Similarly, the gearbox, while based on the 915-style five-speed, has different gearing than a 911. Innards for the 923 box, as it's called, are also unobtainium.

Any 912 is a pleasant driving car, with the 911's wonderfully tight structure, communicative steering and strong brakes all present. With a bit less weight hanging out behind the rear wheels, handling is more forgiving, and fuel economy is excellent—up to 30 mpg is possible. Where it comes apart is in comparison to the 911. 912s (especially the 2.0 liter 912E) have excellent low-end torque characteristics. But by 4,000 rpm, just when the 911 is giving you a tremendous shove in the small of your back, the 912 is done, its pushrod-four essentially out of breath.

The market

912s have recently doubled in value, no doubt riding the coattails of the 356, which has become quite expensive. Soft window Targas and sunroof coupes are particularly desirable. Four-speed cars and those with the three-gauge dashes are less so, along with long wheelbase 1969s and emission control-challenged 1968s. A 912 owner is probably someone who wanted a 356, but acted a bit too late. A later 911, like an SC, although priced similarly these days, is simply not vintage enough for someone considering a 912. 912Es, while rare, are visually similar to 911SCs and generally trade at about a one-third discount over the six-cylinder car.

Case study

1976 Porsche 912E		
Purchase Price $6,800	**Sale Price** N/A (Still owned)	**Owned for** 2.0 years

For a car that has been derided as "pathetic" or "beneath contempt" and "for losers only" by snotty, opinionated Porsche weenies, I've grown inordinately fond of my 912E. And why not? When the car was new, it was well-liked, garnering praise from a persnickety David E. Davis helmed *Car and Driver* who said: "Leaping into and driving the 912E after thundering around in the Turbo Carrera is not nearly so disappointing an experience as one might imagine. The 912E is comfortable where the Carrera is harsh, and rational where the Carrera is excessive….It's so sensible yet enjoyable that you begin to wonder whether Turbo Carreras are necessary at all."

Obviously, Turbo Carreras are both necessary and desirable, and the 912E certainly lacks the excitement of an extra 150 hp. Although there are plenty of 912 apologists around, I'm not one of them—comparing a 912E to a 930 or a 911 is sheer folly. 912s are a compromise; a decent one, but still a compromise.

Compared not to a 911 but to an Alfa 2000 GTV or a BMW 2002tii, however, the car stacks up quite well, with 0-60 times and top speeds in the same range (*Road & Track* got a pokey 912E that did 0-60 in about 11 seconds. *Car and Driver's* did it in 9.7 seconds). Ultimately, a 912E appealed to me because I wanted another 911, but with an E-type and a Maserati Mistral to feed, I just wasn't prepared to spend potentially serious money on a car without any potential upside. A 912E seemed like a relatively painless way to enjoy an air-cooled Porsche again.

When I bought the car, I was still flying back and forth between Portland and St. Louis, using the MGC as my Portland car. After I bought an E-type roadster, I wanted to put some money into the Jaguar, and I thought the C was probably worth a decent amount more than I had in it. The idea was to sell the MG, replace it with something cheaper, and spend the surplus on the E-type. It all worked out quite well, I sold the MGC for $10,500 and bought the 912E for $6,800.

I found the 912E on the Seattle Craigslist. After talking to the owner, who seemed like a quite decent fellow, I was on my way up there the next day. Again, it was apparent quickly that this was another right car. It drove flawlessly, had only two previous owners, and all records from new.

Most of the paint was the original factory applied Porsche Light Yellow, a popular Carrera RS color that suited the mid-seventies Porsche quite well. The car had been in Seattle its whole life, and the cork vinyl

interior was as well preserved as one would expect in a car that lived in a place that gets just 56 sunny days a year. The working electric sunroof was a nice bonus; my understanding is that only 500 of the 2099 912Es built had this option. There were no 912E Targas.

On one of my trips back to Portland from St. Louis, I flew into Seattle instead and picked up the 912E and headed back down I-5 to Portland. In 170 miles, I used less than a quarter-tank of gas. With a 21.5-gallon gas tank and 30 mpg a reality on the highway, I could have easily made it well into California without filling up.

The 912E is a supremely capable highway cruiser. Without the low profile tires and sport suspension of a 911, the ride is quite decent. Because of its relatively slippery shape, it builds momentum in fifth gear far better than one would expect of just 90 hp; it'll do 75 to 80 mph all day while returning excellent fuel economy.

It's a car I had absolutely no qualms about driving across the country, doing just that when I left the magazine in May of 2008. Bringing my never-used-in-ten-years emergency bag of cheap Chinese tools, a flashlight, flares and a tow rope, I added a spare alternator, voltage regulator, cap, points and fuel pump. And as usual, the better prepared one is for a roadside breakdown, the less likely it is for one to occur. I did the 2,000 mile drive from Portland to St. Louis in 2 ½ days averaging 29 mpg.

As of this writing, the 912E continues to be my daily driver. In two years, I've replaced the coil and a thermo-switch that controls the warm up. That's it. At this point, the car has over 200,000 miles on it and the engine rebuild performed 100,000 miles ago is probably getting a bit tired. In a 911, this would be a matter of great concern, but since the estimate for a full rebuild on my 912E is just under $2,000, it's a much easier expense to justify and deal with. With an engine that can be reasonably rebuilt over and over, plus a fully galvanized body, the 912E has the makings of a perpetual motion machine.

chapter six

oddballs

Yes, you can get parts for them,

most are better than you might think

and you won't see yourself coming and going

THERE IS A BIT OF A HERD MENTALITY in the collector car world. My friend Donald Osborne calls certain cars "belly button cars" because as he says, "everyone has one." Over the years, I've had fun owning some pretty obscure cars. Among the disadvantages are constantly having to explain the car, and answer questions like "who makes that?" Or, "is that a kit car?"

Surprisingly, getting parts has never been particularly problematic. It seems that virtually every oddball make has at least one patron saint—a committed person who has put the good of the marque ahead of profit and worked to make the necessities (and sometimes much more) available to those in need. The Internet has made it quite easy to find the savior of whatever oddball car you have.

Oddball cars do trade in a thin market, when you decide to move on and sell the car, your pool of available buyers will likely not be what it would be for a Corvette. It's less of a concern in the Internet era with websites like eBay and BringATrailer.com that put you in touch with other iconoclasts and eccentrics.

Daimler

SP250 1959-64		
Parts availability ✪✪✪½	**Inexpensive to maintain** ✪✪✪½	**Investment potential** ✪✪½
Fun to drive ✪✪✪✪	**Price category** **$$$** Nice driver, $19,000; Show winner-, $35,000	
Performance 0 to 60 in 9.1 seconds; ¼ mile in 16.9 seconds at 83 mph (*Road & Track* 3/60)		

Parts New England Automotive Restorations, www.daimler-sp250.com
Club Daimler & Lanchester Owners Club, www.dloc.org.uk

History

By 1960, the British sports car market in the U.S. was a crowded one indeed. Aside from MG, Triumph, Austin-Healey and Jaguar, there were bit players like Sunbeam, AC, Morgan and Lotus. Even though it was late to the party, the venerable English firm Daimler—best known at the time for making limos and hearses for the Royal Family—thought it could carve out a niche in between MG and Jaguar.

Its entry into the fray, the Daimler SP250 (briefly called the "Dart" until Chrysler complained) could have been a contender in the British sports car scene in the U.S. had circumstances been different. The specs were certainly impressive: A high-revving 2.5 liter hemi V8 designed by motorcycle engine genius Edward Turner, four-wheel disc brakes and a fiberglass body. Total weight was a little over 2000 lbs.

The biggest problem with the car—other than its moribund parent company—was the fact that it was just plain odd looking. Perhaps the illegitimate child of a Sunbeam Alpine and an MGA with more than a little 1958 Packard Hawk thrown in. With its giant gaping maw of a grille and a pair of long whisker-like bumper overriders, only a hook stuck in the grille could have made the SP250 look more catfish-like. Removing the front bumper or at least the overriders improves things considerably.

Huge front overriders and gaping fish-like mouth gave the SP250 its "angry catfish" nickname.

141

Left: Honey, I shrunk the 426 Hemi—little 2.5 liter V8 is a jewel.
Above right: The SP250 after rescue from bankrupt body shop now wearing fresh maroon paint.
Right: SP250 interior is typical 1950s British sports car.

After the unconventional body and engine, Daimler ran out of creativity and cribbed blatantly from the Triumph TR3. Ladder frame and gearbox were nearly exact copies of the Triumph bits. The reputation of the car was tarnished out of the box when road testers found the whole thing to be so flexible, that the doors would fly open in hard corners on bumpy pavement. The lack of rigidity was quickly remedied by a very beefy square tube hoop that ran under the cowl and connected to both sides of the frame. These "B" Spec cars were actually quite stiff, but the old reputation persisted.

Little Hemi V8 best engine in its class

Had the car been more successful, the little V8 would have been remembered as one of the all time great sports car engines. Although a pushrod design, it loved to rev. It was redlined at 6,200 rpm but 6,400 could be used without harming anything. It would pull from 1,500 rpm in fourth gear all the way up to 124 mph without complaint. The exhaust note was unique, starting out like a small block Ford up to about 4,000 rpm, when it turned into a much more exotic sounding howl.

ran when parked...

Great brakes, stone age steering and gearbox

The Girling four-wheel disc brakes were up to the task of hauling the car down from two-mile-per-minute speeds. Unfortunately, the gearbox was simply mediocre. Based on the TR3 box, it had a crash-first and synchros that were easily beaten. Still, it was considerably better than the Neolithic Moss-box that Jaguar was using. Steering was also inspired by the TR3, with a similar cam and peg system—impossibly heavy at low speeds, while comically vague at higher speeds.

Around the time it became clear that the car was not going to make Daimler's sales projections, Jaguar began to covet the Coventry-based Daimler for its production capacity. A deal was finalized and Jaguar became the owner of Daimler. Immediately, Sir William Lyons' thoughts turned to whacking the SP250, which he though was both unattractive and a potential sales siphon from the E-type.

A half-hearted attempt was made to float a restyled version, but the new management wasn't interested. In late 1963, production was quietly ceased after just 2,645 cars were produced. Unsold cars were still sitting on dealers lots almost a year later. A pity; in spite of its shortcomings, the SP250 was quite a decent car, better in most ways than a 1955-62 solid-axle Corvette.

With such limited production numbers, the logical assumption is that parts are very difficult to come by. Strangely, this isn't the case at all. There are at least three patron saints of the SP250—David Manners and Bryan Purves in the U.K., and New England Auto Restorations in Ipswich, Massachusetts. I was even able to buy reproduction chrome tail-light surrounds when my originals proved unrestorable. Had I needed them, even body panels were available.

The market

SP250s trade in a thin market, but their performance, rarity and hemi V8 make them interesting to those able to get past their controversial looks. If you really want one, they're not impossibly rare—in fact, as I write this, there are two on eBay in the "Other Makes" section. Nicely restored cars bring low thirties, drivers high teens, and basket cases around $9,000 to $10,000. Prices are up perhaps 20 percent over the last five years. Again, Hemi 'Cuda-like appreciation is highly unlikely, but I would expect that nice SP250s will appreciate at a modest rate for the foreseeable future.

Case study

1961 Daimler SP250		
Purchase Price $5,400	**Sale Price** $26,000*	**Owned for** 2.5 years

*amount allowed in trade toward Jaguar E-type

My SP250, fresh off the truck and still wearing a bad 1970s vintage respray.

David Slama

Left: Hard to believe, but the U.S. Marshals and the Bankruptcy Trustee left my beloved SP250 behind. Right: September in the Colorado Rockies.

My '62 SP250 came to me as the result of a trade I made with a New Hampshire dealer. It was an even swap for a very nice MGC roadster I'd bought for about half-price at $5,400. The Daimler was a relatively unmolested car that had one ancient respray and a lovely worn-in but not worn-out original black leather interior.

The car was a mystery to me when it showed up. I'd never driven the car (nor any other SP250 for that matter) nor had I ever even seen one in the flesh. The car arrived with the bumper removed; the car was considerably better looking without it. I was delighted by the exhaust note and the car's excellent performance. The four-wheel Girling discs were excellent and unexpected in a car of this vintage.

Also unexpected was the solidity of the car. Mine was a "B" Spec car with the cowl and frame reinforcements. They were well engineered and did their job. The car was tight with no perceptible cowl shake. Not so wonderful was the vague and very heavy cam-and-peg steering. A rack-and-pinion conversion would do wonders. The gearbox was slow with sychromesh that could be beaten in every gear.

I soon tired of the faded red paint, deciding to deal with it as an "easy" winter project. There was little to remove from the car. Rear bumper, lights, windshield and interior were bagged and tagged in a weekend with the help of my friend Cliff Pass. Since the old paint was cracking and crazed in numerous places, my body shop recommended that I have the car media-blasted.

SP250s were among the first fiberglass cars made in large numbers in Britain. The glass itself was quite thick in places, but was of variable quality with numerous air bubbles in which the resin was unreinforced and paper thin. It came back from the media-blasting with an appearance beyond mere surface of the moon, looking more pockmarked than Manuel Noriega's face. The blasting had opened all of the small air bubbles on the body; dermabrasion wasn't an option.

Numerous coats of catalyzed sprayable polyester and blocking later, the body was relatively smooth and near ready for the spray booth. This is when the body shop's creditors moved in and seized everything but the shell of my SP250. My simple cosmetic freshening was going downhill fast. I had a flatbed collect the car, but my efforts to collect the balance of my deposit on the job were thwarted by the U.S. Bankruptcy Code and my status as a "general unsecured creditor."

I found a new (and hopefully more solvent) body shop to finally shoot color on the car. Rather than the incorrect orangish-red that it was, I decided to paint it the original deep maroon. The mid-job collapse of my body shop had put things considerably behind schedule.

Time was of the essence; the company I worked for at the time was one of the sponsors of a vintage rally called the Colorado Grand. Since I was going to use the car to participate in the event, it was a race against the clock to put the car back together. I had to pack the last pieces of the car into my luggage—they went back on the car in the parking garage of the Vail Cascade Resort.

Aside from the door-lock mechanism failing, necessitating the use of a bungee cord to keep the door shut, the unproven car did the 1,000 miles through Colorado without incident. Its tight-sealing top and effective heater were especially welcome when we encountered a September blizzard at the top of eleven-thousand-foot Red Mountain Pass.

ran when parked...

I took the car on numerous other rallies and tours, never once having a problem with it. I parted with it reluctantly when the opportunity to trade it toward a Series I Jaguar E-type came up. While I have enjoyed the E-type immensely, there isn't a time I drive it that I don't wish it sounded more like the SP250.

Studebaker

Avanti 1963-64		
Parts availability ✪✪✪½	**Inexpensive to maintain** ✪✪✪✪	**Investment potential** ✪✪✪½
Fun to drive ✪✪✪	**Price category** **$$$**	Nice driver, $16,000; Show winner, $30,000
Performance (R2) 0 to 60 in 7.3 seconds; ¼ mile in 16.2 seconds at 88 mph (*Road & Track* 10/62)		

Avanti II 1966-85		
Parts availability ✪✪✪✪	**Inexpensive to maintain** ✪✪✪✪✪	**Investment potential** ✪½
Fun to drive ✪✪½	**Price category** **$$**	Nice driver, $6,000; Show winner, $12,000
Performance 0 to 60 in 8.8 seconds; ¼ mile in 17.5 seconds at 85.7 mph (*Road & Track* 8/66)		

Parts Avanti Parts and Restorations, Inc., www.avantiparts.biz; SASCO, www.studeparts.com
Club Avanti Owners Association International, www.aoai.org

Shawn Dougan/Hyman, Ltd.

1963 Studebaker Avanti displaying the most controversial aspect of the car's styling.

History

It truly pains and mystifies me that in early 2009, I'm writing about Avantis in a book on affordable classics. They're unique and striking cars that come closer than anything built in America in the 1960s to a true European GT. Yet for whatever reason, the market just doesn't seem to care. The muscle crowd couldn't care less, and neither could the European car crowd. Pity, in a day when a common '65 Mustang fastback is a $35,000 car, most Avantis struggle to make $20,000.

The mere fact that a car like the Avanti could have sprung from the loins of the moribund Studebaker Corporation was amazing, considering the company was just a few years away from oblivion. The car itself was a desperation move from day one, a Hail Mary to save Studebaker. Time was of the essence, and in the

Left: 289 Studebaker V8 in non-supercharged R1 form.
Above right: Rear ¾ of the Avanti undeniably attractive.
Right: Avanti interior has all the ingredients of a great GT.

Like something out of a vintage fifties 707, roof mounted red-lit rocker switches control lighting and heat.

spring of 1961, Tom Kellogg, Bob Andrews, and John Ebstein holed up for five weeks in a modest rented bungalow in Palm Springs near the palatial residence of famed industrial designer Raymond Loewy.

Ordinarily, three guys and a rented bungalow in Palm Springs is a recipe for empty beer bottles and Chinese takeout cartons, plus some complaints from the neighbors—and little else. But the Avanti design team, created a coke-bottle-sided coupe with a minimum of chrome trim, two porthole-like rounds head-lights and a unique air intake below the bumper. It looked like nothing else before or since. The team returned to South Bend, sketches in hand, and proceeded to turn them into clay models. In less than a year, there was a running prototype.

Unfortunately, failing Studebaker had no money to engineer a chassis befitting the car, necessitating a thoroughly conventional Lark frame and suspension. Front disc brakes were thoroughly unconventional—an oddity on an American car of the time. The Avanti had them two years before the Corvette did.

After several delays and quality control issues related to the assembly of the bodies by the Molded Fiber-glass Corporation of Ashtabula, Ohio, production commenced. Reviews in the magazines were generally good, although import-biased *Road & Track* called it "a Lark in a gilded cage."

Avanti interiors were ergonomic nightmares, but at least they had style. Blower and interior light functions were controlled by rocker switches located on the roof just behind the windshield. Other climate control functions were handled by a set of chrome levers on the console reminiscent of aircraft throttle controls. Soothing red lights helped the driver locate things.

ran when parked...

Front seats were comfortable enough by the standards of the day; both *Road & Track* and *Motor Trend* commented favorably on them. Back seats were even tolerable by adults for short trips.

Power courtesy of Studebaker's 289 V8 was more than adequate, with 240 hp available in normally aspirated R1 form and 289 hp available in supercharged R2 form. A four-speed manual transmission was available in addition to an automatic. In modified form, the Avanti set several speed records with Andy Granitelli in charge of a program with a virtually non-existent budget.

Avanti expert Dave Kinney advises to buy an Avanti that has either air conditioning or a supercharger, and expect to pay considerably less for one that has neither. Studebaker also did a good job of choosing a limited range of colors that all complemented the car's unconventional styling. There are no bad choices among them. 1964 cars are distinguished by the shift-to-square headlight bezels from round.

As everyone knows, the Avanti didn't save Studebaker, who discontinued the Avanti and the Hawk when it shifted all production to Hamilton, Ontario in 1965 before shutting out the lights for good in 1966. Ordinarily, when the parent company kills a car and then goes out of business itself, the car in question becomes a permanent addition to the automotive fossil record. But in the case of the Avanti, no one in South Bend remembered to drive a stake through its heart.

Resurrected as Avanti II after the death of Studebaker

Two local dealers, Nate Altman and Leo Newman bought the rights to the Avanti name, a considerable stock of parts, the tooling and one of the Studebaker plants in South Bend where they put the Avanti back into production as the Avanti II. Early IIs which bore the serial prefix RQA, were essentially Studebakers with Chevrolet motors—many of the parts such as steering wheels, seats and wheel covers and frames were essentially NOS Studebaker items. The only difference visible from the outside was the loss of the car's nose-down, tail-up rake. In order to fit the taller Chevy 327 motor, the front end had to be raised. This necessitated the fitting of a small filler-piece at the top of the front wheel well.

Recognizing that they couldn't compete in the volume production sport coupe market, Newman and Altman repositioned the car as a bespoke luxury car, allowing the customer to choose whatever combinations of colors, interiors and carpets that he or she liked. Unfortunately, the old adage that "money can't buy taste" often held true with cars being ordered in outrageous versions of school colors with shag carpet. My recollection from a factory visit in 1977 was a lime-green metallic car with space-suit silver leather seats.

By the late 1970s, Newman and Altman were producing essentially the same Chevrobaker they'd been building since 1966—minus the horsepower. The car was in danger of becoming America's Morgan. Worse, after the death of Nate Altman in 1974, his brother Arnold instituted cost-cutting measures that affected the quality of the car. In 1983, nice guy Steven Blake stepped in and bought the company and set out to make some much needed improvements. A higher horsepower 305 V8 was inserted, along with an available Doug Nash 5-speed and various chassis improvements were made.

Blake even revised the front-end of the car by substituting body color bumpers and square headlights. Blake got out of the car business in 1987, and the saga of Avantis that you'd want to own pretty much ends there.

Left: 1977 Avanti II with square headlight bezels introduced on the 1964 Studebaker Avanti. Right: Avanti II of undetermined year. No matter; they all look the same.

Mechanically, whether it's Studebaker or Chevrolet powered, Avantis are quite tough, and there are still many parts available at your local NAPA store. Just become familiar with an interchange manual so you can avoid what Dave Kinney terms the "we don't stock no Avanni parts" dilemma.

Body rust is not a problem for a fiberglass car, but like Corvettes, the frames can and do rust. Particularly problematic are the "hog troughs" sheet metal stiffeners located between the frame rails. They're replaceable, but it's a nasty and time-consuming job. Frames can be repaired, but if you go that far, you're into a major restoration, the costs of which will not likely be recouped. Save yourself the aggravation and pay up for a solid car.

As drivers, Avantis are quite pleasant and should have some cross-over appeal between European GT people and muscle car guys. Unfortunately, to date, the only cross-over appeal demonstrated by the Avanti has been from the "iconoclast" market to the "eccentric" market.

All are V8-powered; the power steering is a cut above the usual no senses, no feeling Detroit offering. A manual transmission and a supercharger were offered on the Studebaker-built cars. All this should give the car at least some cred with the Big Three-obsessed muscle car market. Unlike most muscle cars, however, the Avanti could stop as well as go. Even in 1966, *Road & Track* still counted the Avanti's brakes as among the best in the world.

But the powerful brakes are a moot point if you get into trouble on a slick surface. With 59 percent of its weight in front, it takes very little coaxing to un-stick the rear-end of an Avanti. All this can be great fun on a dry road, but having seen the results of an icy spin in my Dad's Avanti, I think it's safe to say that any Avanti should be considered a fair-weather driver.

The market

Inexplicably, the Avanti was left behind in the great collector car price run up of 2003-2006. Since other Studebakers (most notably Golden Hawks and President Speedsters) have surpassed it value, it can't be a general disdain for orphan makes—or orphan makes with funny names. No, I think it must be accepted that a sizable portion of the car collecting population simply finds the Avanti unattractive. Consequently, even the very fast supercharged R2s are hard-pressed to approach $30,000. Nice R1s can still be had in the mid-teens, with air conditioned four-speed cars being the most desirable.

Avanti IIs are all over the board, but seem to be priced based on year, condition, options and colors. The early cars with Chevy 327s, and four-speeds are rare and desirable especially when fitted with optional Italian Borrani wheels. No Avanti (even the ultra-rare R3s) seems poised for any serious appreciation. And really, that's good news for anyone who just wants to enjoy a unique piece of automotive history. Buy a well cared for or competently restored example and you shouldn't have any significant expenses while the car appreciates at the rate of a certificate of deposit.

TVR

2500M/3000S/Taimar 1973-79		
Parts availability ○○○○○	**Inexpensive to maintain** ○○○○○	**Investment potential** ○○○○○
Fun to drive ○○○○○	**Price category $$** Nice driver, $9,000; Show winner, $17,000	
Performance (2500M) 0 to 60 in 9.3 seconds; ¼ mile in 17.3 seconds at 79 mph (*Road & Track* 8/77)		

Tasmin/280i 1983-87		
Parts availability ○○○○○	**Inexpensive to maintain** ○○○○○	**Investment potential** ○○○○○
Fun to drive ○○○○○	**Price category $$** Nice driver, $8,000; Show winner, $13,000	
Performance 0 to 60 in 11.5 seconds; ¼ mile in 18.0 seconds at 74 mph		

Parts Classic Motor Works, www.cmw-tvr.com

Club TVR Club of Northh America, www.tvrna.com

TVR 2500M has a long hood to accomodate TR6 six.

Cozy 2500M interior, as a result of the wide transmission tunnel, won't let you get cold.

History

TVR took its name from three letters of its founder Trevor Wilkinson's first name. The first TVR was constructed in 1947. A small number of club-racing specials were built over the next decade, but "production" didn't really begin until the late 1950s, when TVR hit on the formula of a light fiberglass body mounted on an even lighter tubular space-frame.

Early TVRs were sold as finished cars and as kits, the latter to take advantage of a loophole in British tax laws. But even the factory-built cars resembled kit cars, exhibiting fit and finish reminiscent of a high school shop project. It scarcely mattered, as most early TVRs were turned into race cars anyway. A young Mark Donahue was among the early campaigners of TVR club racers. Engine choices were a confusing jumble of Ford, Coventry Climax and MG four-cylinders.

The most exciting early TVR was the brainchild of a Long Island car dealer named Jack Griffith. Griffith saw what Carroll Shelby had done with the Cobra, and reckoned that a small block Ford V8 could do the same thing for TVR's humble Grantura. With a curb-weight of just 1850 pounds and up to 271 horsepower, the car was sensationally fast.

Rear shot of 2500M displays huge glass window. It's fixed in the 2500 and opens in the Taimar.

Very pretty, very rare 300S roadster.

Unfortunately, with a wheelbase of just 85.5" and suspension, brakes and rear end scarcely changed from the four-cylinder car, the resulting Griffith 200 was about as nervous as a badger on PCP.

To make matters worse, the cars overheated, and the tremendous torque of their engines broke stub-axles with regularity, causing wheels to fly off—but even with all four wheels attached, Griffiths were nearly uncontrollable. Difficult to keep from spinning out in corners, they didn't care to go in a straight-line either—one had to be positively suicidal to attempt to drive a Griffith in wet or slippery conditions. Ironically, the Griffith is by far the most valuable TVR, far out of the realm of affordable classics.

In 1965, then twenty-three year old Martin Lilley bought TVR after a dock strike in New York nearly bankrupted the company. Lilley put an end to the Griffith madness, but not before attempting to tame the car, renaming the improved version the Tuscan V8. To no avail—*Road & Track* magazine called the car "a ferret with an oversupply of Y chromosomes."

Overall, Lilley's sixteen-year stewardship over TVR was quite positive; he certainly had a flair for showmanship. TVR's UK and European motor show displays were legendary—and infamous—featuring topless models (women, not convertibles). In 1972, he introduced what would become TVR's most popular model to date (car, not woman), the 2500M.

As a small volume manufacturer, TVR had to look to the parts bins of larger companies for major components. In the case of the 2500M, things like steering columns, engines and transmissions came from the popular Triumph TR6 sports car.

In a project no less ambitious than decoding the human genome, dedicated TVR club members have attempted to discover the origin of all the parts used to build the 2500M. And while it has conclusively been determined that the door hinges are sourced from a Ford Anglia and the hood latches come from a Hillman Imp, no one has yet determined the origin of the radiator overflow bottle. But it's all part of the fun of being part collector car owner and part automotive archaeologist.

The 2500M was the first TVR that could actually have been called attractive. Like all TVRs up to that point, it had a fiberglass body covering a welded space-frame. Strangely, though, it weighed about the same as the Triumph TR6; performance was comparable although the TVR had a lower center of gravity and better suspension giving it a better ride and handling. Nearly every U.S. 2500M came from the factory with a neat folding fabric sunroof.

In January of 1975, a fire in its Blackpool factory again put the company on the ropes. Through Martin Lilley's dedication and a loyal customer base, the company survived. Continually at the mercy of other manufacturers, TVR's next models, the Taimar and 3000S came about when Triumph discontinued the TR6 and its 2.5 liter straight-six. A British Ford 3.0 liter V6 was quickly substituted. The Taimar had the distinction of being the first British built turbocharged car. It was blindingly quick and had few of the bad habits of the Griffith.

Along with the Taimar Turbo, the pretty 3000S roadster is also quite collectible. Essentially a convertible Taimar, the 3000S was defiantly built at a time when it looked as though the U.S. would outlaw convertibles.

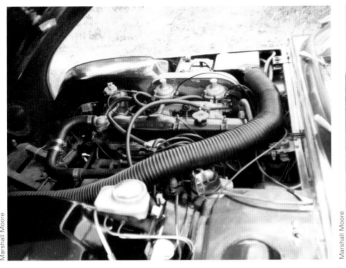

In another example of TVR spitting into the wind, the pugnacious little car also incorporated a feature that had been abandoned by British sports cars in the early 1960s—the 3000S had no rollup windows, instead using removable "side curtains" like those in an MGA, among other vintage British sports cars. They're quite rare, but generally sell for under $20,000 when they do pop up.

By the end of the 1970s, inflation and exchange rates were pushing TVRs further upmarket; Lilley thought it was time for something different, more comfortable and more contemporary than the long-in-the tooth Taimar. Oliver Winterbottom a former Lotus engineer was brought in to work on what became the Tasmin, or 280i, a dart-like two seat coupe and convertible.

Unfortunately, the development of the 280i was drawn out. By the time TVR introduced the car, the wedge-styling fad had run its course, and inflation had pushed the 280i into competition with cars that it had neither the quality nor the performance to match. Consequently, the "wedge" cars, as the Tasmin and its derivatives became known, were nearly sale-proof at anywhere near their $25,000+ sticker price. Large numbers accumulated at dealers.

In 1987, TVR pulled out of the U.S. market, awash in unsold cars and unfulfilled warranty claims. Then-owner Peter Wheeler vowed never to return. Although they're interesting convertible sports cars, 280i prices have never recovered—good examples are still under $10,000.

As a fun occasional driver, TVRs are not without their merits. Both the 2500M and the 280i are sharp handlers and good performers. The 2500M is rather claustrophobic but its styling (kind of an odd combination of Triumph GT6 and first generation Mazda RX7) has aged better than the wedge-shaped 280i.

The 280i, however, was available with a full convertible top that was one of the cleverest ever designed. The center section was a rigid piece of fiberglass covered in canvas that had two tabs in front and two in back,

Top left: 2500M engine compartment is straightforward TR6.
Top right: 280i is as drastic an expression of wedge-trend of the 1970s as you're likely to see.
Left: Short tail of the 280i.
Right: Sharp angles outside carry over inside.

fitting into the windshield frame the folding rear section. Releasing the tension on the rear section allowed it to be removed. The rear section could be either folded down to make the car a full convertible or left up, making the car essentially a targa.

The market

The only TVRs that have made the A-list as real collectibles are the Griffith 200 and 400. They've gained a following as a sort of poor man's Cobra Daytona coupe. Although not an A-lister, the 3000S roadster, is a very desirable car in its own right. Silly anachronistic side curtains aside, they're beautiful, quite fast and very rare. High teens to mid- twenties is the norm for a roadster.

2500Ms and Taimars go for about half the money of a roadster, while the 280i lags considerably behind. Perfectly acceptable 280is sell for as little as $6,000 and ultra-low mileage cars still turn up and struggle to bring more than $10,000. Marshall Moore, the president of the TVR Club of North America, is convinced that new ones are still hanging around out there unsold.

Case study

1985 TVR 280i		
Purchase Price $4,800	**Sale Price** $5,400	**Owned for** 1.0 years

My silver 280i—A nice car from New York City? Fuggedaboutit!

This car illustrates why I'm far better off sleeping on a plane than reading. While on my way to New York, I read an ad in *Hemmings Motor News* placed by a guy on Long Island who had three TVRs for sale. I was traveling with my dad who was ever the good sport and didn't hesitate to jump on the Long Island Railroad with me to go look at some obscure British sports cars out in Massapequa.
Ordinarily, a history that includes a registration in the State of New York is something that is an instant turnoff for me, like an automatic transmission. New York (especially the City) is hard on cars plain and simple, but I'd never driven a 280i before, and here were three for sale.

I instantly gravitated toward the worst/cheapest one of the bunch; a silver and blue car that had a chunk of fiberglass missing from the corner of the air dam and, like all 280is, a completely shot leather interior. But it was cheap and drove quite well. We jacked it up and the space frame looked straight enough, not rusty, so I bought the car. I regretted it instantly.

To say that my 280i appeared "homemade" does a disservice to the bakers of pies and the makers of delicious jams and jellies everywhere. Much of the interior was vinyl covered plywood—the actual walnut dashboard face fell off when I was driving the car. The driver's side power window dropped into the bottom of the door with a thunk, the interior door handle came off in my hand, and the ancient Smiths mechanical oil pressure gauge piddled oil on a pair of my favorite khakis. The headlights also had an interesting habit of raising and lowering themselves when going over bumps. Not even in unison mind you, but one at a time, like a crowd of two doing The Wave.

Still, the car did have its merits. The 2.8 liter Ford V6 had adequate torque and power, and the Oliver Winterbottom-designed space-frame chassis was very good indeed. The car was a very entertaining handler, and the convertible top was quite brilliant. I recovered the seats and fixed the corner of the air-dam, gradually becoming less horrified by my purchase. The car never actually did anything particularly bad (although I always had this feeling that it was just one significant repair away from being a donation to the Kidney Fund).

Eventually, I simply tired of the car's poor construction and constantly having to explain it. I sold it to a local dealer for approximately what I had in it. Occasionally, some low production oddball cars (the Daimler SP250 for example) will surprise you with how unexpectedly good they are. The TVR 280i, however just missed the mark for me (although I'll admit the fact that mine was a substandard example probably had much to do with this). If I decide to revisit TVRs in the future, it will likely be with a 2500M or 3000S.

Jensen-Healey

1972-75		
Parts availability ✪✪✪	Inexpensive to maintain ✪✪✪	Investment potential ✪½
Fun to drive ✪✪✪✪	Price category $$	Nice driver, $7,000; Show winner, $11,000
Performance 0 to 60 in 9.7 seconds; ¼ mile in 17.3 seconds at 80.5 mph (*Road & Track* 3/73)		

Parts Delta Motorsports, www.deltamotorsports.com; Dave Bean Engineering, www.davebean.com
Club The Jensen Healey Preservation Society, www.jensenhealey.com

1975 Jensen-Healey with factory hardtop.

History

The 1970s have been called "the decade without quality control." Alas, the Jensen-Healey was a product of that era. While it should have taken the sports car world by storm, much the same way the Datsun 240Z swept aside mediocre competition like the MGB-GT and Triumph GT6, the Jensen-Healey was instead gone in just three years. It was a better car than most of its British contemporaries, and it deserved a better fate.

The car has its genesis in the late '60s, when Kjell Qvale, noted British car importer and then-owner of Jensen, enlisted the help of Donald and Geoffrey Healey to fill the gap left by the 1967 demise of the Austin-Healey 3000. The resultant Jensen-Healey debuted in March 1972.

Left: Very attractive late J-H interior.

Above right: Slant of the Lotus 907 engine evident here.

Right: Jensen-Healey is a handsome if non-descript design. "Roulette wheel" nickname for factory alloys is apt.

Paul Duchene

Following the standard practice of swiping as many volume-production sedan components as possible, front suspension came from the estimable Vauxhall Firenza; the four-speed gearbox was a Chrysler U.K. product. The engine , however, was a new Lotus 907, a 2.0-liter, 16-valve, alloy four-cylinder with a novel cogged-belt driving twin overhead-camshafts. After decades of cast-iron pushrod lumps, a modern powerplant in a mid-priced British sports car was a revelation. Even fitted with twin Zenith-Strombergs in emissions trim, the engine produced 144 hp, 35 more than the Triumph TR6's 2.5-liter six-cylinder.

Unfortunately, the engine testers (also known as "customers") discovered, much to their chagrin, the engine's propensity for prematurely eating timing belts and tensioner bearings. The results were predictably dire, with valves meeting pistons and such. In all fairness, the Lotus 907 was among the first interference-type engines with a timing belt, and the notion that these had to be changed regularly was probably not ingrained in most owners or service providers.

Adding insult to injury, the slant of the engine meant that when the inevitable cam-cover leaks developed, gravity conspired to direct the errant petroleum straight onto the hot exhaust-manifold. The resulting smoke and smell made driving a Jensen-Healey a lot like following an asphalt paving truck. But road testers universally praised the Jensen-Healey as an excellent handler. Its rear-axle was live, but its four-link location meant that it behaved quite well most of the time.

Road & Track even pitted one against the vaunted BMW 2002 tii, finding that while the cars were evenly matched in a straight line (both cars did 0-60 mph in around 9.5 seconds), the Brit scampered away from the Bavarian in the corners, in spite of the Bimmer's more sophisticated independent rear suspension.

Owing to the short production run, lasting until just 1976, changes to the Jensen-Healey were few. Some new colors, a less austere interior, impact bumpers on post-1974 cars, and a five-speed Getrag gearbox on

ran when parked...

the last cars about sums it up. An odd wagon-esque fixed-head coupe was offered as simply the Jensen GT, mercifully dying along with the whole firm in 1976.

The appalling quality of early examples and styling perceived as bland quickly tainted the Jensen-Healey; the car's reputation never recovered. But as is so often the case, committed aftermarket suppliers can offer fixes for most factory gaffes, and a well-sorted Jensen-Healey can be a really satisfying sports car. Delta Motorsports in Phoenix (www.deltamotorsports.com) has long been in the business of catering to owners of Jensen-Healeys and Interceptors—it's the place to start when improving or restoring these cars.

Ignore timing belt changes at your own risk

Mechanical issues center mainly on the Lotus engine. Stock timing belts should be changed every 18,000 miles, or after two or three years, and timing belt tensioner bearings should be changed at the same time. An upgraded timing belt and adjustable-pulley gears are available from Dave Bean Engineering (www.davebean.com) for about $300—these should last 30-40k miles. If no receipts are present for a belt change, do it. It's cheap insurance. Rubber cam cover-gaskets are also available to take care of those annoying leaks. Finally, beware of burned valves and bad head gaskets.

Even more so than most old cars, rust is a concern with a Jensen-Healey, almost as if the factory took perverse pride in building the most horribly rust-prone bodies. Certainly, it was part of Jensen's heritage, as Interceptors have the same reaction to moisture as an Alka-Seltzer tablet. This means that even Jensen-Healeys that have lived all their lives in the California desert are often found with floor rust, which is no laughing matter, as this is a structural part of the car.

As for the styling, beauty is in the eye of the beholder, but at worst the Jensen-Healey is inoffensive. In the right color—darker colors tend to hide the rubber bumpers—a Jensen-Healey can look quite handsome. Its long, slim profile and Kamm tail are somewhat reminiscent of a TR6, but the Jensen-Healey is a much better car. More comfortable seats, a wider, roomier interior, stiffer unibody construction, a better-controlled ride, and a modern engine make it no contest.

The market

Why, then, are Jensen-Healey values about half that of a comparable TR6? A nice Jensen-Healey can be bought with enough change left from $10,000 to purchase upgrades such as 14- or 15-inch Panasport or Revolution wheels, modern rubber, and twin Weber or Dell'Orto carbs. Add sway bars and lowering springs and you can go Miata hunting with confidence.

But old reputations simply die hard. The collector car world is littered with potentially excellent cars that gained bad reputations when new, and while specialists often develop fixes, the word rarely seems to get out to the public. Fear of problems and general obscurity have kept Jensen-Healey values low. Several years ago, offering anyone money for a Jensen-Healey was like offering to lance a boil on their backside, and the best one on the planet could be had for $4,500. Lately, however, it appears that prices are on the upswing. Now it takes about $7,500 to bring home a nice Jensen-Healey, still just mediocre MGB money. I'll take mine in black.

Jensen

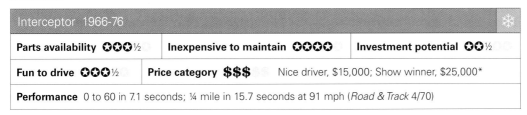

Interceptor 1966-76		❄
Parts availability ✪✪✪½	**Inexpensive to maintain** ✪✪✪✪	**Investment potential** ✪✪½
Fun to drive ✪✪✪½	**Price category** $$$	Nice driver, $15,000; Show winner, $25,000*
Performance 0 to 60 in 7.1 seconds; ¼ mile in 15.7 seconds at 91 mph (*Road & Track* 4/70)		

*Convertible values roughly double

Parts Delta Motorsports, www.deltamotorsports.com; D & K Engineering, www.interceptor.com

Club Jensen Owners Club, www.joc.org.uk

The Jensen Interceptor was as much an artifact of the early 1970s as Hai Karate cologne and quadraphonic stereos. Built to cruise across any continent with paved roads in absolute comfort and safety—with single digit fuel economy under most conditions— it became increasingly irrelevant as the decade wore on.

Jensen Motors of West Bromwich, England has a long history of both producing cars under its own name and for other manufacturers. Jensen used its overflow capacity to produce cars for Sunbeam and Volvo, but its most interesting products have to be the large GTs—the 541, CV8 and the Interceptor.

Most of Jensen's pre-Interceptor product was RHD home market stuff that is quite rare in the U.S. But new owner Kjell Qvale decided that the U.S. market would be a fertile one for his new V8 powered GT which would be a 180 degree turn from the UK-styled, rather grotesque fiberglass CV8.

Jensen employed the Italian styling house of Vignale to both design and build bodies for the Interceptor. Its giant fishbowl opening-glass rear-hatch presaged the Porsche 924 by over ten years; it was the only styling element of the car that was controversial. Build quality and rustproofing by Vignale, however, was as bad if not worse than what Jensen had done to Volvo with the P1800. What goes around surely comes around.

Mark I and II Interceptors were powered by 383 cubic inch Chrysler V8s. With minimal emission controls, these were the most powerful and best-performing cars. Later cars acquired the 440 V8 which became steadily emasculated by emission controls as the 1970s dragged on. Almost every Interceptor came fitted with a Chrysler TorqueFlite 727 automatic transmission.

Interiors came in three basic designs—Mark I and Mark II cars had rather plain but handsome black vinyl-covered dashes with full instrumentation, no wood trim and a rather cool drilled steering wheel. Early Mark III cars had a bit of wood in the console and a new padded two-spoke "safety" steering wheel that seemed to have no purpose other than to stimulate Nardi sales. Late Mark III cars added more wood to the main dash.

All were comfortable and covered in enough Connolly Brothers cowhide to make a sofa, a loveseat and several club chairs. Because of the expense of re-doing an Interceptor interior versus the values of the car, many people skimp and use vinyl. It just kills the character of the car. Try to find one with a well-preserved original interior.

Mechanically, the Interceptor was obviously not as sophisticated as a Ferrari or Aston Martin of the day, lacking the overhead cams, exotic sounds and independent rear-suspension of A-list exotics. However, unlike a Ferrari or an Aston, the majority of mechanical parts were as close as the corner auto parts store. And under most conditions, the Interceptor was a match for a standard Aston V8 or a Ferrari 330 or 365 2+2.

Where the comparison falls apart is on twisty uneven roads where the live-axle of the Jensen makes itself apparent and the slightly numb Adwest power steering makes the car more difficult to place in a corner.

ran when parked...

Shawn Dougan/Hyman, Ltd.

Jensen Motors, Ltd.

Jensen Motors, Ltd.

Above left: Giant fishbowl-like rear hatch lifts to gain access to the trunk.
Right: The Chrysler 440 V8 as fitted to the Interceptor. Don't damage or lose one of the bespoke valve covers.
Left: Rare Interceptor III convertible with its massive "hideaway in plain sight" top.

There's also a bit of squirminess in the way the rear axle is located; under extreme conditions, that can result in torque steer from the back end. But again, crossing continents on Interstates, Routes Nationales, Autostradas and Autobahns and not twisty secondary roads is what the car is all about. When it tested an Interceptor III in 1973, *Road & Track* thought it to be one of the best cars in the world.

Seeking to broaden the Interceptor's appeal, Jensen introduced a full convertible in 1974 and an odd notchback coupe for 1976. The convertible—which makes a truly credible alternative to an Aston Martin V8 Volante—along with the ultra-rare all wheel-drive FF and 440 SP models (three two-barrel carbs) are the most collectible Jensens. The big thirsty convertible was no bulwark against the fuel crisis, crippling taxes and recession of the early 1970s. Jensen entered receivership in 1976 and was liquidated.

The two most frequently cited problems with an Interceptor center around wiring and engine compartment heat. Ordinarily, I don't subscribe to the view that there is anything inherently wrong with the wiring on English cars. Most of the electrical problems I've seen over the years have come from owner "improvements" or lack of maintenance when wires and connectors age. But having been around enough Interceptors when they were new, personally witnessing an unprovoked dash fire in one, I'd have to say that the Jensen folks were in somewhat over their heads when it came to wiring harness design.

In all fairness, Interceptors are complicated cars with air conditioning, power windows, and rocker switches for everything, including dual tone horns. You would do well to check the wiring thoroughly on any Interceptor. Other issues are leaky power steering racks and rampant body rust. Both should be reasonably obvious. The racks can be easily rebuilt; they share most parts with a contemporary Jaguar XJ6.

Shawn Dougan/Hyman, Ltd.

Shawn Dougan/Hyman, Ltd.

Left: Wood, wool and leather Interceptor Interior. Right: A shame this photo isn't a "scratch and sniff" as this much Connolly hide smells like nothing else.

And while most mechanical parts are dead simple, things like wheels, minor trim and non-windshield glass are tough indeed to source. Heaven help you if you need a rear window for a coupe. Body rust is another issue entirely. A few places can supply some Interceptor sheet metal, but it's best to avoid a rusty car to begin with. Fortunately, California was a large market for Jensen. Do yourself a favor and find a California car, perhaps with its original blue license plate.

Engine compartment heat was also paint-bleaching fierce on these cars. Louvered hoods alleviated things somewhat, but the heat could cause even more severe problems. Engine compartment fires were also not unheard of, the result of heat-perished fuel lines. Interceptors were also known for overheating in traffic. An oversized radiator and modern efficient electric fans timed to stay on after shutoff are a big help.

The market

Until recently, there had been little to no interest among collectors in the Interceptor. Part of the reason is the fact that decent ones were rarely seen at public auctions, while ratty cars were quite common. But as Mopar muscle and Aston Martins began to climb in value, some began to take a second look at the big Interceptor, which could be seen as kind of a combination of the two. Unfortunately, since there is little to no intersection between the Aston Martin and Mopar muscle market, Jensens trade in a thin market indeed.

On the rare occasion that a good coupe or convertible shows up, bidders will respond with respectable bids of the high teens to low twenties for a coupe and about twice that for a convertible. It makes little to no sense to try to restore an Interceptor—the cost of paint and interior alone will put you far underwater. Again, spend a little more and get the best one on the market. It will be far cheaper in the long run. A fine Interceptor can be expected to appreciate modestly, perhaps at the rate of a certificate of deposit, while costing very little to maintain. And what's wrong with that?

ran when parked...

acknowledgements

aT THE RISK OF JINXING MYSELF (and no doubt to the chagrin of some readers) I've never suffered from writer's block—until now. Giving credit where credit is due is a daunting task--and as a first time book author, it's difficult to know where to start. I was certainly the child left behind when it came to English—I left high school, college and law school as a woefully deficient writer. Thankfully, Peter Hamilton, the "cool" partner at my first law firm, took an interest in helping me improve. Peter bought me a copy of Strunk and White's *Elements of Style* and would occasionally beat me with it, but only when I deserved it. He helped me, belatedly, acquire some solid writing fundamentals.

I might be back in a suit and tie everyday, marking my life in quarter-hour increments but for a piece of very sage advice given to me by McKeel Hagerty about six years ago at a Scottsdale auction. Thankfully, I listened.

Keith Martin and *Sports Car Market* magazine gave me the opportunity to write things that began with phrases other than "may it please the court". Keith was also responsible for beginning my relationship with *The New York Times*; I will forever be thankful to him for opening that door.

I'm also grateful to Paul Duchene and Cliff Pass, great friends with whom, over the years, I've looked at and worked on a good number of "Ran When Parked" old cars. Thanks to Jim Cobb, Norman Mayersohn and Jim Schembari at *The New York Times* for continuing to tolerate me; and thanks to Tim Parker for believing that I could string together more than a thousand words.

By far, the nicest images you'll see in this book came from Bob Lichty at Motorcar Portfolio, Charlie Kuhn at Chicago Classic cars, and Mark Hyman and Shawn Dougan at Hyman, Ltd. I greatly appreciate their help in rounding them up. Kathleen Donohue is the talented editor who foolishly took on the challenges of editing my manuscript, including excising the "moreovers," "howevers," and "aforementioneds" that are the remnants of my legal career. Thanks to Dave Kinney of Hagerty's *Cars That Matter* for helping me with values and for talking me off the ledge numerous times. And thanks to Donald Osborne, one of the more insightful old car people that I know, who always makes me think twice before dumping on Italian cars. And special thanks to Fred Garcia, part mechanical maestro and part therapist, without whom my hobby would grind to a halt.

Finally, my parents Joyce and Richard have never once questioned my decision to give up a promising legal career to do something that I actually enjoy. Where other parents might not be able to resist an occa-sional subtle dig by mentioning Sheldon, "that nice classmate of yours" who made managing partner at some fancy schmancy downtown law firm, my folks simply enjoy seeing my byline and e-mailing stories to friends and family.

To my daughter Rachel and wife Michele, thank you for giving me the time and space to get this done—and for tolerating my laptop to the dinner table. And of course, thanks to you for purchasing this book. It's my hope that reading my adventures may inspire you to begin one or two of your own.

index

Alfa Romeo
    Giulietta Sprint Coupe, 106
    Spider, 39-41, 52, 55-60, 63
    GTV(s), 62, 106, 138
AutoTrader Classics, 15
Aston Martin(s), 37, 110, 157, 158
Austin Allegro, 54
Austin-Healey
    3000, 49, 92, 110, 153
    Sprite, 49, 65, 66
Automobile Quarterly, 79

Bentley
    Continental GT, 28
    Mulsanne, 27, 28
    Turbo R, 27, 28
Bloomington Gold, 16
BMW
    2002/2002tii, 8, 109, 122-124, 138, 154
    2800CS, 21, 72
    3.0 CS, 21, 23, 47
    633i, 22
    635i, 22
    630CSi, 24
    633CS, 24
    L6, 24
    M6, 24, 25
    E9, 21, 22, 23
    E24, 25
    Z3, 106
Buick Riviera, 68-71
Buyer's Services, LLC, 13
BringATrailer.com, 15

Chevrolet
    Cadillac Eldorado, 68, 70, 79-80, 102
    Corvair, 82-84
    Corvette(s), 16, 37, 75-76, 143, 146
Car and Driver, 83, 137
Citroen, 73, 109, 132
Clarkson, Jeremy, 30, 37
Comer, Colin, 130
Cord, 8, 72, 73, 74
Cotter, Tom, 130
Craigslist, 7, 8, 15

Daimler SP250, 140-144
Datsun
    240/260/280Z, 76, 91-96, 103, 153
DeLorean, John, 102, 103
Delta Motorsports, 155
De Tomaso Deauville, 46
Duchene, Paul, 10, 32,53, 66, 96, 122

eBay Motors, 7,15

Ferrari, 8, 37, 70, 76, 90, 103, 109, 119, 126
Fiat
    Spider, 48, 52, 58-60
    X1/9, 61
Ford
    Mustang, 87-89
    Mustang 5.0 Convertible, 112-114
    Falcon, 113
    Thunderbird, 77-78, 85

Garcia's Restorations, 42

Hagerty, McKeel, 7
Hagerty Insurance, 9
Hemmings Motor News, 15, 152

Iacocca, Lee, 87

Jaguar, 19, 33
    3.8S, 46
    420G, 45
    E-type, 8, 33-39, 45, 49, 90, 138, 143, 145
    XJ Coupe, 46
    XK120, 105
    XJ6, 45-47
    XJS, 41-43
    XJ-SC, 42
    XK8, 43
Jaguar-Daimler Heritage Trust, 37
Jensen-Healey, 55, 153-155
Jensen Interceptor, 155-158

Kinney, Dave, 14, 28, 147, 148
Kruse, Dean, 9

Lancia
    Beta, 8, 60-61
    Fulvia, 61

Lamborghini, 42, 103
Leno, Jay, 74
Lincoln Continental, 74, 85-87
Lotus, 109, 154
Lyons, Sir William, 41, 45, 46, 47, 143

Martin, Keith, 9, 56, 63, 129
MG
    MGA, 52, 126, 141
    MGB, 13 48, 53-55, 59, 60, 66, 92, 105-110, 112, 126, 143, 154
    MGC, 105-110
    Midget, 12, 48, 49, 54, 64-67, 112
    TC, 103
Maserati
    Merak, 103
    Mistral, 138
    Quattroporte, 46
Mazda
    Miata, 40, 53, 55, 66, 113, 155
    RX7, 103-104
Mercedes Benz
    230/280/300/350/380/ 560SL, 43-45
MidAmerica Motorworks, 76, 118, 134
Mini Cooper, 65, 73
Mitchell, Bill, 70, 71, 74, 79, 80
Morgan, 65
Morris
    Ital, 54
    Minor, 132
Moss Motors, 107, 129
Motor Trend, 79

New York Times, 8, 129

Oldsmobile Toronado, 8, 68, 70, 72-75, 80
Opel GT, 13, 92
Osborne, Donald, 14, 64, 140

Pegaso, 90
Pontiac
    Grand Prix, 101-103
    GTO, 102
Porsche
    911, 8, 12, 29, 30, 31, 117, 136
    911 Carrera, 8, 28, 29, 30, 32, 33, 76

911S, 12, 29, 123
911SC, 29, 32, 52
911T, 32, 92, 115, 123
912, 912E, 115, 135-138
914, 114-118, 136
924, 103, 156
944, 103
928, 19, 48
356, 12, 136

Roadster Factory, 100, 128
Road & Track, 21, 44, 45, 60, 61, 74, 87, 103, 104, 107, 117, 132, 133, 138, 146, 147, 148, 150, 154, 157

Sports Car Market, 8, 10, 56, 63, 96, 109, 125, 129
Studebaker
    Avanti/Avanti II, 81, 145-148
    GT Hawk, 78, 80-82
    President Speedster, 148
Sunbeam
    Alpine, 111-112, 141
    Tiger, 112

Tatra, 83
Top Gear, 30
Toyota 200GT, 92, 105
Triumph
    Herald, 49
    Spitfire, 13, 48, 49-53, 112
    TR250, 77-101, 127
    TR3, 126, 142
    TR4/TR4A, 53, 125-130
    TR6, 92, 97-101, 127, 153, 154, 155
TVR
    2500M/300S/Taimer/ Tasmin/280i, 103, 148-153
    Griffith 200/400, 150-152
Tuscan V8, 150

Uniform Standards of Professional Appraisal Practice (see USPAP), 13-14

Vintage Air, 90
Volkswagen, 83, 117, 131-135
Volvo
    P1800/P1800E/P1800ES, 8, 118-122, 156
    P1900, 119